**This book is to be returned on or before
the last date stamped below.**

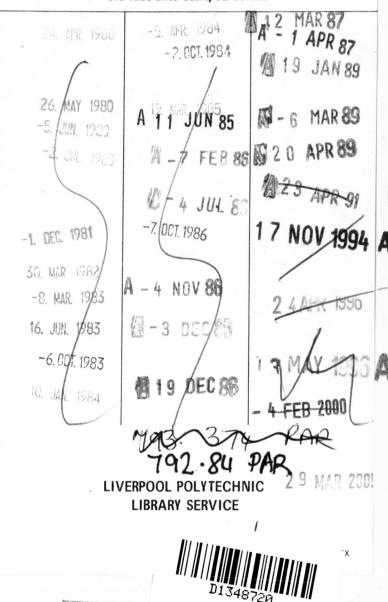

A Garland Series

OUTSTANDING
DISSERTATIONS
IN THE

FINE
ARTS

"Parade":
Cubism as Theater

Richard H. Axsom

Garland Publishing, Inc., New York & London

1979

All volumes in this series are printed
on acid-free, 250-year-life paper.

Library of Congress Cataloging in Publication Data

Axsom, Richard H   1943-
   "Parade", Cubism as theater.

   (Outstanding dissertations in the fine arts)
   Reprint of the author's thesis, University of Michigan,
1974.
   Bibliography: p.
   1. Ballet--Stage-setting and scenery. 2. Cubism.
I. Title. II. Series.
GV1782.A94 1979   792.8'4   78-74361
ISBN 0-8240-3950-5

PARADE: CUBISM AS THEATER

by
Richard Hayden Axsom

A dissertation submitted in partial fulfillment
of the requirements for the degree of
Doctor of Philosophy
(History of Art)
in The University of Michigan
1974

Doctoral Committee:

Associate Professor Joel Isaacson, Chairman
Professor Marvin Eisenberg
Professor Victor Miesel
Professor Glenn Watkins

To my loving father and mother,

Russell and Vera Axsom

TABLE OF CONTENTS

ACKNOWLEDGMENTS

I am deeply indebted to three individuals who fostered my art historical interests in Parade and who closely followed me through many phases of research on the subject. Specifically, I should like to thank my chairman, Professor Joel Isaacson, for his unstinting generosity and for the advice and encouragement he gave me at every stage of the work. Special thanks are due to Professor Victor Miesel, whose provocative course on Cubism generated my initial curiosity about Picasso's work for the theater. And, I extend my gratitude to Professor Marvin Eisenberg, who suggested and encouraged the expansion of my original ideas on Parade into a dissertation. My obligations to these men really cannot be measured.

In the world of scholarship, I would further like to thank Professor Glenn Watkins, whose ideas on the relationships of the arts were a helpful guide, especially for the formulation of my comments on Cubism and Satie. Also, I wish to acknowledge Professor Marianne Martin for the influence her research into the interchanges between Cubism and Futurism exerted upon my own arguments. During the first year of research, my activities were greatly facilitated by a Chester Dale Fellowship which was awarded by the National

v

Gallery of Art in Washington, D. C. For the support this
fellowship provided I should particularly like to express
my gratitude to the Gallery's Director, J. Carter Brown,
Douglas Lewis, and the late Professor Wolfgang Stechow.

I owe a special debt of appreciation to Edouard Dermit,
who graciously received me at Cocteau's residence in Milly-
la-Forêt and kindly placed at my disposal Cocteau's Cahier
romain as well as a collection of sketches affiliated with
the original production of Parade.

To Leonide Massine I offer my sincerest gratitude
for hospitably permitting me to talk to him about Parade
and for allowing me to attend several rehearsals of the
City Center Joffrey Ballet during which he set the choreography for Parade's New York revival in 1973. Of course,
the invaluable perspectives made possible by a revival of
Parade must be credited to Robert Joffrey, who sponsored the
production. I would like to thank Mr. Joffrey not only
for the interviews he arranged for me with Massine but also
for the sustained interest he has shown in authentic resto-
rations of major repertory from Diaghilev's Ballets Russes.
During the period of rehearsals for the Joffrey revival,
two company administrators, Ruth Hedrick and Jane Hermann,
unfailingly responded to many requests for information.
Their generous assistance was helpful in more ways than I
can enumerate. In the world of dance, I must additionally
acknowledge Lincoln Kirstein and Gigi Oswald, the former
for personally encouraging my research and the latter for

allowing me to examine many important and unpublished documents in the Lincoln Center Dance Collection.

Finally, I want to thank my devoted sister, Susan Axsom Smith, for typing the dissertation and for her patience and concern during the final stages of preparation. And, with great affection, I offer my gratitude to Steven May for his confidence in my project and for his determination to see my work brought to a successful close.

LIST OF ILLUSTRATIONS

INTRODUCTION

Even before the final curtain fell on the Ballets
Russes' matinee performance for the War Benefit Fund in the
spring of 1917, the Parisian audience had audibly begun to
express its disfavor with the third and concluding ballet.
Serge de Diaghilev, the company's impresario, had knowingly
paced the afternoon's program with the conservative Les Sylphides and the pre-war Petrouschka before unleashing the pre-
mière of Parade, a Cubist ballet. For the new production,
Diaghilev had recruited Jean Cocteau, Pablo Picasso, Erik
Satie, and Leonide Massine (Figs. 1, 2, 3, 4). Parade's sched-
uled debut at the Théâtre du Châtelet had led the conservative,
right-bank audience to anticipate a theater piece which would
be a polite introduction to Cubism. Unfortunately, Cubism's
appearance that afternoon--immediately ostensible in the set
and costumes of Picasso--was less than courteously received.
Parade was no mere artifice of the theater for the audience,
but moral effrontery, an outrage perpetrated by an impudent
avant-garde. If the audience expected Cubism, they saw only
Kubismus. The indignant cries of sale boche from the spectators were directed against a war-time, political conspiracy,
a German Bolshevik plot. The ballet Parade was quickly ush-
ered into the notorious company of two other early-modern
theatrical scandals--Ubu Roi and Le Sacre du Printemps.

1

Such is the history of taste, though, that when it was
revived four years later in Paris, Parade was the fashionable
hit of the season. Parade has since assumed the figurative
role of a raucous overture to the entre-deux-guerres. With
this reputation in hand, Parade has been tucked away into the
annals of social rather than art history. Until only recently,
other considerations have been negligible. One dance historian
in 1954 dismissed Parade as "an unsuccessful work which was
hampered by some cubistic customs that did not come off."[1]
Relegated to footnotes in dance histories, ignored by theater
historians, Parade has survived as a disembodied ghost in
Picasso's extant overture curtain and in Satie's score.

What lies at the source of Parade's previous critical
fate at once indicts certain attitudes which have sheltered
Parade from any serious consideration and exposes the problems
which arise for the historian who undertakes comparative studies between the visual and performing arts. Conventional histories of painting and sculpture offer little to suggest any
relationship to the history of performance. Where does one
read art-historical studies of the theatrical contributions
of Bernini, Matisse, or Braque? The development of performance has been similarly treated as a self-sufficient disci-
pline. The plastic arts may be drawn into the discussion of
theatrical productions, but only as they decorate the stage.
More rigorous inquiries into the aesthetic and philosophical
connections and cross influences between the stage and the
studio have been few.[2]

The art historian's indifference to the role of the

visual arts in the history of performance may be attributed primarily to a concern for the pure forms of painting and sculpture. Parade was an event whose significance has been overlooked by the art historian in his desire to analyze painting and sculpture in terms of formalist criteria. For the art historian, Parade properly belongs to Picasso, whose contribution, however, is usually commented upon in parenthetical references in histories of the artist's work. Picasso's scenic designs are not easily accommodated into conventional categories of artmaking. Picasso's Cubist costumes in Parade are not "sculpture"; the 1500 square feet of Picasso's overture curtain do not constitute a stretched and framed "painting." The components of Picasso's scenic designs for Parade are not autonomous works of art, they function in a theatrical setting. They cannot be fully explicated without reference to other aspects of the spectacle: namely, the scenario, the music, and the choreography. All the various arts which are brought to the level of synthesis in a theatrical production lose their individual integrity as pure form in order to co-operate in a collective scheme. Picasso's scenic designs for the theater have recently been given separate and extensive treatment in Douglas Cooper's Picasso Theatre. Although the book is rewarding inasmuch as Picasso's theater work has been gathered for special consideration by itself, the study is ultimately anecdotal and descriptive. No effort is made, specifically in the case of Parade, to characterize the function of the scenic design within the context of the spectacle.

The particular formalist approach of the art historian--

the concern for pure form divorced from other contexts--is
paralleled in critical evaluations of Parade made from the
point of view of other art forms. In music histories, readings of Satie's Parade are made as though the score's ultimate haven is the concert hall rather than the orchestra pit.
Parade has been designated Cocteau's first theater piece.
Others view it as Massine's ballet. The damage of critical
partisanship is subtle. It is not that the assorted critical
entrances to Parade do not acknowledge the contributions of
the other artists involved. Yet the result of isolated cele-
brations of individual contributions to Parade quietly and
successfully inhibits broader perspectives which could di-
vulge new information.

Critical ballet literature is thin. What little exists is essentially social history: autobiographies of celebrated dancers and balletomane's appreciations of favorite
ballets. There is, for example, no satisfying critique of
Massine's career as a choreographer. Ballet has not been over-
ly self-conscious about its historical development. The first,
serious iconographical investigation of ballet viewed as a historical sequence was only recently published.[3]

Parade was intended by the man who conceived its theme,
Jean Cocteau, to be experimental theater. The art of the ballet was the means for realizing a contemporary French theater.
Parade was one of the first distinguished experimental theater
pieces of the twentieth century and submitted a notion of
theater which opposed traditional western drama. To ask the
question why Parade is ostracized from histories of modern

theater is to expose a basic assumption of western theater criticism. Conventional theater is dramatized literature written by a playwright. It is verbal, psychological, acted; and, the script may be studied apart from actual performance.[4] Cocteau's early stage pieces, beginning with Parade, were essentially non-narrative and non-psychological and offered, in the place of acted drama, a ritualized theater of effects. There is no script for Parade, only a general synopsis of the action. Parade's primary impact is visual, not literary. Consequently, it is excluded from discussion of drama because it remains unconventional. Cocteau considered Parade his first mature work as a poet and wished others would forget his earlier "juvenile imbecilities." And yet, unfortunately, Cocteau's early experimental plays--Parade, Les Mariés de la tour Eiffel, and Le Boeuf sur le toit--do not appear in the edition of his collected works.

If one reads separately about Cocteau's Parade, Picasso's Parade, Satie's Parade, and Massine's Parade, the task of establishing an integrated overview cannot be initiated simply by collecting and synthesizing the various commentaries on the production's component parts. Assumptions and attitudes underlying art historical, theater, music, and dance criticism have prevented not only a collective assessment of Parade, but they have, moreover, protected the individual scenic, dramatic, and choreographic dimensions from serious scrutiny.

One problem for the historian of the performing arts is the inevitable intangibility of an original theatrical performance. As persisting events, a painting, a piece of sculp-

ture, a novel, or a building are tangible entities. The
performing arts--concert, dramatic, operatic, and balletic--
however, are more precarious events in time. Each new performance will be different because of the variables of performers, audiences, period styles of interpretation, and the
shifts in technical virtuosity. Scores and scripts may, at
least, be studied independently of performance. Dance events
are more elusive. The only records left are verbal descriptions, the music, and possibly photographs of the mise en
scène. The choreography itself is handed down orally from
one choreographer to the next. Even then a ballet may be
lost. Nijinsky's great setting of Stravinsky's Le Sacre du
Printemps for the Ballets Russes in 1913 survives imperfectly
in the memories of those associated with the original production. Dance notation--the writing down of the movements
of a ballet--still remains an imprecise method of suggestion
and recall. This lamentable situation is being remedied through
the use of film and video tape to preserve choreographies and
performances. The dance world in the past has been slow to
adopt modern technology for its own ends. The loss is a
grievous one. Although the motion-picture camera was available to document the first season of the Ballets Russes in
1909, there is not one film of any original Ballets Russes
production performed during the company's twenty-year ex-
istence.

The topic of this dissertation was originally undertaken with the knowledge that no record existed of any performance of Parade. Critical judgments were to be based upon

the ballet's remains--a synopsis of the action, the musical score, photographs of the mise en scène, and descriptions and evaluations of others. Parade in performance would have to be imagined. It was this writer's good fortune, however, that during the preparation of the dissertation Robert Joffrey of the City Center Joffrey Ballet in New York invited Leonide Massine to supervise an authentic revival of Parade for the company's 1973 spring season. The opportunity to see Parade in actual performance, with recreations of Picasso's costumes and sets, was a much needed corrective to any hypothetical reconstruction of the ballet. A series of interviews conducted with Massine during the setting of the choreography for the Joffrey company in September 1972 and during final preparations for Parade's New York debut in March 1973 served as an important primary source for the casting of my arguments.

In this dissertation the critically balanced overview was not meant to be the major thrust or goal. There have been four critical entrances to Parade--literary, musical, scenic, and choreographic. What has been sorely missing in the critical literature for each frame of reference is the awareness not only of the other contributions, but of how the four dimensions of Parade worked in ensemble. Obviously, a single component of Parade was not created in isolation but in response to demands exerted by other components. The relationship of parts was the crucial aspect of Parade to be uncovered. The evaluation of each contribution, seen as a working part of a larger whole, permitted a clearer focus of Parade's totality.

Relationships between the elements of the spectacle became
more readily discernible.

The insights gleaned from a consideration of all parts
of Parade's production aided immeasurably in the working out
of the central issue of this dissertation: the relationship
of Parade to Cubism. The formalist critical perspective in
the arts, which has been the dominant mode of inquiry in modern art, has addressed itself to the histories of pure forms.
Intermedia performance has been ignored because it is a max-
imal mode which utilizes several art forms in one work of
art. Since Cubism was originally a pictorial form, formalists
have hesitated to transfer their discussions of Cubism to
other media.[5] Formalist interests have not only steered art
historians away from Parade and from the question posed in
this dissertation about the relationship of Cubism and the
theater, but they have ironically prevented formal and iconographical analyses of Picasso's mise en scène, both of which
are mandatory in considering the problem of Cubism in the
theater.

To be explored in this dissertation are the ways in
which Parade functioned as a vehicle for the placement of a
pictorial mode of behavior, Cubism, within a theatrical setting. Consequently, the critical emphases--ideally not biases--
will be placed upon the theatrical and pictorial dimensions
of the production: namely, Cocteau's scenario and Picasso's
mise en scène. The aims of this inquiry also necessitate a
preliminary consideration of Diaghilev's concept of ballet
theater, a theoretical attitude which presented Parade's

collaborators with a pre-set theatrical formula within which
to generate their ideas. A primary source of information
that significantly influenced the direction of the dissertation was the Cahier romain of Jean Cocteau, which was graciously
offered for my examination by the literary benefactor of Cocteau's estate, M. Edouard Dermit. Cocteau's ideas for Parade,
written and drawn within the pages of this notebook, warrant
special attention to Cocteau's role in the original production
and aid in establishing an accurate theatrical context.

What was the nature of Parade's Cubism? Was it innocently decorative, or was it the controlling sensibility?
It is submitted that Parade bore the stamp of Cubism not only
in the look of Picasso's scenic designs, but convincingly in
the aesthetic underpinnings of the entire production. The
transposition of Cubism from the canvas to the stage was
subtly and effectively carried out. Armed with notions of
the workings of Cubism as a pictorial style, the investigator can uncover new levels of meaning in Parade, which in
turn may effect a broadened understanding of Cubism as a range
of phenomena and as an aesthetic strategy.

A discussion of an application of Cubist ideas to a
non-pictorial form, the theater, quickly immerses one in
theories of style. What are the assumptions which allow a
work of art to be Cubist? To compound the problem, Parade
has been variously observed to be a Futurist, a Surrealist,
and a Realist ballet. If Parade is a serious repository of
Cubist proposals, what new types of attentiveness are required
of the viewer? Do the complexity of the cognitive demands

run counter to the expectations asked of a fifteen-minute,
self-styled divertissement? How is the category "style"
used by the historian to describe a work of art? Do accepted
notions of style prevent us from accounting for Parade as
richly as we could otherwise? Wittgenstein suggested that
how we talk about something is how we think about it. The
amassed critical writings on Parade offer evidence that as
an event it begs to be rethought. If this is, in fact, the
case, how we talk about, or better, how we rephrase our talking of Parade and Cubism must be diligent.

CHAPTER I

DIAGHILEV AND THE BALLETS RUSSES

On the eve of his seventy-fifth birthday, Igor Stravinsky, in conversation with Robert Craft, recalled Serge Diaghilev as "a kind of Oscar Wilde," and then continued his description with a line of adjectives: "well-dressed, elegant, chic, smiling, protective, and distant."[1] The popular image of the theatrical producer as the dashing European, posturing with the rakishly placed fedora and the heavy black coat worn over the shoulders, must find its source in the figure cut by Stravinsky's first patron. The very name, Diaghilev, conjuring ambitious theatrical projects, begs for another, more distinguished, title: impresario (Fig. 5). Diaghilev was neither a creator nor an intellectual, but he did display keen talents as a critic and a coordinator. Diaghilev's supporters pointed out his determination to set new art before the public. Theater productions necessarily cost more than the painter's simple request for paint and canvas, and Diaghilev needed great sums of money to realize his spectacles. Rather than pandering to the upper classes to advance his social position, as he was often criticized for doing, Diaghilev discreetly manipulated the elite to advance his artistic goals.[2] For those closest to the man, Diaghilev was a shrewd and discerning critic, a friend and

11

a patron, and a unique judge and ally in art. In another
discussion about the impresario of the Ballets Russes, Stravinsky queried, "Has anyone ever had so much taste as
Diaghilev?"[3]

Diaghilev's goal was to bring before a larger audience
the contemporary art of composers, painters, and choreographers.[4]
Diaghilev was an ardent promoter of modern art. Constantly
on the alert for originality and fresh expression, he proclaimed:

> One of the greatest merits of our time is to recognize
> individuality under every guise and at every epoch...
> The desire to make a science out of criticism will
> never solve the importance of the relative merits of
> talent. One must sing art, hail every new manifesta-
> tion triumphantly.[5]

The twenty year tenure of the Ballets Russes in western Europe
from 1909 to 1929 exerted extraordinary influences on intellectual and artistic life. And all initiated by a Russian
dilettante who knew from the start where his talents lay.
In a famous statement, Serge Diaghilev wittily and honestly
estimated his own worth:

> I am: 1) an unusually enthusiastic charlatan. 2) a
> great charmer. 3) an insolent man. 4) a man possessing
> great logic and few biases. 5) a being, it would appear,
> afflicted with a total absence of talent. Furthermore,
> I believe I have found my true vocation: patron of the
> arts. For this, I have everything that is necessary,
> except money. But that will come.[6]

Diaghilev and "The World of Art"

Parade was one of many realizations of what Diaghilev
saw ballet theater to be: a collective whole of dance, scenic
design, and music. A central attitude implicit in the shaping
of Parade--the assumed integration of parts--issued from a

notion of ballet which he had encouraged during the first
seasons of Ballets Russes. 1909, however, did not mark its
initial formulation. The opening season of Russian ballet
in Paris was a dramatic culmination of the impresario's previous activities in Russia and in Europe. Diaghilev, thirty-
seven years old at the debut of Ballets Russes, could look
back over a period of fifteen years of intense participation
in the arts.

Diaghilev arrived in St. Petersburg in 1890 to enroll
in the law school at the University.[7] The same year, he was
introduced by a cousin to Alexander Benois, who had organized
a literary group of university students called the Nevsky
Pickwickians. Diaghilev, whose interests were sympathetic,
joined the society and attended its frequent lectures and
discussions on painting, literature, and history. A primary
goal of the group was to become acquainted with western modernism in the arts. With the exception of Diaghilev, whose
background although literate was provincial, the young men
of the literary circle came from upper middle-class families
of St. Petersburg's intelligentsia--a cosmopolitan stratum
of Russian society which had maintained contact with the
new ideas of western Europe.

During their years as students at the University of
St. Petersburg, the Pickwickians continued together and
further pursued their enthusiasms. Slowly forming in the
minds of the young members was the sense of a two-fold mission: Russia must break her isolation from the west and re-
vitalize her traditions with modernism; and, the artistic

heritage of Russia must be presented to the west. The one member of the group who gradually assumed leadership and galvanized the others into action was Diaghilev.

By 1898 the Nevsky Pickwickians had expanded the function of their society, under the direction of Diaghilev, into an exhibiting organization and into an arts periodical, whose name, The World of Art, now identified the group as a whole, which had grown to include about a dozen men. Exhibitions were held to expose new trends in painting and to acquaint Russians with their own art historical heritage. But it fell to the magazine, The World of Art, to reveal to subscribers a fuller picture of the European avant-garde. Works of the French Impressionists and Post-Impressionists and of the English and German schools were discussed and illustrated in the pages of the periodical. Articles were additionally published on literature, music, architecture, and interior design, with critiques on the works of Baudelaire, Verlaine, Mallarmé, Scriabin, and Wagner, and on the Art Nouveau movement. Benois considered the men of The World of Art as forming

> a kind of community which lived its own life, with its own peculiar interests and problems and which tried in a number of ways to influence society and to inspire in it a desirable attitude to art--art understood in its broadest sense, that is to say including literature and music.[8]

By 1904, with the last issue of The World of Art released and with the satisfaction that he and his friends had successfully introduced modern art to Russia, Diaghilev turned to other enterprises. Taking into account the aims of The

World of Art and the intellectual milieu in which its members were active during the 1890's, it is no surprise that
Diaghilev should have been led to the theater. Theater was
the perfect vehicle for bringing several arts together in
one public event.

The World of Art in 1900 had managed to become involved with the official theater world in St. Petersburg.
Although Diaghilev was appointed to a post within the Imperial
Theater Administration, he soon fell out of favor and was
barred from any further activity. Benois, however, continued
to work successfully within the Imperial Theater and collaborated
with Michel Fokine and Nijinsky on a ballet, a work which
was the product of The World of Art, but which was not over-
seen by Diaghilev. But Diaghilev, thinking of how he might
publicize Russian art in the west, began to promote a season
of Russian ballet and opera in Paris. However, before this
was accomplished, he had already begun to take Russia to
Paris.

Two and a half years before the Ballets Russes made
its debut in Paris, Diaghilev arranged a Russian art section
for the Salon d'Automne of 1906. The result was a unique
opportunity for the public to see a broad spectrum of Russian
painting, which ranged from medieval icons to the recent
experiments of Gontcharova and Larionov. As an indication
of Diaghilev's inherent sense of dramatic presentation--a
sense which informed all of the productions of the Ballets
Russes--Léon Bakst was enlisted to create a properly Russian
setting for the paintings; the walls and rooms of the Grand

Palais given to Diaghilev for his exhibit were papered and transformed into gardens. During the 1907 fall season, Diaghilev coordinated a schedule of six concerts introducing the works of recent Russian composers. Not until these concerts had the music of the Russian Five and Tchaikowsky been heard in the west. Finally, in 1908 Diaghilev sponsored a production of Moussorgsky's Boris Godunov.

Diaghilev and the Ballets Russes

The Paris Opera in the later nineteenth century and during the early years of the twentieth century was the center of an impoverished ballet in western Europe. After the flowering of the great Romantic ballets in Europe during the 1830's, the dance had declined into a second-rate entertainment. With the exception of a few full-length productions, ballets were now fashionable divertissements for the elite Jockey Club and often only brief inserts between the acts of an evening's opera.[9] The Romantic ballet, however, if moribund in Europe during the later nineteenth century, had been flourishing at the Maryinsky Imperial Theater in St. Petersburg. Marius Petipa, a French dancer, arrived in St. Petersburg in 1847 to become dance master of the Imperial Ballet. During his tenure as artistic director from 1870 to 1905, Petipa developed and sustained a remarkably vital ballet tradition. Swan Lake, Sleeping Beauty, and The Nutcracker, staples of contemporary ballet companies, were the inspired creations of Petipa in collaboration with Tchaikowsky and Ivanov. Surprisingly, western Europe knew nothing of these developments.

The first evenings and matinees of the Ballets Russes
in Paris were not samplers of the repertory of the Czar's
Imperial Ballet. Diaghilev did import a group of dancers
from the St. Petersburg and Moscow theaters, but Ballets Russes
was not exactly the Russian Ballet proper. With the exception
of one ballet the repertory of the Ballets Russes was created
expressly for western European audiences; it was never seen
in Russia.[10] Still, by virtue of the sheer technical virtuosity of its dancers and by the aesthetic seriousness it
accorded its activities, the company of the Ballets Russes
proudly claimed its Russian heritage. The debut of the
Ballets Russes in 1909, taking place in a season shared with
Russian opera, was a tumultuous success. The combined effect
of superb dancing, dazzlingly colorful sets, and the melodic
exoticism of the musical scores astounded Parisian audiences.
The seeds were planted for a Russian craze. Ballets Russes
became the rage. In the history of popular French taste,
things Spanish and Japanese were about to be replaced with
things Russian. In her memoirs, Lydia Sokolova, a dancer in
the original Ballets Russes, recalls that what thrilled the
first audiences was not that they danced ballet, but that
they were so Russian.[11] The public acclaim which met the
first and subsequent seasons of Ballets Russes encouraged
Diaghilev to continue his sponsorship for twenty years. The
exportation of Russian arts to the west, integrated for
breathtaking effect in the form of ballet theater, made the
Ballets Russes the most satisfying expression of The World

of Art. Diaghilev also managed to see to the emergence of ballet as a legitimate category of the arts, one ready to assume an identity squarely within the twentieth century.

What were the reforms headed by Diaghilev which made the early productions of the Ballets Russes so revolutionary in contrast to both European and Russian ballet? The most striking quality was the coordination of the various components of the spectacle: dancing, music, set, and costumes. The notion that the theatrical facets of a ballet production should be planned together and display relationships was an idea foreign to nineteenth-century ballet. The choreographer, the composer, and the scenic designer did not usually generate their ideas together. Rather, their individual contributions were brought together during the later stages of production. Diaghilev took the very opposite approach. A theme was chosen for a ballet. Appropriate music was selected or specifically commissioned. The composer or the conductor helped the choreographer set the choreography to the music. So that a decorative unity would be apparent in the mise en scène, the scenic designer was responsible for both the set and the costumes. The collaborators on any one production worked intimately with one another, and often their roles tended to blur. For example, the choreographer and the composer could accept suggestions from each other, or the choreographer might pull body gestures from the style used by the scenic designer. All components of the production were corralled to express the spirit of the narrative or theme. Ballets were created in committee.

Diaghilev and his first balletmaster, Michel Fokine, established the shorter ballet. Until the advent of the Ballets Russes, a complete ballet was an evening's affair, traditionally requiring three acts to move through the narrative. Instead of a full-length ballet, a typical program of the Ballets Russes presented three one-act ballets.[12] Diaghilev set the precedent for the modern, one-act dramatic, comic, and abstract ballet. Lincoln Kirstein suggests that Diaghilev, in his choice of the one-act ballet, was bowing to French tastes and the predilection for shorter theatrical works, specifically, vaudeville acts and the nineteenth-century ballet divertissement.[13]

Michel Fokine shared Diaghilev's view that ballet theater should be an unbroken alliance between dancing, music, and painting. And he was directly responsible for the choreographic reforms and the modification of the strictures of the classical danse d'école. Part of Fokine's rethinking of conventional ballet movement was influenced by Isadora Duncan, who traveled to St. Petersburg in 1905.[14] Duncan based her new dance on natural movement. She felt that the orthodox ballet costume of tutu, tights, and toe-shoes was too confining. Barefoot, hair loosened, and wearing chiffon tunics, she brought a refreshing spontaneity to theatrical dancing. Music was chosen for her dances not because it conformed to "ballet music," but because it was sufficiently expressive. Fokine's incorporation of Duncan's reforms into the Ballets Russes is confirmed in a letter Fokine wrote to the London Times in 1914.[15] The choreographer, Fokine stated,

was "not to form combinations of ready-made and established
dance-steps, but to create in each case a new form corresponding
to the subject." Fokine went on to say that the new ballet
"in contradistinction to the older ballet...does not demand
'ballet music' of the composer as an accompaniment to dancing;
it accepts music of every kind, provided only that it is good
and expressive." Fokine also agreed that dance costume should,
when warranted by the subject matter, dismiss traditional
dress. Another practice of Fokine in the Ballets Russes, one
which appeared to western European audiences to be a reform
but which was actually a standard element of the Russian
tradition, was the preeminence given to the male dancer, who
had suffered near extinction on the late nineteenth-century
French stage. As electrifying for the Parisian as any other
aspect of the Ballets Russes was the athletic virtuosity of
Fokine on stage, as well as the passionate movement of the
one figure who embodied the mystique of the early seasons
of the Ballets Russes: Nijinsky.

The twenty-year phenomenon of the Ballets Russes in
Europe may be categorized stylistically and thematically in
a variety of ways. The most useful distinction is made between
the productions mounted before and after the outbreak of
World War I. The pre-war phase was the Russian period. It
was characterized by Russian and orientalizing themes, de-
cidedly romantic in their presentation. This was the period
of Fokine, Nijinsky, Pavlova, and Karsavina. For his <u>ballets
d'époque</u>, Fokine chose subject matter which ranged geo-
graphically from ancient Greece and the Middle East to India

and Russia. Although there were ballets which were western
in mood--Carnaval, Papillons, and Jeux--twenty-three of the
thirty-six ballets introduced between 1909 and 1917 drew
their inspiration from the east. Eleven of the eastern ballets
took Russian themes.

For the ballets of the pre-war Russian period, Diaghilev engaged the talents of nine scenic designers who had
been involved with The World of Art in St. Petersburg.[16]
The most celebrated artist, and the one whose designs were
the visual signature of the early Ballets Russes productions,
was Léon Bakst. Bakst's drop cloth for the set of Schéhérazade (Fig. 6) and his costume sketch for the ballet Narcisse
(Fig. 7) exemplify the magical and richly flamboyant quality
of this first phase of Ballets Russes history. The visual
style of these ballets was a combination of the linear ex-
cesses of Art Nouveau and the saturated palette of Fauvism,
a brocaded world of Moreau and Wilde. Or as Erik Satie would
have innocently said, "An art with lots of sauce."[17]

Although a theoretical violation of Diaghilev's concept of total theater, the visual splendour of the early
Ballets Russes outweighed in popular appeal other components
of the spectacle. The heavy orientalism of this period caught
the fancy of Parisian couturiers; fashionable women began
to costume themselves in turbans, peacock feathers, and yards
of silk brocades. The spill of bright colors over the exotic
figures on the stage encouraged one critic for Le Temps to
call the Ballets Russes "a magic lantern for big children."[18]
The public fury over Petrouschka, Le Sacre du Printemps, and

Jeux was elicited not by the sets and costumes, which the audiences adored, but by the music and the choreography.[19]

The second phase of the Ballets Russes, which began during the last year of the war and extended to 1929, was the French period, a sequence of urbane and experimental productions intimately affiliated with the artists of the School of Paris. During the interruption of World War I, Diaghilev, in seclusion with friends in Switzerland, turned his thoughts from opulent spectacle to the formulation of a new style of ballet, which was to be invigorated with modern art. In this second period, Diaghilev would incorporate into a series of ballets every new "ism" available: Cubism, Dadaism, Surrealism, and Constructivism. The first authentic statement of Diaghilev's new artistic strategy was the ballet Parade, which was presented during the late spring of 1917.

The French period broke into two moods. The first, which marked the seasons until 1926, was the result of Diaghilev's efforts to establish a new era of modern realism in ballet. Productions such as Les Biches, Le Train bleu, and Les Matelots were light, topical, and witty. Towards the end of the 20's, Diaghilev apparently sensed that it was time to cut short the satire and the ballets of manners.[20] The last ballets Diaghilev commissioned, represented in Balanchine's choreographic settings for La Chatte, Apollon Musagète, and Le Fils prodigue reflected in their restraint and seriousness a period trend of the entre-deux-guerres broadly identified as neoclassicism.

The Ballets Russes and Symbolism

Dance criticism repeatedly observes that the Diaghilev revolution lay in the ideal integration of first-rate dance, music, and scenic design. It asserts that the history of modern ballet issued from the Ballets Russes. According to Lincoln Kirstein, the reforms of Diaghilev were more momentous in their impact on the development of the dance than the ballet de cour, the ballet d'action, and the ballet romantique.[21] In some respects, this is a puzzling statement because trends after 1929 pointed in the direction of an increasingly abstract ballet, in which the notion of ballet as a collective whole was superceded by a concept of pure dance which dominated productions. Total ballet theater was revived during the 1960's by Robert Joffrey and Maurice Béjart, an indicator of renewed interest in multi-media performance. But the productions of these men, popularly received by the public, were slighted by the dance world, in part because the works were considered too rich and offered devices which some felt competed too aggressively with the choreography. And so, if the Ballets Russes did initiate a vital period of comtemporary ballet by according the dance a new seriousness and self-esteem, its very theatrical essence does not speak for modern ballet as a whole. For the purpose of establishing the theatrical context in which Parade was conceived, it is more informative to see the Ballets Russes as a unique manifestation of later nineteenth-century aesthetic theory and theater reform than to perceive Diaghilev's productions posed only to the future.

Who formulated the idea that the Ballets Russes would be total dance theater? It is difficult to attribute precise authorship within the circle of The World of Art. Diaghilev, Bakst, Benois, and Fokine must have worked it out in lengthy discussions in St. Petersburg. But the following remarks of Diaghilev indicate his concern to be credited with its discovery and his active insistence on coordinating productions:

> The more I thought of that problem of the composition of ballet the more plainly I understood that perfect ballet can only be created by the very closest fusion of three elements--dancing, painting, and music. When I mount a ballet, I always keep these three elements in mind. That is why almost daily I go into the artists' studios, watch their work and the active execution of the costumes, examine the scores and listen to the orchestra with close attention, and then visit the practice rooms where all the dancers practice and rehearse daily.[22]

Diaghilev's ideas on the theater are directly traceable to French Symbolism, a set of motivating attitudes for writers, artists, and composers, which originated in the early 1880's in conversations between Mallarmé and a circle of young writers. New ideas of what art should be, put forward within a literary milieu, significantly inflected several decades of advanced painting, literature, theater, and music. One tenet of the new art was the insistence, in reaction against realist modes, that the artist have the right to explore the inner life. Not through a literal description of the world but through allusion and suggestiveness, the arts could potentially uncover an ideal reality which lay behind appearances. The theory of the correspondences of the senses and the arts, one posited earlier by Baudelaire, was critical to Symbolist thought. The very possibility of metaphor, which allowed one event to be experienced in terms of another, hinted at an interconnectedness of things that suggested an invisible unity. Man's perception of the world had become fragmented and his senses blunted. It was the responsibility of the arts to provide a return to a purer and originally undifferentiated reality. This might be accomplished within one art form: in poetry, for example, through multi-evocative metaphor; in painting by means of arbitrary pictorial equivalents of the artist's feelings before nature. The analogies of experience, be they made through everyday mundane sensations of the world or elevated in art through metaphor, was the pivotal idea of Symbolism. Angelo Bertocci's concise definition of an exceedingly complex moment in the history of ideas intelligently articulates the issue. Symbolism was the aspiration

> toward a thoroughgoing poetic unity conceived in terms of the metaphor of "color"...in a philosophical context which permits interflow and interglow of meanings...between areas of experience formerly maintained distinct.[23]

In Symbolist thought, an emphasis was placed on the reciprocal spiritual and aesthetic influences in the arts. If man's reintegrated senses might allow for a purer perception of nature's unity, the theoretical correspondence of the various arts to each of man's senses implied that a synthesis of the arts might reveal that same wholeness of a lost spiritual reality. Symbolist aims might be achieved within one art form, but because of its ability to deal effectively with several art forms simultaneously, the theater

was the true Symbolist platform. The two men who responded
to Symbolism and took western theater in a completely new
direction were Adolphe Appia and Edward Gordon Craig.

Adolphe Appia, profoundly influenced by Richard Wagner's
Gesamtkunstwerk, enhanced the theatrical unity of the music-
drama when he discerned and implemented the expressive potential of the visual elements of production which Wagner had
neglected. Illusionistic sets and fixed lighting were dis-
carded and replaced by geometric and monochromatic platforms
and variable lighting patterns. The musical design of a
work established the manner in which component elements were
to be integrated. Appia was concerned with musical drama
not with traditional dramatic theater and its emphasis on
the spoken word. "The art of staging can be an art only
if it derives from music," Appia observed.[24] Musical dyna-
mics could be used to structure the movements of the actors,
and Appia searched for a new style of acting. In close
collaboration with Jacques Dalcroze, the originator of
Eurhythmics--a rhythmically oriented system of movement--
Appia developed a manner of stage movement which could be
integrated with the music for any particular work. The Appia-
Dalcroze production of Orpheus and Eurydice in 1913, the
climax of Appia's efforts, took place in the same year that
Dalcroze, indirectly through Marie Lambert, helped Fokine
and Nijinsky map out their angular and disjointed choreography
for the Ballets Russes' Le Sacre du Printemps.

Gordon Craig, inspired by the ideas of Appia, promoted
his concepts from Florence during the early years of the new

century. In <u>The Art of the Theatre</u> (1905), Craig, like Appia, insisted upon the pivotal role played by the director. He alone must unify and imaginatively coordinate movement, scenic design, and costume to reveal the inner soul of the play. In this manner, Symbolism was at the heart of Craig's theories. Further, the human actor's traditional imitation of everyday behavior would be replaced by symbolic gesture. In his early theories, Craig called for the <u>Übermarionette</u> to perform the former role of the human actor.[25] The stage movements of the mechanical puppet could be far more strictly controlled than the vagaries of human gesture and gait. The integral task of music did not assume the importance it did in the productions of Appia, but both Craig and Appia strove for an anti-natural stage movement, which was to be a primary source of theatrical expression.

In terms of traditional theater practice, the heresy committed by Craig and Appia was their insistence upon the sovereign control of the director and upon his prerogative to order all elements of a production in which the historically all-powerful script was now but one aspect of a larger whole. All elements of production were subordinated to the joint revelation of what the director considered to be the soul of the play. The Symbolist Theater of Maeterlinck and others was thought far too literarily structured by Appia and Craig, who observed their own theatrical efforts to be, more pointedly, Total Theater.

Such, very sketchily, was the theoretical framework in which the Ballets Russes evolved. The aesthetic orientations of the Symbolists, Craig, and Appia constituted the intellectual milieu in which Diaghilev and members of The World of Art developed their ballet reforms. Indeed, the conception of the Ballets Russes was thoroughly Symbolist.[26] Diaghilev saw himself as a director who must coordinate and oversee all aspects of production so as to create a successful composite work of art. Scenic design, costumes, music, and choreography were all pulled into an intimate relationship to convey a powerfully unified and sensuous effect in support of the theme of the ballet. The ultimate theatrical impact of the Ballets Russes was a spectacular non-verbal appeal to the emotions. The new one-act ballet was perfectly in tune with the suggestiveness promoted by the Symbolists; the aim of the shorter ballet was to evoke a mood rather than to develop a naturalistic narrative through three acts. It is puzzling that the relationship of the Ballets Russes to Symbolism and Total Theater has been ignored in the critical literature to date. Diaghilev's company, in these writings, appears historically to have been born sui generis as a bourgeois crowd-pleaser, removed from the serious aims of the fine arts. If Total Theater was the most complete Symbolist statement, then the popularity and vitality of the Ballets Russes made Diaghilev's productions exceedingly satisfying manifestations of Symbolism. And yet, Craig disliked Diaghilev's notion of a collective ballet theater. He regarded the ballets as too visually sumptuous and saw them as repositories for booty from the other arts.[27]

The negative criticism that the Ballets Russes re-

ceived from its very sources resulted, I believe, from the
Symbolist correlation of theater and religion. Mallarmé,
the major exponent of Symbolism, evinced a strong interest
in the theater. Wallace Fowlie states that: "The experience of religion for Mallarmé seems to have been completely
merged with that of art, and particularly joined with the
experience of the theater and of music."[28] Mallarmé held
the drama sacred and a potential source for communal religious experience in face of a depleted Christianity. The
theater offered its audience, or congregation, the opportunity for ecstasy and social catharsis--ancient goals of
the religious service. Mallarmé called the symphonic concert a religious service and contrasted the passive and mys-
tified audience with the orgiastic activity on stage.[29] The
unwillingness of Gordon Craig to support the Ballets Russes
may find its source in the historical and social status of
the dance in the west, best described by Maurice Béjart in
the following: "The dance's rejection by the medieval church
deprived it of its ancient ritual status and reduced it to
secular entertainments in the courts."[30] Fokine alluded to
an undesirable element of triviality in the dance's current
social status when he stated that he wished "to lead ballet
away from the narrow circle of balletomanes and its situation
as a court entertainment."[31] Danced movement was central to
the theories of Appia and Craig, but the associations of
ballet with secular and aristocratic entertainments demoted
the Ballets Russes to frivolous social divertissements, devoid of any high religious significance. Still, Mallarmé's

prescription for an orgiastic religious theater seems to have
been filled far more splendidly by the early ballets of the
Ballets Russes than by the stark and somber productions of
Appia and Craig.[32]

Symbolist ideals of a Total Theater were by no means
historically unique. Men of the Renaissance were intent upon
reviving a unity of the arts, which they felt had once existed
in antiquity.[33] What distinguished European nineteenth-
century and early twentieth-century Total Theater projects
was the emphasis placed on the revelation of a mysterious and
invisible reality and the attempts to make it visible through
the joint collaboration of scenic design, music, and the dance.
Music was the great unifier of effects, the one component
whose spirit the other arts were to reflect. Within the context of Symbolist theory, the importance put upon music derived from the purity of musical form. In the eyes of a
generation who saw the other arts subservient to descriptions
of the real world, music was closer to invisible truths, un-
encumbered as it was with mundane description. Music was
ideal poésie pure and a model for artists and writers who
wished their works to evoke rather than to document.

If the Ballets Russes were situated within a Symbolist
ethos, there was yet another historical precedent for the
form the productions of Diaghilev took. Michel Fokine,
Diaghilev's first balletmaster, was no mere passive imple-
menter of the impresario's ideas. Actively involved in the
productions of the Ballets Russes and well-versed in painting,
music, and literature, he was as insistent as the others upon

a unified ballet which gave equal attention to dance, decor, and music.[34] But Fokine, the ballet reformer, if responding to the aesthetic pressures of Symbolism, could also point with pride to another formative source outside the intellectual confines of fin-de-siècle Europe.

Within the history of European ballet, an art form whose development began in sixteenth-century France, the idea of a collective form in which the arts were equally represented has been an occasionally voiced ideal of what ballet should be. Fokine's reforms were inspired by Jean-Georges Noverre, the man who made ballet an independent spectacle of theatrical dancing by removing the hitherto conventional elements of declaimed or sung verse. Noverre's reforms, proclaimed during the early eighteenth century, urged the dismissal of plotless Rococo entertainments and the reorganization of ballet into a dramatic whole in which scenery, costumes, music, mime, and book would be effectively integrated. Noverre's concept of ballet theater, brought to fruition in his ballets d'action, was ignored in France until Fokine. And so, Fokine could claim that the model of contemporary theater reformers was of no mean significance and influence, but that what distinguished the enterprise of the Ballets Russes was its cutting back to and restoration of the original concept of ballet.

The above discussion of Diaghilev and the Ballets Russes has characterized the intellectual and aesthetic milieu in which Parade was generated, an environment rich in the exchange of ideas. Diaghilev's production of Parade appeared in 1917 to be radical and to herald a new period in ballet; but its mold was long in the making. <u>Parade</u> was a brilliant manifestation of Diaghilev's previous efforts to realize a total ballet theater. In pursuance of his ideal, Diaghilev reminded others of the difficulty of its achievement when he said that "This form of art does not admit of mediocrity."[35] The potential danger of the second-rate, however, was effectively combatted when Diaghilev, for the production of <u>Parade</u>, enlisted the talents of Jean Cocteau, Erik Satie, Pablo Picasso, and Leonide Massine.

CHAPTER II

JEAN COCTEAU AND THE "NOUVEAU THEATRE CONTEMPORAIN"

Lorsqu'une oeuvre semble en avance sur son
époque, c'est simplement que son époque est
en retard sur elle.

Jean Cocteau[1]

Cocteau's Scenario for "Parade"

To date, the majority of critical opinions on Parade
inadvertently leave the impression that Parade's authorship
should be attributed to Picasso and Satie. This critical
bias unfortunately shifts attention away from and often entirely neglects Parade's very maker, the young poet Jean
Cocteau, whose idea it was to create a circus ballet for the
Ballets Russes. Cocteau's role in the production of Parade
was unusual from the start. Only rarely did Diaghilev employ
the services of a separate scenarist. The theme of a ballet
was most often worked out by Diaghilev in conference with his
balletmaster and intimates. For the most part, the company's
repertory did not include ballets with elaborate scenarios.
Rather, the slenderest narratives were pretexts for highly
suggestive evocations of moods. The brevity of the story-
lines, however, did not preclude dramatic interest; the themes
chosen for the Ballets Russes were often exquisitely turned
conceits.[2]

33

The dominant information in a ballet production, of course, is its theatrical implementation, not the theme itself, which is usually little more than an excuse for kinetic, aural, and visual elaboration. A ballet's scenario cannot assume the importance of the script in traditional theater. This standard aspect of ballet helps explain why a ballet scenarist may be overlooked in criticism, especially if the scenario is as innocently deceptive of complications as Cocteau's Parade. But, the crucial problem in an evaluation of Cocteau's contribution arises from the fact that his responsibilities as ballet scenarist for Parade were originally expanded well beyond the writing of a synopsis. Cocteau chose his collaborators, wrote verbal and noise inserts to be used in performance, and was to oversee the production. Unfortunately, Cocteau's control over Parade was severely curtailed during the actual collaboration. Yet, Cocteau was always to be fiercely possessive of his ballet, and he indicated at every turn that he alone, in spite of the brilliant contributions by Picasso, Satie, and Massine, deserved the claim of authorship. After seeing the 1921 revival of Parade, André Gide made the following snide comment, which if jealously hostile nonetheless underscores Cocteau's concerns:

> Found Cocteau walking up and down in the wings, older, tense, and uneasy. He is perfectly aware that the sets and costumes are by Picasso, and that the music is by Satie, but he wonders whether Picasso and Satie aren't by him.[3]

To seek an elucidation in Cocteau's own writings of the role he played in the collaboration can be exasperating.

Cocteau's lifetime self-aggrandizement resulted in autobiographical commentaries which are sprinkled with contradictory statements and a string of suspicious corrections and
revisions that counter earlier and later observations. Des-
perate guardian of his reputation, Cocteau incarnated his
fundamental insecurity in the theme of Parade.

The world of Cocteau's ballet was the forain or
traveling fair, which reached its apogee in France during
the nineteenth and early twentieth centuries.[4] It was anx-
iously awaited each year by French towns and might include
a market fair or the always popular circus. An integral
part, however, of every forain was the côté 'aller' des
attractions, which consisted of a series of baraques--tempo-
rary wooden shanties--erected along each side of a city street
(Figs. 8 and 9). Here were situated the théâtres, attractions,
and jeux--theaters, lotteries, shooting galleries, demonstrations, and amusements. Immediately alongside the facade of
the théâtre was an elevated platform or parade, which became
identified in name with a short theatrical act performed upon
it by the company. Not to be confused with the American parade
or circus procession, the French parade was performed at the
entrances of the théâtres forains to attract a crowd inside.
A come-on for the public, the parade was comprised of snippets
of comic acts to be later seen in their entirety within the
theater (Fig. 10).

The subject matter developed by Cocteau in his ballet
scenario and chosen for the title of the ballet was the parade.
The action is very simple. The setting is a Parisian boulevard

on a Sunday afternoon. In front of a little théâtre forain,
three abbreviated acts or numéros are performed in turn by a
Chinese Magician, a little American dancer, and an Acrobat.
Each preview is announced and ballyhooed by three managers.
But, much to the growing frustration of the shouting managers
the crowd outside somehow believes it is seeing the actual
show--not a preview--and refuses to enter the theater. Despite
the pleas and mounting hysteria of managers and performers,
the momentarily gathered crowd drifts away from the little
sideshow and leaves the pathetic company, which has collapsed
in anguish.

For the understanding of any topical allusion in a
work of art, historical context is necessary, especially for
later audiences upon whom the original associations may be
lost. Cocteau's Parade was accurately drawn from contemporary
experience, and this fact is exceedingly important when
ferreting out the nuances of the dramatic situation. Of
the five categories of théâtre forain, Cocteau chose the
Théâtre de Magie-Variété-Music-Hall for his scenario.[5] The
numéros he included were well known, and the importance assigned
to the Chinese Magician by Cocteau is explained by the fact
that the magic act was the main attraction on the programs
of the variety theaters. The number of acts performed in
Cocteau's Parade also indicates that his little company's
enterprise was extremely modest in comparison to the more
established théâtres forains, which often presented as many
as ten acts. Finally, and significantly, Cocteau's Parade
is Parisian, not en province. A common sight in Paris during

the winter months were the baraques lined up along the grands
boulevards. These théâtres forains were often individually
owned and were not affiliated with the permanently housed
cirques stables of Paris: le Cirque d'hiver, le Cirque
Médrano, and le nouveau Cirque. And yet, the théâtres forains
and the cirques stables together comprised that circus milieu
which was so important in the imaginations of the Parisian
vanguard during the early twentieth century.

The subject matter of Cocteau's ballet, the théâtre
forain, was a familiar one in nineteenth and early twentieth-
century French art (Fig. 11). The identification of the
socially estranged individual with the setting and characters
of the traveling fair traces its pictorial beginnings to
the wistful airs of Watteau's displaced comedians and fully
establishes itself in the art of Baudelaire, Flaubert, Degas,
Rimbaud, Verlaine, Seurat, Toulouse-Lautrec, Rouault, and
Picasso. The circus environment held a certain fascination
for both the Realist, who documented it as a part of contemporary life about him, and for the Symbolist, who discovered
in it metaphors for the human condition ranging from the
monstrous to the defeated. Cocteau's association of mystery
and fantasy with the théâtre forain was also a popular one.
This attitude may account for the barbaric qualities of
Rimbaud's Parade and for Seurat's Parade, whose eerie and
disturbing mood should be viewed as intentionally instilled
by the artist rather than as inadvertent.

Picasso's concern for the worlds of the circus and
traveling fair during his Rose Period was never directed to

actual performance. ⅄ The lower class acrobats--the Saltimbanques--
which Picasso portrayed are removed from the stage and arena
and are shown either behind the scenes or in undifferentiated
settings.[6] The dominant moods are apartness and resignation.
Cocteau may have desired Picasso's contribution because of
the sensationalism his presence and that of Cubism would
cause, but a more insightful examination of Cocteau's choice
suggests the spiritual affinity between the poet's theme
and the earlier statements of the painter. In the same manner
that Picasso chose the Saltimbanques--the "failures of the
profession"[7]--for an added dimension of pathos, Cocteau chose
the fragile identity of a small théâtre forain, apparently
separated from a collective fair setting and functioning
alone.

Such was the deceptively simple theme which Cocteau
submitted to Diaghilev for balletic elaboration in 1916. By
this time, Cocteau had been affiliated with the Ballets
Russes for six years. A charming young man who delighted
others with his quick wit, Cocteau was brought into the
Diaghilev entourage in 1910 and became active within the
company.[8] He designed posters for the Ballets Russes (Fig.
12), and in 1912 he wrote the scenario for the subsequently
poorly received Le Dieu bleu. The scenario for Parade was
actually Cocteau's third proposal for a theater piece à la
cirque. The first project, initiated in 1914 for Ballets
Russes, held the promise of a score from Stravinsky. Never
produced, this ballet, entitled David, contained the beginnings
of Parade, clearly identifiable in a later description by

the poet.

> On stage, in front of a booth at a fair, an acrobat
> would be doing a come-on for DAVID, a spectacle in-
> tended to be given inside the booth. A clown, who
> is later transformed into a box (theatrical pastiche
> of the phonograph played at fairs--modern form of
> the ancient mask), was to celebrate David's exploits
> through a loudspeaker and urge the public to enter the
> booth and see the show. In a way it was the first
> sketch for PARADE, but unnecessarily complicated by
> biblical references and a text.[9]

The other abortive project which Cocteau headed was

an adaptation of A Midsummer Night's Dream for performance

within a circus setting, specifically the Cirque Médrano in

in Paris. The Cubist painter Albert Gleizes was asked to

create the sets and costumes, and Erik Satie was invited to

provide the music. Both the plans for this production and

for David indicated a specific theatrical direction Cocteau

was following: the development of dramatic themes within

the lighter forms of popular entertainment. The idea for

Parade was set shortly after plans for Dream were abandoned

in the late fall of 1915. By early May 1916, during a leave

from the War Front, Cocteau left the first notes for Parade

with Satie in Paris. With the approval of Diaghilev, Cocteau

chose the two men he wanted to costume and to score his

ballet: Pablo Picasso and Erik Satie.

A ballet scenario is usually a simple synopsis of

the narrative, often included in programs to clarify the

action for the audience. Cocteau's work as the scenarist

for Parade, however, was considerably more ambitious than

thinking up an idea and realizing it in a few paragraphs.

The collected literary evidence of Cocteau's contribution,

which may be loosely termed a libretto, consists of two

sketchbooks, and assorted loose pages, which reveal character descriptions, verbal segments, choreographic indications, drawings, and aphorisms on art.[10] The major primary source for an evaluation of Cocteau's role in Parade is the Cahier romain, a sketchbook presented to Cocteau by Massine and partially filled with notes and drawings during rehearsals for Parade in Rome in the spring of 1917. Reproduced here in its entirety for the first time, the Cahier romain will be frequently referred to in this chapter and during the remainder of the dissertation (Figs. 82-115).[11]

Cocteau's original implementation of his theme and many of the additional suggestions made during rehearsals were eventually dismissed by the other collaborators and Diaghilev. Had they been used, Parade would have been a very different theatrical event. If the distinction is lightly drawn, Cocteau's original Parade would have been more a theater piece and less a ballet. Of course, the finished version of Parade must be the basis for the interpretive arguments advanced in this dissertation, but Cocteau's original proposals may, like synopia or preliminary sketches, enrich or even direct our responses to the final product.

In addition to providing the storyline for Parade, Cocteau intended the ballet to have a verbal dimension. Using the idea of a megaphone from his ballet David, Cocteau planned a spoken monologue to describe the various acts and to hint at the personalities of the performers. The two dancing managers of the final ballet did not exist in this first version, only a disembodied voice "singing a typical

phrase, gathering the perspectives of the character, opening
a porthole on a dream."[12] Another plan was to have two voices--
a young boy's soprano and a contralto--singing the character
descriptions. A musical libretto for the duet was written
and sent to Satie, but later abandoned. The megaphone, "an
amplifying orifice, theatrical imitation of the circus gramo-
phone, antique mask in the modern style,"[13] was probably to
be placed directly on the stage, much in the same way that
the two boxes and large victrola horns flanked the stage for
the production of Cocteau's Les Mariés de la tour Eiffel in
1921. Their function was undoubtedly similar to the one
envisioned for Parade. Cocteau's character descriptions
voiced by the megaphone were comparable to the ballyhoo
shouted through the megaphones of actual fair hawkers. But
unlike their real-life counterparts, Cocteau's verbal résumés
were far more bizarre and fantastic and were meant "to expand"
the personalities of the performers. The descriptions were
catalogues of free-associations the poet made with each
character.

Before returning to ambulance duty on the War Front
in May 1916, Cocteau left Satie a sheaf of notes with the
original megaphone monologues to help the composer imagine
the characters while he wrote the score. The character résumé
for the Little American Girl is perhaps the most remarkable.
An act like that of the Little American Girl (La Fille
américaine)--a combination of dancing and pantomime--was
frequently seen at the théâtre forain. One of the more
prestigious théâtres de variété in 1904 closed its program

with an audience favorite: Bib et Bob--la très amusante
Pantomime américaine.[14] The character outline for the Little
American Girl listed a series of images which wonderfully
evoked a special setting: The United States seen through
the eyes of a Frenchman.

> ...THE NEW YORK HERALD--dynamos--airplanes...palatial
> cinemas--the sheriff's daughter...the silence of
> stampedes...the telegraph operator from Los Angeles
> who marries the detective at the end...beautiful
> Madame Astor--the declarations of President Wilson...
> huge automobiles of enamel and nickel--Pullman cars
> which cross the virgin forests...Nick Carter--Helen
> Boodge--the Hudson and its docks...my room on the
> seventeenth floor...(See Appendix 1)

The America Cocteau saw was one gleaned from the early
American cinema. In fact, the Little American Girl, according
to Massine in conversation with this writer, was based upon
Mary Pickford.[15] During World War One, the European film
industry virtually collapsed, and the American movies were
the only films available to the French. The favorite stars
of Cocteau were Chaplin and Pickford. Apparently, the Little
American Girl is a direct allusion to "America's Sweetheart."

Frederick Brown, Cocteau's least affectionate biographer, complains that the lines of the résumés--later to
survive partially in Cocteau's collection of poems, le Cap
de Bonne Espérance--plagiaristically derived their form from
Mallarmé and Apollinaire.[16] The actual source, inventively
made fresh, was Walt Whitman and his cataloguing of images
in The Leaves of Grass.[17] After a reading of Cocteau's lines
for the Little American Girl, she can never again be quite
as one-dimensional. Her character is, indeed, "expanded."
Cocteau was infatuated with America and embodied his affection

in the Little American Girl:

> The United States evokes a girl more interested in
> her health than in her beauty. She swims, boxes,
> dances, leaps onto moving trains--all without know-
> ing that she is beautiful. It is we who admire her
> face, on the screen--enormous, like the face of a
> goddess.[18]

Cocteau's profile of the Little American Girl indicated

an astute and popular awareness of a romanticized and mythical

United States. The fascination of the French for America,

first manifested in the pantomimes and demonstrations of the

cakewalk performed in the théâtres forains, had its beginnings

on the legitimate stage in the ballet Parade. One member

of the Ballets Russes' corps de ballet fondly recalls that

"Parade discovered America."[19] Caricatured in several draw-

ings in the Cahier romain, Marie Shabelska was originally

chosen to dance the Little American Girl (Figs. 113 and 114).[20]

In a letter from Rome, Cocteau raved about the dancer assigned

to radiate things American: "You will love my little Sha-

belska, who dances the American Girl and looks like Buster

Brown's dog."[21]

During rehearsals for Parade in Rome, Cocteau's con-

cept of the invisible speaking manager was transformed by

Picasso into three dancing managers on stage, who would

ferociously advertise the three acts. Cocteau met the change

in his scenario by placing three actors in the orchestra pit

who would stridently scream out their come-ons and character

descriptions of each act. From several pages of possible

lines for the managers in the Cahier romain, e.g.,

> Enter...the most beautiful spectacle in the world.
> Enter...the most beautiful theater in the world.
> Enter...the most beautiful stage in the world.
> Enter...the most beautiful footlights in the world.
> (Figs. 110-111),[22]

a page of script emerged which indicated three simultaneous, almost contrapuntal, speeches for the managers. These come-ons made extraordinary offers to the potential audience of the _théâtre forain_:

> If you never want to be sick,
> If you want to be all powerful,
> If you want to have a beautiful chest,
> If you want to be loved (Fig. 127).[23]

Ultimately, all of Cocteau's suggestions for a spoken or sung element in the ballet were overridden by the objections of Picasso and Satie, who felt that the literary aspect would interfere with the music, choreography, and decor. Cocteau's plans for an aural enhancement of his characters were reduced in the end to a series of recommended sound effects placed in Satie's score: sirens, typewriters, trains, aeroplanes, dynamos, gun shots, lottery wheel, klaxon.[24] Even then these sounds were, for the most part, suppressed by the other collaborators for the first performance of _Parade_, although they were somewhat restored for the 1921 Paris revival. Cocteau was always to feel that Satie's score should have served as a musical base for suggestive noises and patter. Satie could only innocently observe that

> I only composed a background to throw into relief
> the noises which the playwright considered indis-
> pensable to the surrounding of each character with
> his own atmosphere.[25]

With the removal, however, of most of the sound effects, Cocteau bemoaned the fact that _Parade_ "was performed incomplete and without its crowning piece."[26]

An extremely important role Cocteau played in the shaping of Parade was his close collaboration with the young Massine in the setting of the choreography. Massine and Cocteau decided that a strong element of pantomime was called for by the subject matter of the parade. Conventional balletic movement alone could not accommodate the many actions demanded by the Chinese Magician, the Little American Girl, and the Acrobat if they were to suggest their separate circus stereotypes.

The needed movements would be derived from a French setting--the théâtre forain--which was a new experience for the young Russian, Massine.[27] So, Cocteau contributed dance outlines and demonstrated certain movements which were used as a basis for Massine's choreography. Cocteau later wrote that his "...role was to invent realistic gestures, to exaggerate and order them, and thanks to the science of Leonide Massine, to elevate them to the level of the dance."[28]

An example of Cocteau's choreographic role was his outline for the Chinese Magician (Fig. 93). The nine-part sequence included bows, gestures with an oriental fan, blowing fire from his mouth, and the egg-swallowing trick.[29] In the Cahier romain (Fig. 95), Cocteau paradoxically counseled Massine: "My dear Massine, you will never be tacky, so take tackiness as your point of departure. Long live tackiness!"[30] The vulgarity Cocteau requested was bold, non-balletic, everyday movement which because of Massine's theatrical stylization could never be in bad taste.

The most pointed moment of collaboration between poet and dancer occurred in the Little American Girl's <u>Steamboat Ragtime</u>, for which Massine concocted a balletic pantomime frantically intercut with the following stage directions of Cocteau:

> ...riding a horse, catching a train, cranking up and driving a Model T Ford, peddling a bicycle, swimming, driving away a robber at gunpoint, playing cowboys and indians, snapping the shutter of her new Kodak, doing a "Charlie Chaplin," getting sea-sick aboard a transatlantic luxury liner, almost drowning, and finally relaxing at the seashore.[31]

Although Cocteau's part in the choreography of <u>Parade</u> was apparent and acknowledged by Massine, his sound segments barely survived, notwithstanding the valiant efforts he made to incorporate them within the production. However, the idea and conceit for <u>Parade</u> was inarguably Cocteau's. The sound effects which did remain in the score added a convincing note of fantasy in the production. And, not to dismiss in any way the mastery of <u>Parade's</u> implementation in dance, music, and design, the expressive armature of the ballet was the poignancy of Cocteau's sad theme.

The "Nouveau Théâtre Contemporain"

Although Cocteau's ostensible purpose behind <u>Parade</u> was the creation of a new ballet for the Ballets Russes, his more serious intent was nothing less than a renovation of the current French stage and the creation of a <u>nouveau théâtre contemporain</u>. With the glaring exception of Jarry's <u>Ubu Roi</u> (1896), French theater had been a conservative institution for over two decades. French tastes in 1916 still preferred the elaborately plotted narratives and highly realistic mise

en scène first introduced in the productions of Antoine's
Théâtre Libre in 1887. Cocteau reacted against the prevailing
naturalistic theater, whose intent was literally to duplicate
natural environments on stage and whose aesthetic marked the
apogee of the theater conceived as an illusion of the real
world (Fig. 13). The impact of Craig and Appia had scarcely
been felt in France during the early century. As an indication of the failure of modernism to inform legitimate
theater, Feydeau and Rostand were the popular playwrights
during World War I. In place of a Theater of Naturalism,
Cocteau wished to establish a Theater of Effects, one which
would rely upon a synthesis of dance, music, and scenic
design to engender formalized worlds of fantasy and delight.
For Cocteau, traditional western theater was merely staged
literature; what Cocteau wanted was staged magic. Diaghilev's
Ballets Russes, whose theatrical aims were similar and established in practice, was the perfect vehicle for Cocteau's
ideas. In Cocteau's own words: "Ballet was a machine to
produce a poem."[32] The first manifestation of Cocteau's
ideas for a new theater was the ballet Parade. One year
after its premiere, Cocteau, still disappointed that many
of his ideas had been overlooked, insisted that his ballet
remained "a window opened onto what contemporary theater
ought to be."[33]

Parade and the subsequent productions of Le Boeuf
sur le toit (1920) and Les Mariés de la tour Eiffel (1921)
were Cocteau's first major essays for the theater--all realized
within the context of ballet theater. The text for Les Mariés

de la tour Eiffel was published in 1924 with a Préface
written by Cocteau.[34] The Préface, which Pierre Dubourg
considers the most intelligent manifesto written on modern
theater,[35] was a polemical essay that outlined Cocteau's
philosophy of the theater. The crucial distinction made in
the Préface was between a "poésie au théâtre" and a "poésie
du théâtre."[36] The staging and elevation of the written word,
at its best, was poetry in the theater. But Cocteau's secret
for a new theatrical form was to forget literature and to
exploit the visual resources of theater in order to bring
forth a poetry of the theater. Cocteau would have been
sympathetic with a recent writer who, in reference to the
manner in which the Classic Chinese Theater fused movement,
speech, scenery, sound, and music into a balanced unity,
stated that: "The play is not the thing--it is the playing
which is."[37] In fact, Cocteau seems to have been attempting
to enliven French theater with an aesthetic which governed
Asian theater. The theaters of the East were both realistic
and stylized. They were feasts for the eye as well as for
the mind in contrast to the nineteenth and twentieth-century
western theater which has remained oriented to issues, to
dramatic literature: a theater of listening.[38]

Cocteau's efforts to remake western theater within
the world of ballet mirrored the pivotal position accorded
the dance in eastern theater. Eastern theater encompasses
a variety of forms--the Chinese Opera Theater, the Japanese
Kabuki, the Balinese dramas--but the one shared element is
stylized movement. The Kabuki actor, for instance, bases

his movements, even the most realistic, on dance. [39] Cocteau indicated the pre-eminence he gave stylized movement, specifically balletic, when he stated: "As far as I am concerned, dancing is the language in which I would prefer to express myself, and my favorite theatrical formula."[40]

If Cocteau desired an experimental theatrical format, reminiscent of Eastern theater, he sought occidental and contemporary subject matter. In reaction against the veiled mists and exotic themes of Romantic and Symbolist art, Cocteau, like Daumier, insisted: "Il faut être de son temps." The Symbolist-early Modern sequence of attitudes recalls the earlier Romantic-Realist shift. The new art of the twentieth century should give image to the experiences peculiar to it. "Don't forget that the _parade_ takes place in the streets," Cocteau insisted in the _Cahier romain_ in regard to the necessity for observed, everyday detail (Fig. 90).[41] Cocteau acknowledged Apollinaire's imperative for an _Esprit Nouveau_, but he chose to fill Apollinaire's demand with a clever and original amalgam of Symbolist and Realist ideals. Subject matter was selected from everyday experience. Cocteau was an anti-romanticist when he stated: "Poetry must be looked for not in the exotic but in the familiar."[42] And so, in this respect, the poet was behaving like a proper Realist. However, what the poet sought in the everyday actually transgressed realist modes. Cocteau claimed in his _Préface_ to _Les Mariés_:

I'm the one who rejuvenates the commonplace, places it, presents it from a special angle so that it becomes young again. A generation of obscurities, of tired-

out realisms is not so easily disregarded. I know
that my text may appear too simple, too <u>clearly</u>
<u>written</u>, like children's alphabets. But really,
aren't we still all in school? Aren't we still
deciphering the primary symbols?[43]

Cocteau presented the familiar in such a way that

he would reveal the latent and unobserved magic it possessed.

His aesthetic creed was a symbolism of the mundane. But

how did he present the familiar so that mysterious worlds

might open up? Cocteau counseled the poet to pull "objects

and emotions out from under their veils and their mists,

to display them suddenly, so stark and so quickly that one

scarcely recognizes them."[44] This was accomplished by

exaggerating a situation and placing it in an absurd con-

text. "The spirit of buffoonery is the only one which author-

izes certain audacities," Cocteau claimed.[45] The audacities

lifted the object and situation into new realms of meaning.

"Let us be vulgar!"--the poet emblazoned across a page of

the <u>Cahier romain</u>--"Because it is impossible" (Fig. 96).[46]

This seemingly contradictory demand meant that vulgarity

offered in certain ways was actually not a negative quality

but rather allowed for additional and unexpected meanings.

<u>Parade</u> was a poem of ordinaries phrased less farcically than

<u>Le Boeuf</u> or <u>Les Mariés</u>, but articulated nonetheless in an

exaggerated manner. <u>Parade</u> has been hailed as one of the

first theater pieces offering a modern iconography of the

everyday. What has been consistently overlooked is that

the action in <u>Parade</u> is utterly absurd. No Parisian crowd

would ever mistake a <u>parade</u> for the actual show, especially

if the managers kept screaming that what it saw was a <u>parade</u>.

And yet, this conceit immediately removes the story from the ordinary.

The new theater envisioned by Cocteau was a combination of lightheartedness and the extraordinary. Wallace Fowlie, another American biographer of Cocteau, succinctly sums up his artistic attitude, which was first manifested in Parade and underlay much of the poet's oeuvre: "Art must be a collaboration between seriousness of themes and a lightness of form which is almost a disguise of the theme."[47] The last part of this statement is a perceptive insight into a certain artistic strategy. To embrace the decorative, the sentimental, the popular, the serious artist runs the risk of being superficial, or even worse, of being perceived as superficial when in fact his statement is more substantial. The stakes are high. The enterprise can topple. This particular dialectic between the unassuming and the serious underlies much of French art and is particularly acute in the works of Watteau, Manet, Matisse, Satie, Poulenc, Cocteau, and Truffaut. Cocteau hoped the public would discern his ironic formula. In a statement which appeared in the Excelsior the day after the premiere of Parade, Cocteau wished that audiences would see Parade "...as a work which conceals poetries under the wrappings of guignol."[48]

Claims are often made that Parade was the first modern ballet. Like most epithets this designation can be qualified by isolating what aspect of Parade one is talking about. Picasso's Cubist designs for the mise en scène have been responsible for most of the assertions that Parade was the

Demoiselles d'Avignon of the dance world. Parade's own
choreographer, Massine, considers Le Sacre du Printemps
to be the first modern ballet, choreographically speaking.[49]
The music by Satie, however appropriate, was conventional,
and it certainly was not as daring as Stravinsky's earlier
scores for the Ballets Russes. Had Cocteau's scenario been
inflected with his original ideas, Parade would have been
far more strikingly a new ballet form. Even in its final
version, Parade still holds the distinction, often ignored,
of being the first vanguard statement of the twentieth-century
French theater. The cryptic form, yet richly nuanced content,
of Parade's contemporary scenario was an innovation in both
ballet and theater history. But, the basic use per se of
contemporary subject matter, unquestionably not new to conventional theater, had been precedented in ballet theater
by the 1913 Ballets Russes' production of the Nijinsky-
Debussy Jeux, delightfully subtitled a "tennis-ballet" and
a "plastic vindication of the man of 1913."

From the above description of Cocteau's concept of
theater, it may be appreciated to what extent Cocteau's
reforms within the French theater reflected general European
trends. If Total Theater can be defined as "the intersection
of symbolic meaning with music and movement,"[50] then Cocteau's
choice of the Ballets Russes was an appropriate one for his
own goals and one which indicated sympathy with, and knowledge of, contemporary attempts to realize a Total Theater.
There is no doubt that Cocteau was fully exposed to the ideas
of Gordon Craig, the major proponent of Total Theater during

the early century, in theoretical writings and in discussion with men and women active in Ballets Russes.[51]

The one element, however, which distinguished Cocteau's efforts from European Total Theater as a whole, and it should be added from the Ballets Russes, was the emphasis placed upon the absurd and farcical. The examples confirming and directing Cocteau's own innate sense of wit and irony were Alfred Jarry, Guillaume Apollinaire, and Futurist Theater. Jarry's production of Ubu Roi at the Théâtre Nouveau in 1896 negated the theater as a vehicle for the precise reproduction of the details of everyday life and offered instead a theater of madness. The first men to continue the implications of Jarry's theater were Jean Cocteau and Guillaume Apollinaire.

The younger Cocteau had long been a faithful admirer of Apollinaire. The extent, however, to which Apollinaire influenced Cocteau has long been the issue of partisan debate. Apollinaire's Les Mammelles de Tirésias was a clipped and nonsensical play about the need in postwar France for a baby boom. Cubist sets and megaphones through which many speeches were shouted were used in performance. Although Cocteau saw the production of Parade make its debut four-and-a-half weeks before Apollinaire presented Les Mammelles at the Théâtre du Vieux Colombier, Apollinaire claimed that his play had been mostly written in 1903.[52] Apollinaire protested against the "realistic theater," saw the stage theater possibly replaced with a circus theater,[53] and yet, he designed Les Mammelles as a drame à thèse, or message play. Cocteau deemed the drame à thèse too conventional and literary for his new total theater.

The most interesting evidence of Apollinaire's and Cocteau's shared interests is found in a lecture Apollinaire gave at the Théâtre du Vieux Colombier in November of 1917, a talk outlining guidelines for an _Esprit Nouveau_ in poetry.[54] The essential demand was for the embracing of new, contemporary subject matters, a request which had already been met in French poetry in the works of Cendrars, Jacob, and Apollinaire himself. Three other prescriptions for the contemporary poet are more informative for the Cocteau-Apollinaire argument:

1. "...the poet of the future will direct large, multi-media works"
2. "The new spirit will cast off a heavy Germanic romanticism"
3. "...our modern poet [will] attempt to amplify the art of the dance and outline a choreography whose performers would not confine themselves to entrechats..."[55]

Cocteau may have been encouraged by Apollinaire's plea for a contemporary subject matter, but Apollinaire's three requests of the modern poet were made somewhat after the fact. Cocteau had splendidly realized them six months earlier in _Parade_.

What is extremely important in an understanding of Apollinaire's and Cocteau's formulations for a new theater was the example set by the Italian Futurists. Apollinaire, initially unenthusiastic about Futurism, was soon influenced by the ideals of Tommaso Marinetti's Futurist theater, and he indicated their impact upon his own ideas in his _Antitradition Futuriste_ (1913). The Futurist's theater program was itself heavily dependent on the reforms of Craig; but unlike the Total Theaters of Appia and Craig, the Futurists promoted

an anti-realist theater based upon theaters of variety,
music-halls, the circus, and café-concerts. Marinetti's
manifesto In Praise of Variety Theater, written in 1913 and
published in Craig's theater periodical The Mask, was certainly a source for Cocteau's ideas on theater. Through
the spontaneity, hilarity and absurdity of variety theater,
the Futurists hoped to achieve in their theater a new mar-
velousness. The Futurists' call for a Synthetic Theater in
1915 further emphasized non-verbal and visual modes of communi-
cation, which suggest Cocteau's later designation of a
poésie du théâtre.

Another Futurist aspect of Cocteau's anti-realist
theater was its direct appeal to the audience in emulation
of popular entertainments like music-hall or circus where
there existed no aesthetic "footlight" barrier between the
audience and the illusions of another world perpetrated on
the stage. But the spontaneity of the variety theater,
instilled so successfully into Parade, Le Boeuf sur le toit,
and Les Mariés de la tour Eiffel, did not indicate that
Cocteau wanted simply to elevate popular entertainments to
the level of serious art. Cocteau qualified his use of
the popular theater:

> When I say about certain circus and music-hall shows
> that I prefer them to everything that is done in the
> theater, this is not to say that I prefer them to
> everything that could be done in the theater.[56]

Cocteau's statement directly paralleled Futurist strategy,
whose concern was with the spirit and content of variety
theater forms--music-hall, cabaret, nightclubs, circuses--

not specific details. Aside from Futurist variety theater, an interesting, little known confirmation of the theater proposals of Apollinaire and Cocteau was the fact that the war years in Paris had seen a decline of interest in conventional stage drama and an almost manic fondness for vaudeville.[57]

The way in which Cocteau wanted to present his Parade to the public--in the spirit of Diaghilev's demand of Cocteau, "Etonne-moi!"--was closely allied to the publicity-seeking forms of Futurism. In the most boisterous and startling ways, the Futurists shouted their ideals to the public and drew up their intentions in innumberable manifestoes. Like the Futurist serate, Parade was conceived by Cocteau as a geste scandaleuse, a brazen proclamation of the new. The series of critical essays by Cocteau written after the premiere of Parade should be taken as the equivalent of the many manifestoes published in support of early Modern art. If the tactics of Dada, Futurist, Surrealist, and Abstract Art manifestoes were keenly political and self-serving, Cocteau's life-time dedication as a promoter of himself and his art in innumerable writings was Machiavellian.

The sound and verbal segments of Cocteau's scenario were undoubtedly inspired by earlier Futurist experiments. Yet, it should be granted that Cocteau made of his sources something special and all his own. Cocteau's "amplifying orifice, theatrical imitation of the circus gramaphone," bore a striking resemblance to Luigi Russolo's intonarumori (Fig. 14). The intonarumori were rectangular wooden boxes

with acoustical amplifiers or megaphones projecting from
the front. These "noise-intoners" created bizarre sounds
which were a manifestation of Russolo's theory--proclaimed
in The Art of Noise (1913)--that everyday sounds, as well
as newly fabricated sounds, should be a part of music.
Cocteau's megaphone in Parade was originally to project the
characters' résumés in addition to nonsense syllables and
everyday sounds. For example, the following phrases were
to emerge from the megaphone in a description of the Little
American Girl:

> Cube tic tic tic tic on the hundredth floor an angel
> has made its nest at the dentist's tic tic tic Titanic
> toc toc Titanic sinks brightly lit beneath the waves...
> ice-cream soda Pullman tic tic.[58]

The nonsense syllables which were to be interspersed
into the character glosses appear in the Cahier romain and on
several loose sheets tucked in the notebook (Figs. 106, 108,
116, 117, 118). These vowel salads are reminiscent of
Marinetti's parole in libertà and have their pictorial
counterparts in the paintings and collages of Carrà and
Severini (Fig. 15), as well as in lines from the Futurist
Synthetic plays (Fig. 16).

For all the ways in which Futurism impinged upon
Cocteau's shaping of a nouveau théâtre contemporain--and
the full extent of that influence in Picasso's work has yet
to be discussed--Cocteau was wary of crediting the Italians.
Perhaps in an effort to claim originality for his ideas in
Parade and to obscure his obvious borrowings, Cocteau, in
his Cahier romain (Fig. 97), pointed out one way in which he

wanted _Parade_ to differ from Futurist behavior:

> Work with three colors--too many colors look like
> Impressionism (Picasso)...The Futurists are the
> Impressionists of ideas...Beware of ideas.[59]

Quoting Picasso, whose request for economy is critical of

Impressionism, Cocteau likened the Futurists to the Impression-

ists. Concerned with too many ideas in their many proclama-

tions, the Futurists were criticized by Cocteau for being too

hypothetical. And yet, this slight to Futurism almost begged

the question of how telling the impress of Futurism was upon

Cocteau's ideas. To qualify, however, Cocteau's debt to the

Futurists, it is important to repeat that if the ideas of

Futurism were profitably taken up by Cocteau, they were

means which ultimately led in a very different direction.

The idea of coaxing mystery from mundane situations

and objects would have sounded strange to the Futurists. A

convincing piece of evidence for this point and one which

catches Cocteau in the act of lifting an idea is found in

the poet's _Préface_ to _Les Mariés_. Marinetti in 1913 stated

in his document _In Praise of Variety Theater_ that efforts

must be made to prevent traditions from settling into the

variety theater.[60] The stupid Parisian revue must be abolished

with its wisecracks, political personalities. It was as

"tedious as Greek tragedy with [its] _Compère_ and _Commère_

playing the part of the ancient chorus."[61] Cocteau rather

liked the associations, and eleven years later in his _Préface_

he compared the human phonographs flanking the stage in _Les_

Mariés to the classical chorus, to the "_Compère_ and the _Commère_

who, without the least literature, describe the absurd action

which is unfolded, danced, and mimed in the center."[62]
Cocteau reversed the judgment of Marinetti and described his
own theater, which in contrast to Futurist Synthetic Theater,
tended to refer rather than to be.

The Meaning of Cocteau's "Parade"

For Cocteau, the scenario of Parade was "a simple
roughly outlined action which combines the attractions of
circus and music-hall...Just a big toy, why search for crime,
mystery, and secret intentions in this little divertissement
which has been so much trouble for Satie, Picasso, Massine
and me."[63] These are deliberately ironic words for a writer
whose major themes were persecution, alienation, and personal
liberty. Responding to Apollinaire's call for an Esprit
Nouveau, Cocteau sought the poetic in the objects and situations of everyday life. By mythologizing the mundane, by
giving expression to "the intense forms of minor beauty,"[64]
Cocteau created a literature, theater, and film of magic
and mystery. Early in August 1916, Cocteau wrote to Stravinsky about his new project: "May it [Parade] distill all
the involuntary emotions given off by circuses, music-halls,
carousels, public balls, factories, seaports, the movies,
etc., etc. It is very short and develops in depth."[65]
Cocteau from the start considered Parade more than a theatrical
trifle.

One inarguable aspect of Parade's narrative, one
exposed like a nerve end, is the view of a scornful public
which does not understand the artist's work and which refuses

to "enter in." <u>Parade's</u> metaphor of the modern artist's
condition is straightforward and is couched within a tradition
which regarded the fair and circus as worlds for the estranged.
But, the unsuccessful <u>parade</u> as a symbol for social alienation
was far more richly handled by Cocteau. With an understanding
of the autobiographical dimensions of the narrative, the
implications of Cocteau's <u>Parade</u> may be seen to reach deeper.

Francis Steegmuller, Cocteau's most distinguished
American biographer, forwards the interpretation that Cocteau's <u>parade</u> represents the artist's work of art which is
passed over by an indifferent public, whose perception of
the artist's accomplishment is superficial and ignores the
inner complexities of the artist's imagination.[66] Until
<u>Parade</u>, Cocteau's accomplishments as a poet had been rather
thin, a fact he sorely realized. Steegmuller sees in the
crowd's indifference to a mere suggestion of the real show
inside the theater, a parallel to the reading public's in-
comprehension of Cocteau's true sensibilities. An astute
connection is thus made by Steegmuller to Cocteau's fortunes
as a young poet. The role and symbol, however, of Cocteau's
<u>parade</u> is more complex.

Jacques Guicharnaud sees additional biographical
information given in the theme of <u>Parade</u>. It may stand for
the whole of Cocteau's works and his attitude toward his
public.[67] The public is invited to understand, but is kept
at bay. Moreover, this feeling may describe the ambivalence
of the modern artist to society. The inner circus or soft,
vulnerable inside of Cocteau remains inaccesible and is

protected with an evasive and glib social exterior, perceived
as a hard shell or parade. A corollary to Guicharnaud's
view, one which elaborates upon his idea and connects it to
Cocteau's oeuvre, should be posited here. Although the
hijinks of the Little American Girl, pantomimed for the audience,
were comical, the actions out front of all three performers
were abbreviated suggestions of what was to occur inside
the theater, happenings more frightening and sublime. Cocteau
claimed that his aural segments and character résumés

> ...had nothing humorous about them. They insisted,
> on the contrary, on the mysterious, on character
> expansion, on the inside of our fair booth. The
> Chinaman was there capable of torturing missionaries,
> the Little American Girl of sinking with the Titanic,
> the Acrobat of being in confidence with the stars.[68]

The occult and mysterious interior of the théâtre forain in
Parade, which signifies the realm of the poet's imagination,
is guarded by a superficial and summary display. It marks,
I believe, the prototype in Cocteau's work of the "forbidden
zone." Here is offered, for the first time, an image which
is repeated throughout Cocteau's art: the photographer's
camera in Les Mariés de la tour Eiffel, through which the
personages emerge and exit; the room in Les Enfants terribles;
Hell in the film Orphée; and the Pavilion of Diana in La
Belle et la bête. The Pavilion of Diana was the source of
the Beast's magical powers and could only be opened with a
strange, golden key, which the Beast jealously guarded.
Although Rimbaud's Parade, in distinction to the Beast's
Pavilion, was a sanctuary for black rather than white magic,
the last line of Rimbaud's prose poem recalls Cocteau:

"J'ai seul la clef de cette parade sauvage."

The paradoxical nature of Cocteau's stance in
Parade was the simultaneous plea for understanding and
acceptance and for isolation and apartness. Parade made
a most ambivalent and contemporary gesture to the outside:
come in, but do not come in. The psychological dissonance
is stated and rationalized in the following theoretical
thinking of the artist: "I'm devastated because you make
no attempt to comprehend my actions, but that is acceptable
because I would not want you to comprehend me anyway." The
parade of Cocteau's ballet exhibited, as a symbol, two
contradictory levels of meaning. And yet, the sharp ambiguity
of symbolic intent complemented Cocteau's theme of the modern
artist's dilemma. The little parade out front stood at
once for the problem and for the solution to the problem.
Cocteau's parade manquée served to signify the misunderstood
artist, and also it was the symbol of a deliberate ploy to
distance the unfeeling. Philosophizing about art and the
theater in his Préface to Les Mariés de la tour Eiffel,
Cocteau warned against what he was about and how his enterprises were mined for the unwary. Written seven years after
the production of Parade and ostensibly in relationship to
a general theory of the theater, these lines allude dramatically to Parade and should substantiate the argument put
forward here that Parade was an intimate and intricate
allegory of Cocteau the artist. The relationship has not
previously been observed and the lines deserve to be quoted
in full:

Every living work of art has its own parade outside the real performance. This parade is only
seen by those who do not choose to enter in. In
the case of a new work, this superficial impression
will often be too shocking, too irritating, too upsetting to bring the spectator in. He is distracted
from its essence by its appearance, by the unfamiliar
expressions which distract him as would a clown
grimacing at the door. It is this phenomenon which
deceives even those critics least enslaved by convention. They fail to realize that they are witnessing a work demanding as much attention as they
would accord the latest popular drama. They think
they are watching a street show, plain and simple.[69]

The sensitive would see beyond the superficial; others would

be duped. Cocteau's theater was in no sense a popular theater,

but elitist to the core. The poet goes on to make this quite

clear:

The secret of theatrical success is this: set a
decoy at the door so that part of the audience can
enjoy itself there while the others take their seats
inside. Shakespeare, Molière, and Charlie Chaplin
do it well.[70]

The price, unfortunately, for personal authenticity

was isolation. The failure of the little sideshow in Parade

reflected the melancholy aloneness of Cocteau who said, "The

goal of every artist must be his own extremity."[71] Neal

Oxenhandler observes that in all of Cocteau's plays fear is

the "protean antagonist."[72] The frivolity of Parade cannot be

convincing because it is progressively forced during the

ballet in the attempts of the managers to lure people in. A

thin scrim of anxiety rests over the ballet from the beginning.

Parade was tragicomedy of the highest order and its pathos

was the creation of Cocteau. Parade is a fragile work of art.

Its conceit bears an oppressive, symbolic freight which, in

contrast to the ostensible gaiety of the setting, creates a

dramatic tension.

Parade was Cocteau. Its characters dramatized the workings of Cocteau's personality. The managers, from the beginning and more effectively in their later transformations into aggressive hawkers, were that part of Cocteau which throughout his life struck bizarre stances, did somersaults, did anything to gain attention to himself. Why did Cocteau choose the acts he did for Parade? The Acrobat, the Chinese Magician, and the Little American Girl represented in their essences those three qualities immediately associated with the art and personality of Cocteau: agility, mystery, and invention.

The idea of the Total Theater director, who coordinated all aspects of production, undoubtedly appealed very much to Cocteau. But the experience of Parade must have chastened his views. From the ideals he based his theater on, it is no surprise that he was so upset with the collaboration. His vain attempts to oversee the ballet were somewhat vindicated later by his personal accounts of the production, embroidered in his favor. His working relationship with Satie, Diaghilev, and Picasso was stormy. Here was no ideal Total Theater situation, but a power struggle. The critical judgments of Cocteau's role have been curious. Cocteau is usually the last personality mentioned in discussion of Parade, if at all. Apollinaire was seriously remiss to exclude all mention of him in his famous program note for the opening production. In face of the evidence, the belittling of Cocteau is puzzling. Parade was his idea. It was conceived in the spirit of a serious exercise in Total Theater for the purpose of renovating the French theater. Cocteau's views on the theater, so thoroughly linked to the most advanced thinking on theater reform, are, without exception, never given their proper context. Because Cocteau envisioned the way he wanted Parade to be implemented by the other arts, he hoped to have control over the other elements in the same way that someone like Craig or Appia coordinated all aspects of their productions. In the beginning it seemed to be this way. Diaghilev approved Cocteau's choice of collaborators. It was Cocteau who re-cruited Satie and Picasso. It was Cocteau who worked so closely with Massine to set the choreography. The appropriateness of the contributions of Picasso, Satie, and Massine is an important aspect of a consideration of Parade as a finely integrated whole. In arguing further on for the intimate relationship between Parade and Cubism, it will be mandatory to examine to what extent Cubism decorated, supported, or stood apart from Cocteau's scenario and his plans for a nouveau théâtre contemporain.

Cocteau was always to prize his Parade. He esteemed it the first work of his oeuvre. The fuss made over Picasso's and Satie's roles in Parade, at the expense of his, was understandably a source of anguish. Parade was part of the Ballets Russes' repertory, but it was not frequently performed. Years later in 1947, Cocteau fondly reminisced about Parade and recalled Diaghilev's reasons for not mounting it more often:

> And when someone asked Diaghilev why de did not allow it to be performed more frequently, he said,"It is my best bottle of wine, I do not like to open it too often."[73]

CHAPTER III

THE MISE EN SCENE: COSTUMES AND SET

...avant lui le décor ne jouait pas dans la
pièce; il y assistait.

                    Jean Cocteau[1]

Picasso's mise en scène for <u>Parade</u> was his first
work for the theater and marked the beginning of an eight
year affiliation with the Ballets Russes, during which the
artist created the scenic designs for six new productions.[2]
Before World War I, Diaghilev, in his search for theatrical
unity, had frequently asked his scenic designers to create
both the decor and the costumes. Following this practice,
Diaghilev commissioned Picasso to conceive for <u>Parade</u> the
stage decor and the costumes for the dancers. Another pref-
erence of Diaghilev, initiated during the early pre-war
seasons, was the gradual abandonment of illusionistic decor
and the development toward large, simplified designs.[3]
Before <u>Parade</u>, the epitome of Diaghilev's decors were the
primitivizing sets, curtains, and costumes of Larionov and
Gontcharova.[4] These two aspects of Ballets Russes stage design--
integration of set and costumes and visual boldness--were
givens for Picasso, ones from which he did not choose to
depart when he undertook Diaghilev's commission. However,

within these parameters, Picasso in the productions he designed for the Ballets Russes asserted an aggressive, new
role for the scenic designer. Until Parade, scenic implementation of the Ballets Russes' productions had been, in
the best sense, splendid, decorative adjuncts to the ballets.
This particular function of decor and costumes was maintained in the majority of productions throughout the twenties.
What Picasso offered to the stage in his designs was not a
visual intrusion upon the spectacle but, rather, additional
commentary made upon the content of the ballet beyond the
establishing of a setting. Diaghilev's formula for ballet
theater, based upon the ideals of Total Theater, was the
equal footing of the various components of the spectacle:
decor, music, and dance. This strategy had been adopted by
Diaghilev from the very first season of Ballets Russes in 1909.
What was so remarkable about Picasso's mise en scène for
Parade was the brilliant tautening of the desired synthesis
into its finest realization.

The Costumes

The costumes which Picasso designed for the three
acts in Parade--the Chinese Magician, the Little American
Girl, and the Acrobats--were conventional in terms of char-
acter-ballet dress, but cleverly apt visual expressions of
Cocteau's personages. The Chinese Magician--seen in Picasso's
final watercolor sketch and in a preliminary drawing--was
outfitted in a mandarin's habit, which consisted of a tunic,
trousers, and skullcap (Figs. 17 and 18). On a saturated

red ground, the side-buttoned tunic with its upturned collar
displayed three quilted motifs: on the front, four white
arabesques with radiating yellow stripes; on the back, a
white sun and a crescent moon with notched, radiating stripes
in yellow. On the right trouser leg, diagonally undulating
yellow stripes of varying widths figured on a black ground.
The left trouser leg opposed this design with black undulating
stripes placed vertically on a yellow ground. The tiara
which the Chinese Magician wore was composed of three peaked
caps in double color combinations of red, yellow, or black.
Accenting the bold colors of the costume was the bright
white of the quilted motifs: the gloves, the stockings, and
the white face of Massine's make up. A final touch was the
long braided queue falling from the skullcap.

　　　Do the moon and sun on the verso of the Chinese
Magician's tunic make any symbolic reference? Complementing
the sources of natural illumination depicted on the tunic was
the mimed blowing of fire from the Magician's mouth during
his routine. Knowing that an everyday object for both Cocteau and Picasso was never entirely mundane but referred to
more fantastic levels of identity, one surmises that Cocteau's figure of the Chinese Magician, visualized by Picasso,
was more than a simple fair magician. The sun, moon, and
fire could have referred to more elemental and mythical
meanings. Important to the identity of the magus is his
control over the natural world. Cocteau's French designation
for his Magician was <u>Presdigitateur chinois</u>. The <u>presdigi-
tateur</u>, or conjurer, is a maker of illusion. He has in

his control the ability to make things appear and disappear, to bring out of the clear air wondrous things.

The two central gestures of the Chinese Magician's routine were the blowing of fire from his mouth and the conjuring of an egg which he swallowed and magically made reappear at his toes. The quilted scroll motif on the front of the Magician's jacket might have been purely decorative or a stylized image of water--yet another elemental force. One witty allusion of the scrolls, apart from any serious mythical reference, was their function as intestines through which the magical egg traveled en route from mouth to toe.[5] Lincoln Kirstein's observation that the Chinese Magician was a "metaphor for the creative spirit"[6] may be substantiated by Picasso's and Cocteau's respective views of the painter and poet as being prestidigitators, namely, manipulators of illusion. A reading of the centrality of the Chinese Magician to Cocteau's allegory of the modern artist is encouraged by the fact that Massine danced the original role and that the Magician made the first and last appeal to the audience in the scenario. Other indications of his significance were the elaborateness of his costume and his compositional prominence in the final tableau.[7] Massine's interpretation of the Chinese Magician--suggested in production photographs of the first performance--was a strange and frightening being, contorted in his movements (Figs. 19 and 20).

Cocteau's original scenario called for one acrobat, and it was for this single male dancer that Picasso worked up a finished watercolor sketch (Fig. 21). The addition of

a second female acrobat, suggested by Massine in Rome for
the purposes of a character pas de deux, was not followed
up by any croquis or formal watercolors. The original male
acrobat and the final male and female combination were called
upon in the Cocteau-Massine choreography to mime the actions
of tumblers, tightrope walkers, and trapeze artists--a collage,
as it were, of the circus movements which transpire above
our heads. Fittingly enough, Massine's choreography for the
Acrobats was, and remained in the Joffrey revival, airborn,
not terre-à-terre. When Cocteau later spoke of the "mysterious
side...of our fair booth," he intimated that the acrobat was
capable of being "in confidence with the stars."[8] Cocteau,
again, makes magical the everyday. The acrobats have become heavenly. And Picasso's costume for the Acrobat comple-
ments this mood. The costume for the original Acrobat consisted of a pair of body tights figured with white stars and
arabesques on a saturated cobalt-blue ground (Figs. 22, 23,
24).[9] The arabesques echoed those in the Chinese Magician's
jacket, and the stars of the Acrobat's costume along with the
sun and moon of the Chinese Magician's costume made for a
truly celestial iconography.

The costume for the female Acrobat was improvised
on the spot, and Picasso was never entirely satisfied with
it (Fig. 25).[10] Picasso's sentiments were conveyed to
Douglas Cooper during rehearsals for the Joffrey revival,
and Picasso gave his consent to execute the female Acrobat's
costume according to his original wishes: an exact duplicate
of the male Acrobat's costume. Marcel Proust attended the

Paris revival of <u>Parade</u> in 1921. His fondest memories were
of the two Acrobats, whom he likened to the twin Roman gods,
Castor and Pollux. How ironically appropriate Proust's
poetic allusion was, although it was made without any knowledge of Picasso's original intentions for the Acrobat's
costumes.

It has been mentioned previously that the effortlessly
aerial movements of the Acrobats signify a facet of the
artist's or poet's creativity, specifically that of Cocteau's, which is associated with a nimbleness of the imagination. Cocteau's social and artistic agility was often criticized for its superficiality. Friends of Cocteau have re-
marked that he was always the center of attention at parties.
The young poet's wit and verbal pyrotechnics were highly
entertaining, although friends claimed that later, after a
winning performance by Cocteau, no one remembered what he
had said.[11] Creative facility can be considered a positive
attribute of the artist. It describes Cocteau's effortless
gestures in his art. In a more negative light it characterizes
what the poet himself was afraid of: aesthetic glibness--
all form and no content. A spiritual relationship can be
observed in this instance between Cocteau and Picasso.
Facility was a trait Picasso fought against from the very
beginning of his career. Learning to draw like a child,
challenging his remarkable ability to ape the numerous modes
of western illusionistic painting--these were the deliberately
chosen and agonizing goals of the artist. And even after
quelling the too facile line, Picasso's incredible prolificness

throughout his life earned him rebukes from critics and
artists alike.[12] One begins to appreciate the affinity
between Cocteau and Picasso. On this one point alone, that
of a breathtaking facility which borders on an empty virtuosity, the grievance was mutual. It was captured in the dazzlingly physical and visual display of Parade's Acrobats

The costume for the Little American Girl was not,
properly speaking, created by Picasso (Fig. 26). The apparel
Picasso thought fitting was purchased, according to Boris
Kochno, the day before the premiere at Williams, a sportswear
shop in Paris.[13] What was bought at Williams was probably
only the little navy blue sailor's jacket. The very short
white pleated skirt and the ballooning muslin bow were comic
exaggerations. The accord of the Little American Girl to
Picasso's own sensibility seems less pointed than that of
the Chinese Magician and the Acrobats. Picasso was never
to exhibit significant interest in the United States. Cocteau's fascination for a modern America was more fittingly
a characteristic of artists like Delaunay, Malevich, and the
Futurists, although American people, objects, and events
were never to be specifically a part of their iconographies.
However, the Little American Girl's ageless and youthful
vigor and cleverness must have exerted its appeal on Picasso,
even if the only pictorial postscript to the Little American
Girl in Picasso's oeuvre, and one which was not specifically
American, was The Girl with a Hoop of 1919 (Zervos, III, 289).

The most startling scenic contributions to Parade
were Picasso's designs for the three Managers: the American,

the French, and the Equestrian. As it has been pointed out,
the cardboard Equestrian Manager, who would have ballyhooed
the Acrobats, was finally removed during rehearsals because
of his precarious position on the Horse. What was left was
a two-man horse, which became an act in its own right (Figs.
27 and 28). In an ambiguous manner, the collaborators let
the Horse intrude into the scenario without clarifying his
exact function in program synopses or in any statements.
The Horse's costume was not as assertively Cubist in appearance
as those for the American and French Managers; the only
Cubist component of the costume was the headpiece (Fig. 29).
Shaped somewhat like an over-sized mandolin, it gave two
aspects of the Horse's head: a frontal view with pointed
ears, and a balloon shape with two eyes and two nostrils
inscribed within a squared forehead and muzzle; and, a profile
view, which revealed a black ridge along the center of the
face with two pairs of dots for eyes and nostrils and a
lower register of piano-key teeth. In a Cubist painting
it is acknowledged that more than one aspect of an object
is given to the viewer. In a piece of sculpture, like the
Horse's Cubist head, the singling out of frontal and profile
aspects may not seem particularly important in light of an
inherent three-dimensionality. What is significant about
the Horse's head is that the two aspects conveyed abrupt
changes in expressiveness. With its pinced eyes echoing
the lower nostrils, the front of the head makes a quizzically
silly expression. Played against this delightful visage
is the fierce expression of the profile, with the teeth

terrifyingly flared. In the head alone, Cubist ambiguity
is displayed: a back and forth between a passive and an
aggressive mood, the latter which was in keeping with the
revised conception of the Managers as frightening presences.
This double reading is apparent in a comparison of the two
production photographs (Figs. 27 and 28) and in the preliminary
sketch (Fig. 29). The Horse in performance, however, posed
little problem for the audiences, who responded enthusiastically
to the show-stopping antics of the Horse's act, executed
with Satie's score momentarily silenced. According to one
member of the corps de ballet, the first audiences received
the Horse as a familiar comic, the two-man horse being a
regular feature of vaudeville.[14] What was unfamiliar and
bizarre for Parade's original audience were the figures of
the American and French Managers.

Picasso's preliminary sketches for the American and
French Managers suggest two initial approaches to the costumes.
The first, typified by an early sketch for a Manager (Fig.
30), shows a contorted and humorous figure with an elongated
neck, top hat, striped trousers, and a body placard. He
carries in his hands a violin and an ambiguous object which
is at once a bow and saw. The only Cubist inflections are
the violin, a box affair with a stylized diagram of a violin
shape, and the printing on the front side of the placard.
The words on this surface offer, like the words in Cubist
collage, a variety of meanings, a punning which, in this
case, is indelicate. It reads: "Grand (ce soir) Concert--
Miss Merd." Aside from the jaunty duple rhythms and rhyme

of the lines, a rather mischievous comment was being made on a certain Mlle. Misia Sert, an influential and monied intimate of Diaghilev, who late in 1916 had unsuccessfully attempted to sabotage the Parade collaboration.[15] She would have paid dearly for her mischief if this design of Picasso's had appeared on stage at the Châtelet. Through a clever placing of words and syllables, we see that the letters "MISS...CERT" kept close company with "GRAND...(CON)" and "MISS MERD."

Picasso's other concept for the Manager's costumes is a type more fully Cubist in its morphology. A good example is seen in one Manager sketch (Fig. 31), whose figure shapes are more complex and ambiguous. The Manager's top hat sits on a face in one plane which contains both a frontal and profile aspect. His torso is inscribed within a single plane which additionally depicts a shape seen either as a body placard or as a publicity poster. Piercing this shape are two holes for the dancer's arms. Another flat shape, which might be contiguous with the torso/sign or placed on another plane to the rear of the figure, could be read as theatrical drapery or reminiscences of proscenium shapes. If the appearance of this Manager reflects Picasso's constructions of 1912, it also betrays a debt to a purely pictorial mode. This latter source is more strikingly apparent in another preliminary sketch (Fig. 32). This sketch does not appear to be a blueprint for a three-dimensional sculptural shape, but rather the working out of a standing figure within the ambiguously planar modes of Synthetic Cubism and collage.

The second design concept was chosen by Picasso for
the final elaboration of the Managers' costumes. The costumes
of the American and French Managers (Figs. 33 and 34) were
·fashioned out of painted cardboard and canvas and were, in
essence, eight-foot "shells" which were placed over the
dancers' bodies, allowing the legs relative liberty of movement. Still, the dancers unlovingly referred to the Cubist
constructions as "carcasses" because their movements were
severely inhibited by the clumsiness of supporting the whole
affair.[16]

In the French Manager's costume, the dancer's legs
were visible, dressed in knee breeches and white hose, and
so were his two arms, which held, respectively, a baton and
large pipe. The costume of the American Manager only allowed
the free play of the dancer's legs, which were dressed in
cowboy chaps. Both arms were papier-mâché constructions
which held a megaphone and a program with the word "parade"
written across the cover. The legs and arms of both Managers
were the only visibly human and real elements of these
toweringly artificial presences.

With his bow-tie, top hat, dicky, breeches and hose,
the French Manager was dressed in the formal evening clothes
of a Compère, the Master of Ceremonies. With his turned-up
moustache, he bore an uncanny resemblance to Seurat's ring-
master in Le Cirque. Above the fragmented torso of the
figure, the French Manager's head, from a frontal view, was
split into a face which accommodated a witty frontal aspect
with a more serious and ghost-like profile. Added to the

head was an actual profile equivalent in its mysterious
mood to the "frontal" profile. The shapes to the rear of
the French Manager appeared to be vestigial body placards
which had been metamorphosed into suggestions of the Manager's ambient surroundings. The French Manager's back, like
a great magnet, attracted to itself architectural motifs
suggestive of the set's proscenium and a swatch of green
shrubbery which disturbingly assumed the shape of a dorsal
fin.

Less urbane than the French Manager, yet more aggressively urban, the American Manager's costume gave several
clues to its national identity. The torso consisted of two
vaguely mechanical cardboard tubes with two vertical registers
of six open-ended tubes that constituted a vest. The negative space of the head offered no features and, consequently,
no psychological expression other than anonymity. The stove-
pipe hat of the American Manager had the look of a ten-gallon
hat, whose western flavor was matched by the pair of cowboy
chaps worn by the dancer. Like the French Manager, the
American Manager's back decoration is carried in the manner
of a publicity placard. Its shapes, too, are transformed
into motifs associated with the set design, but which loosen
other associations and identities. The squared, windowed
shapes were related in design to the architectural panels
of the set, but their vertical emphasis and the little
triangular piece attached at the top suggested skyscrapers.
Another environmental feature which attached itself to the
American Manager was the flag pole which flew five notched

flags. This motif might be identified with fair-booth
decorations of the théâtre forain or, possibly, with nautical
things, the latter appropriately alluding to what the American Manager was ballyhooing: the Little American Girl's
Steamboat Ragtime.

          Certain precedents for the Managers' forms may be
found within Picasso's own earlier work. Unlike the costumes
for the three acts, those for the two Managers, as well as
that for the head of the Horse, may be considered sculpture.
As such, their form derived from Picasso's relief constructions of 1912 (Fig. 35). The Managers' costumes, like the
series of guitars and still-life assemblages of 1912-14,
were "constructed" rather than carved or molded. Although
precedents for constructed stage dress, especially for fantastic effects, do exist in the earlier history of the theater,
the assembled multicolored pieces of cardboard that constitued
the Managers' costumes were technically influenced by Picasso's
earlier constructed sculpture. The style of the Managers'
costumes, as well as that of the relief constructions, was
informed by the syntax of Synthetic Cubism and collage. The
year 1912 marked a major shift in Picasso's Cubist style
toward a simplified morphology of flatter and more opaque
planes. The relief constructions were contemporary with
this shift in style and themselves sprang from Cubist painting.
Figurative images, however, which presaged the Managers
are to be found in Picasso's painting, not his sculpture.
Picasso never had fashioned a human figure using the new
technique of assemblage. Even in Picasso's painting prior

to Parade exact sources are difficult to find. The Harlequin
of 1913 (Fig. 36) was one of the few standing figures realized
by Picasso before Parade in the Synthetic Cubist style.
With its flat planes and pendulum moustache it bears a
curious resemblance to the French Manager. More to the point,
in the way of a pictorial source for the Managers' costumes,
was a painting done two years later and also entitled
Harlequin (Fig. 37). The planes with which the standing
figure was built were more boldly opaque than the 1913 Harlequin, suggesting a model which would have been more easily
adapted to a sculptural construction. Most significant for
the French Manager was the double aspect of the head. Two
different psychological states, which corresponded to the
French Manager's, were given simultaneously: the upturned
Cheshire-cat smile, anticipating the French Manager's moustache,
gave the frontal view an inane countenance, while the L-shaped
profile, identical to the profile of the French Manager, was
more severe and mysterious.

To find earlier expressions of Cubist derived, full-
length figure sculpture, one must look outside of Picasso's
art. Although Archipenko, Lipchitz, and Duchamp-Villon
created their own version of this type, Juan Gris' painted-
plaster Harlequin (Fig. 38), executed in the year of Parade's
premiere, may serve as a good example of a standing figure
modeled in three dimensions with the ambiguous and interpenetrating planes of Synthetic Cubism. This particular
group of efforts by other artists, however, comprised carved
and modeled sculpture, although the materials could be un-

conventional, like Gris' work. Actually, very few assembled
or constructed figures anticipated Picasso's Managers. Archipenko's Médrano of 1914 (Fig. 39) was an important prototype
not only for its diversely assembled materials--painted tin,
glass, wood, and oil cloth--but also because of the reference
to the Cirque Médrano and the world of Parade. One other
little known and important work, which may have possibly
marked the first example in the Modern sequence of constructed
figures, was Vladimir Baranoff-Rossine's Sculpture Symphony 1
of 1913 (Fig. 40). One of two versions, Baranoff-Rossine's
imposing conglomerate of painted wood, iron, and crushed
egg shells was a full-sized figure. Symphony 2, later thrown
into the Seine by its creator, was exhibited at the Salon des
Indépendants in March 1914 and may have possibly been seen
by Picasso. It is interesting to note, with regard to the
Managers' historical precedents, that the constructed
sculptures in the series of standing Cubist figures were
worked on a large scale; the one-piece carved or molded
figures were table-top size.

For a discussion of a significant shaping force
behind the creation of the Managers' costumes, it is necessary
to turn from Picasso and to return to an influence which has
already been shown to have exerted considerable impact upon
the scenario: Futurism. During the rehearsals for Parade
in Rome, Cocteau and Picasso came into contact with the
Futurists Balla and Depero, who were preparing works for
Diaghilev's company. Depero had been commissioned in 1916
by Diaghilev to design the costumes and decor for a ballet

version of the earlier Stravinsky one-act opera <u>Le Rossignol</u>
(1910). Balla had been asked to create an elaborate stage
setting for a dancerless ballet, whose music was another
earlier Stravinsky orchestral work, <u>Feu d'artifices</u>.

The Futurists were a presence in Rome and mingled
with Diaghilev's company. They caused Cocteau in his <u>Cahier</u>
<u>romain</u> to adopt a disparaging, anti-Futurist stance. It
has already been noted that one reason for Cocteau's position
toward the Futurists was his concern to obscure what for
others might appear to be generous borrowings from the
Futurist's experiments and proclamations. In a letter to
Misia Sert, published in Steegmuller's biography of Cocteau,
the poet wrote about Giacomo Balla and the Futurists:

> We see little of the Futurists--too provincial and
> bragging. They have always wanted to travel at top
> speed, which keeps them from seeing the road and in
> effect reduces them to immobility. When they succeed,
> it's very pretty, very graceful, like a toy or a
> poster.[17]

Steegmuller deduces from similar comments by Cocteau--"The
Futurists pursue us like provincials wanting to learn the
Paris styles"[18]--that Picasso thought very little of Futurist
painting. The exact nature of Picasso's sympathy or anti-
pathy toward Futurism is, however, difficult to ascertain.
Still, it is fairly clear that Picasso looked to Futurism
for aspects of the costumes he designed for the Managers.
Picasso's contact with Futurism did not date from <u>Parade's</u>
rehearsals in Rome. Nearly six years earlier in Paris,
Carrà, Russolo, and Boccioni had gained entry into the
studios of Picasso and Braque during their stay in the city

in conjunction with the opening of the Bernheim-Jeune Futurist
exhibition in February 1912.

In any attempt to uncover priorities of aesthetic
discovery, the first half of 1912 poses many knotty problems
of chronology. It is assumed in several major histories of
the period that Boccioni's ideas on sculpture were initiated
by Cubist collage.[19] Boccioni's call for new materials in
his Manifesto of Futurist Sculpture (1912) paralleled the
actual use of non-traditional materials by Picasso and Braque
in their paintings and papiers collés of 1912. The fact
remains, however, that even with Picasso's own redating of
his Still Life with Chair Caning to May 1912, Boccioni's
Manifesto was published in Paris in April 1912. Consequently,
Boccioni's views on sculpture, voiced in early 1912, may have
played a more formative role in the genesis of Picasso's
collages and relief constructions later in the year. In
any event, Boccioni was Picasso's favorite Futurist,[20] and
his influence, whether or not it acted upon Picasso's major
sculptural innovations of 1912, was impressed upon Picasso's
work for Parade. The inclusion of environmental motifs into
the Cubist constructions for the Managers' costumes indicated
an originally Futurist, not Cubist, tactic.

The Futurists, notably Boccioni, worked out a notion
of simultaneity which dealt with the impingement of environmental events and sensations upon the individual. First
developed in painting, the "dynamic sensation," early
pictured in Boccioni's The Noise of the Street Penetrates
the House (1911), offered a pictorial demonstration of

Futurist simultaneity. In 1912, the seated image of
mother realized in both painting and sculpture--<u>Mater</u>
and <u>Head+House+Light</u> (Figs. 41 and 42) attempted to incorporate
into the sitter's body a variety of sensory events both near
and far. In a statement in the Bernheim-Jeune catalogue
for the 1912 Futurist exhibition, the nature of Boccioni's
concern was articulated:

> We must show the invisible which stirs and lives
> beyond intervening obstacles, what we have on our
> right, on the left, and behind us, and not merely
> the little square of life artificially compressed,
> as it were, by the wings of a stage.21

Boccioni's <u>Head+House+Light</u> of 1912, with its use of various
materials, and most pointedly, in its connecting of what
appears to be an architectural panel with windows to the
back of Boccioni's mother's head, must stand as an influential
source behind Picasso's French and American Managers, who
attracted to the back of their bodies architectural and
landscape motifs from their immediate urban setting. Although Picasso displayed scant interest in a Futurist simultaneity of near and far in his works prior to <u>Parade</u>, the
Cubist painter Gleizes, in the very year that Boccioni
voiced his new ideas on sculpture, 1912, painted a standing
portrait of the <u>Man on a Balcony</u> (Fig. 43), which if conservative for its date in the way the figure was separated
from its ground, still meshed, to some extent, the distant
background with the head of the individual. Uncharacteristically,
in Futurist terms, the figure was left psychologically un-
perturbed by the onslaught of his environment.

The first time that Picasso introduced a personal

phrasing of Futurist simultaneity into his painting was, fittingly enough, during his first trip to Italy in 1917 for Parade's first rehearsals. L'Italienne (Fig. 44), worked on in Rome, exhibited a desire to blend a standing figure into an environment whose confines were considerably more spacious than those of the conventional studio of early Cubism. The standing peasant woman, assembled with the interlocking and opaque planes of Synthetic Cubism was also, with these same planes, joined to her environment. Those environmental motifs were identical with those attached to the Managers' costumes: foliate and architectural--in this instance, the red silhouette of St. Peter's and the black, white, and grey meanderings of tree and shrubbery forms. Another point of comparison between L'Italienne and the Managers' costumes was the appearance of the face which accommodated more than one psychological state. Leo Steinberg argues successfully that the two-in-one face, which contained both a facing head and a profile, was refined during World War I.[22] L'Italienne was one of the earliest statements of this device in Picasso's painting. Equally important in Picasso's oeuvre was its sculptural realization in the Managers' and the Horse's heads, where the three-dimensional medium allowed not only a facing head whose visage opposed the expression of an actual profile, as in the head of the Horse, but, more complexly in the French Manager's head, a facing head with dual aspects in addition to a virtual profile, which presented yet another expressive state. Without exception, Picasso's Managers do not appear

in books devoted to the artist's sculpture. Again this is
an instance of prevailing critical attitudes sheltering the
appreciation of certain activities; the result in the case
of Parade's Managers is to obscure a major contribution to
the development of the artist's ideas.

Even though Picasso's debt to Futurism was evident
in the creation of the costumes for the French and American
Managers, the influence of the Italians must be qualified
to the extent that Picasso made of his sources a personal
and an original statement. In comparison to the costumes
of Depero for Futurist performance (Figs. 45 and 46), Picasso's
Managers were far less mechanically robot-like in their
appearance. Whereas Depero's anthropoids belonged to a new
world of technology, Picasso's Managers were more mythical
creatures, whose presences on stage engendered a Cubist
ambiguity of meaning that played upon the witty and the
terrifying. And finally, and perhaps ironically, Picasso's
costumes for Parade's Managers were, in a sense, more Futurist
than Depero's, if Boccioni's sculptural ideas are taken
as a standard. The Futurist "dynamic sensation" as it was
realized in the sculpture of Boccioni was never transplanted
to Futurist stage dress.

Picasso's costumes for the Managers in Parade have
so far been discussed within the context of sculpture.
Another source, however, was pivotal in the shaping of the
Managers' costumes: that of theatrical costume. Again,
Futurist theory played a formative role.[23] A central concern
of Futurist performance was the integration of the performer

with the theatrical setting through the mechanization of
the performer.[24] The notion of a stylistic unity established
between the actor and the stage decor was derived by the Futurists from the theater reforms of Appia and Craig. The
Ballets Russes also adhered to this aesthetic in their
productions dating from the first Paris season in 1909. It
was noted above that Picasso's designs for Parade were influenced by the conventional practice of Diaghilev to commission
boldly colorful and carefully integrated scenic designs for
his productions. In this respect, the coordinated scene and
costumes that the Futurists urged was matched, as a design
pressure upon Picasso, by Ballets Russes tradition. The
innovative Futurist idea which was important for Picasso was
the mechanical integration of the performer with his setting.
Control would be placed upon the performer by dismissing the
human actor altogether and replacing him with a kinetic
decor; the performance or stage movement would consist of
movable scenic elements and animated illumination. This
radical solution was first carried out by Balla in his production of Feu d'artifices for the Ballets Russes in 1917.
Preparations for this work were carried out concurrently in
Rome with the rehearsals for Parade. Another method to control the performer was declared by Prampolini in his manifesto of Futurist Scenography published in 1915.[25] Prampolini's
idea that the actor must be abolished and replaced with a
more controllable agent was influenced by Gordon Craig's call
for the Übermarionette in 1908, although Prampolini himself
spoke out against Craig's super puppets. Two other Futurists,

Depero and Clavel, implemented a marionette theater with their production of <u>Balli Plastici</u> in 1918. The one Futurist solution to the actor problem, however, which impinged most markedly in Picasso's ideas for the Managers was the deformation and mechanization of the human actor through costume rather than replacing the human actor by the <u>Übermarionette</u> or dismissing him entirely.

Picasso's costumes for the French and American Managers, the eight-foot constructions which concealed the dancers almost entirely, were a direct response to Futurist theory, to ideas which had been discussed several years before <u>Parade</u>. It is ironic that Picasso implemented certain Futurist ideals before the Futurists did. Aside from the dancerless performance of Balla's <u>Feu d'artifices</u>, those productions which utilized the <u>Übermarionette</u> or the actor-deforming costuming took place after Picasso's Managers had made their entrances in <u>Parade</u> in 1917.

Picasso "made use" of Futurism in his Managers' costumes for <u>Parade</u>. That Picasso did this not in glib imitation but in a manner which at once brilliantly aped and made utterly personal another style admitted of an amazing virtuosity. Picasso's <u>Parade</u> was not an imitation Futurist performance. It is probable, in one respect, that an element of sophisticated tease was at play on Picasso's part. Marianne Martin, the noted Futurist scholar, views <u>Parade</u> as a satirical gloss on Futurism, perpetrated on the parts of both Cocteau and Picasso.[26] However, with the ambitions of Cocteau understood in an earlier chapter and with a further understanding (sug-

gested below) of the function of Picasso's costumes in performance, the notion of _Parade_ as a deliberate satire of
Italians by Parisians, if successful in illuminating sources
and elements of wit, is limiting as a full explanation of
Parade's dramatic impact and ultimate meanings.

The Futurist aesthetic, sculptural and theatrical, as
it influenced Picasso was only one aspect of his designs. If
the Managers were integrated stylistically with the stage
setting and were virtual demonstrations of Futurist costuming,
they were, however, realized with Cubist forms, and, they
did not constitute the entire cast of actors on stage. The
three acts were outfitted in conventional stage dress, not
in actor-deforming shells. What Picasso did was to establish
between the stage set and costumes a set of dialectical relationships which derived from earlier Cubist ploys and which
conveyed particular dramatic and expressive information.

Already observed is the way in which the costumes of
the French and American Managers corresponded to the stage set
by repeating architectural and foliate motifs. Additionally,
the sharp geometric angles of the set, especially the planes
of the inner proscenium, were echoed in the style of the
Managers' costumes. Prampolini suggested that the actor or
performer be integrated with his stage setting by matching
the movements of the actor with the lines of the setting.[27]
It is perhaps initially difficult to imagine a kinetic counterpart of Picasso's stage setting for _Parade_, but if the abrupt
and angular movements of the Managers were contrasted with
the more fluid, "human" movements of the acts, the Managers'

actions on stage did correspond in their stylization with the lines of the setting.

The relationships available between the Managers and the acts were more complex. Why not outfit the entire company of performers in Parade in constructions? This option, which would have been more authentically Futurist, was not Picasso's choice. For the Managers' costumes were meant to contrast with the other dancers to engender particular meanings, and it is worthwhile to inquire into the expressive function of Picasso's reservation of artificial, actor-deforming costumes for the Managers alone.

Psychologically, the Managers and the acts fall into two groups. Picasso's new conception of the three managers to replace Cocteau's single, invisible Manager was the portrayal of fierce and intimidating figures, whose harangues to the fictional audience in the scenario were to be abrasive and strident. The deformation and physical aggrandizement of the human dancers playing the Managers and the Managers' non-emotional faces--especially the cold anonymity of the American's--visually captured the spirit of the Managers' personalities. The American and French Managers and the acts collectively constituted an entity which was threatened by the apathy of the crowd outside which did not respond to their entreaties. However, the relationship between the Managers and the acts was not meant to be marked by total sympathy. The acts are controlled, owned, and forced to perform by the Managers. The impersonal posture of the Managers characterized a co-ercive force over the performers. The size, style, and movement of the Managers intentionally set them apart from the

three acts.   Cocteau intuitively understood the function of

the Managers' costumes in a statement he made shortly after

the premiere of <u>Parade</u>.

> When Picasso showed us his sketches, we understood
> how effective it would be to exploit the contrast
> between the three "real" characters as "chromos"
> pasted on a canvas (canceled post cards) and the
> more solemnly transposed unhuman, or superhuman,
> characters who would become, in fact, the false
> reality on stage, to the point of reducing the real
> dancers to the stature of puppets.[28]

This statement also betrayed, by implication, a sophisticated

understanding of an important Cubist phrasing of Cocteau's

scenario in the relationship submitted between the Managers

and the dancers.   Cocteau was saying that the false takes on

the real, and the real assumes the false.   When a <u>chromo</u>,

Cocteau's real postcard, was placed within the artificial arena

of a collage, the ostensible relationship of what should remain

real and artificial became unstable--multiple identities were

made available for the various components of the collage.

The same Cubist shuttling of identities occurred in the juxta-

position of Managers and acts and was implied in Cocteau's

statement.   The compounding of relationships between the

Managers and the performers resulted in three possible read-

ings.   First, the Managers represented the real and the acts

assumed a theatrical artificiality in the illusion of a real-

life situation: that is, the managers or hawkers in a real-

life situation stood aside from the stage previews of the

performers in order to comment to the audience about them.

Secondly, the Cubist constructions of Picasso transformed

the Managers into fabricated, non-human creatures which towered

above and in contrast to the human reality and frailty of
the three acts. And finally, the size and stage presence of
the Managers took on a super-reality in performance which
rendered the real dancers nothing more than programmed dolls--
Cocteau's reading. Like the spatial flip-flops of planes in
Cubist illusionism, or similar to the changing aspects of an
optical illusion, only one reading is permitted at a time.
The expressive function, then, of Picasso's costume style for
the French and American Managers was that of establishing
characterization and character relationships, and as such was
a borrowing of Futurist theatrical theory for non-Futurist
performance goals. Those goals corresponded to the dramatic
and expressive aspects of the scenario; and, the articulation
of those aspects was made through the strategies of Cubism.

The Set

The specifications in Cocteau's scenario for the stage
set were simple. Picasso was asked to create an urban setting
for a théâtre forain and to allow for a fair-booth proscenium
through which the acts would enter for the parade. In a
preliminary drawing (Fig. 47), Picasso planned to place an over-
sized, false proscenium at the center of the stage. Flanking
the false proscenium, Picasso situated schematic depictions
of buildings and trees. In the lower right hand corner of
another early sketch (Fig. 48), Picasso attempted to include
the suggestion in silhouette of the crowd described by Cocteau
in his scenario, a narrative aspect of the set which was left
out in the final version.[29] The actual set Picasso designed

for the production was largely similar to the preliminary
drawings, with a few additional touches added (Fig. 50).
The large proscenium was maintained, although its acute
angle was now placed to the left. The architectural elements in the final version flanked the proscenium rather
than surrounded it. The clear indications of trees in the
sketches were replaced with a large shrub to the right, one
overhanging clump of foliage, and the suggestion in silhouette of a tree which flanked the right side of the proscenium.
The false proscenium of the final version was embellished
with scrollwork, a lyre, and to the left a cropped panel
depicting a semi-clothed, running female figure. Before and
to either side of the false proscenium, Picasso positioned
two railings with balusters.

The only remaining evidence of the stage set is a
black and white photograph taken of the original 1917 production at the Théâtre du Châtelet in Paris (Fig. 50). What
appears to be a toile de fond--the customary backdrop in
Ballets Russes productions which allowed the dancers ample
floor space on which to move--was actually a three-dimensional
stage set. Although Picasso reserved room enough for the
dancers downstage, the cityscape and fairbooth proscenium
constituted a series of stage flats (see Appendix 2). If
the style of the set was one of the more startling elements
of Parade for its original audience, the set's physical make-
up was, in some respects, quite conservative. Stage scenery
for the ballet in the nineteenth and early twentieth centuries
had, itself, remained conventional. There was usually a

toile de fond depicting the central scenic motif, be it a
swan lake or a baroque staircase. Flanking the stage from
the proscenium arch to the toile de fond were a series of
framing flats, most usually silhouettes of trees with overhanging branches. Picasso's set did not really violate this
convention, but it did wittily play upon it. The proscenium
arch of the fairbooth was upstage, and although its opened
curtains revealed another expanse of upstage space limited by
a white backcloth, the entire motif served the purpose of
the traditional toile de fond. Picasso's trees, however,
were not positioned in the customary manner. The first pair
of downstage legs, which framed the setting, represented
large tree trunks. The placing of other foliage on the set
has been mentioned and did not conform to the bracketing tree
flats of conventional practice. Rather, Picasso painted the
black legs to each side of the stage--curtains which were
normally used in addition to other flanking scenic elements
to block glimpses of backstage and to provide entrance and
exit ways for the dancers--to represent buildings. He painted
these structural givens of the stage set white and, in an
intentionally gauche manner, inserted large rectangles of
black to represent windows.

The black-and-white photograph of Picasso's set posed
problems for the Robert Joffrey revival of Parade. Some
areas in the photograph read ambiguously in terms of the
separation of planes. A good example of spatial confusion
is the upper right-hand corner foliate shape: to which flat
did it belong--to the forward false proscenium, to one of

the side building legs, or was it flown in alone? A far
knottier problem, however, for Joffrey's scenic designers,
was the original color of the set. There was very little to
go on except the memories of Massine and of others who saw
the original production.[30] Most accounts recalled that the
stage set was considerably subdued in color, although in what
specific manner it was difficult to remember. In a letter
to William Crawford--Robert Joffrey's General Manager--Lydia
Sokolova, a member of the original Ballets Russes who frequently danced the role of the Little American Girl, wrote
that the set was

> ...a monochrome sketch in pale sepia or light brown.
> The lyre gilded over the arch. Not very vividly.
> Some dark green trees but not distinct. More a sug-
> gestion than reality.[31]

It was decided upon by Robert Joffrey and Douglas Cooper,
who was the major scenic consultant, that a grayish-brown and
a scrubbed beige would color the architectural legs, backcloth,
and balustrades. The foliage would be painted a dark green,
the fairbooth proscenium a dark red, and the embellishments
of the scroll, lyre, and female figure in a muted gold.
Cooper, whom Picasso allowed to speak for him in all matters
of color choice,[32] suggested that the red, green, and gold
be matched with the palette of those paintings surrounding
the production of Parade, colors which in these paintings
tended to be of a somber cast.

Along with the costumes for the American and French
Managers, the stage set was the other scenic element in the
ballet which was most blatantly Cubist for the first audience,

and for that matter, all succeeding audiences. And Cubist
the stage set does appear, with its clusters of acute angles
and geometric stylization. What is unusual about Picasso's
Cubist set is the subject matter. Although a cityscape was
specifically requested in Cocteau's scenario, this was the
first time since the early Horta de San Juan townscapes of
1909 that Picasso had created an urban setting within the
general style of Cubism. The city had not been an improper
iconography for other Cubists like Delaunay, Leger, and Gris.
Picasso's Cubist iconography, however, had attended to other
things and events. In fact, there are amusing allusions to
Picasso's major Cubist concern for still life in the set for
Parade. Although the lyre over the proscenium entrance was
not a familiar object in Picasso's Cubist still lives, there
were drawn on the end balusters of the railings to each side
of the fairbooth proscenium two exceedingly familiar Cubist
things: a violin and a mandolin.

In Cocteau's Cahier romain, there are several drawings
the poet made while in Naples (Figs. 115, 120, 121, and 122).
The location of the cityscapes was made clear in one drawing
where Cocteau drew a fuming Mt. Vesuvius in the background.
Not only are these three drawings delightful--especially the
third "Cubist variation" which incorporated Picasso's portrait,
intriguingly enough in dual aspect--but they are informative
for what they indicate about the geographical location of
Picasso's stage setting for Parade. Picasso's architectural
legs in the stage set were curiously non-Parisian. The window ranges ran to the ground, which made the buildings look

more like skyscrapers than the city architecture of Paris.
Cocteau's drawings strongly suggest that although Cocteau's
scenario was specifically a Parisian boulevard on a Sunday
afternoon, Picasso's source for his buildings was Neapolitan,
not Parisian. To further substantiate the generalized setting
of Picasso's Parade, Cocteau wrote in his Cahier romain the
following imperative (Fig. 90):

> You must form streets by combining the perspectives
> of the buildings which bob like buoys in Naples,
> Paris, Montmartre, Clichy, Place Pigalle, etc....[33]

With the impress of Futurism conditioning the making of Parade
on both the parts of Picasso and Cocteau, it seems fitting
that even the setting proper of the ballet negotiated two
spheres: French and Italian.

To what extent, however, was Picasso's stage setting
Cubist beyond Cocteau's metaphor for Cubism, a "chute des
angles?" First of all, the setting in its entirety is not
as ambiguously conceived in the placement of its planes as
the majority of Picasso's Cubist paintings. This must have
been a function of the necessity that a theatrical setting
be easily readable for its audiences. But, there are ways
in which the set was tied more intimately to Picasso's Cubism.
One self-referential gesture was made in the architectural
and foliate motifs. Their pointilist pattern, bold in the
former, more delicate in the latter, made a visual pun upon
the stippled patterns in Picasso paintings done during 1914
and 1916, which bear the phase marker "Rococo Cubism." Most
important, however, in a subtler Cubist reading of the setting
was the distortion and disjunction of the scenic elements.

The fairbooth proscenium was far too large, looming as impressively as the flanking architectural legs. As an even stylized depiction of the scene as it might have appeared in real life, the placing of the motifs was awkward. Is it to be assumed that the six architectural legs in depth offered the spectator a view down a street which ends in a fairbooth, or even, that the two sets of buildings held the fairbooth proscenium in something of a vice? These questions may be answered in the negative. In true Cubist fashion, Picasso has gathered reminiscences of a real situation into a montage of aspects. Cocteau, in the Cahier romain, wrote poetically about what must have been the spirit informing the creation of Picasso's stage set (Figs. 83 and 84):

> The choreography of Perspectives is inspired not by what moves but by immobile objects, around which one moves, especially by the way buildings turn, combine, stoop, get up again, and buckle according to one's walk down a street. [34]

In Picasso's stage set there were only glimpses of that hypothetical boulevard where the drama of the parade was played out. Inasmuch as Picasso was working with an outdoor urban setting and brought together near and far, small and large, side and front in one image, it is submitted, although less insistently than in other cases, that Picasso was looking at and personally responding, once again, to Futurism.

Picasso's stage set was built up of opaque planes which may be associated with Synthetic Cubism. On the other hand, a correspondence of Picasso's style here with that particular phase in his art was qualified by the monochromatic color, which was more appropriately affiliated with the earlier,

Analytic phase of Cubism. Another aspect of Picasso's scenic
designs, however, suggests the reasons for this particular
choice. Stylistically, the Managers' costumes were joined
to the set in the angular Cubism of their forms. Together
they formed a unified part of the scenic design. It has
already been posited that the Managers and the acts established
two psychological groups, the latter controlled and manipulated
by the former. Another way in which this dramatic separation
was stressed was through color discrepancy. Massine indicated,
in conversation that the set of Picasso was intentionally
made monochromatic so as to put into relief the bold colors
of the costumes of the three acts.[35] This proved true in
Joffrey's performance of Parade. The saturated colors of the
Magician, the Little American Girl, and the Two Acrobats were
put into dazzling relief by the subdued palette of the stage
set. Cocteau spoke of the acts being opposed to the Cubist
Managers like chromo elements in a Cubist collage. Another
crucial feature of the dialectic Cocteau perceived was the
very background for this relationship--the stage set itself.
The stage set was figuratively the flat surface upon which
Picasso "pasted" in the manner of a collage the real elements
of the Chinese Magician, the Little American Girl, and the
Two Acrobats. In addition to the psychological readings
possible between the Managers and the acts, the three acts
received further dramatic emphasis by being sharply punctuated
in their presence on stage by the stage set before which they
performed.

CHAPTER IV

THE MISE EN SCENE: THE OVERTURE CURTAIN

Le rideau rouge se lève sur des fêtes qui boule-
versent la France et qui entraînent une foule
en extase derrière le char de Dionysos...

Jean Cocteau[1]

The overture curtain or rideau de scène was a second

curtain, more accurately, a painted stretched-canvas flat,

which was revealed after the red-velvet house curtain or

rideau rouge was either parted or raised. It was exposed

briefly during the overture to the ballet or during the first

bars of the score if the music did not include an overture

proper. Overture curtains for productions outside of the

Ballets Russes often displayed purely decorative designs.

When Diaghilev, however, used an overture curtain for a produc-

tion, it depicted a representational scene which was affilia-

ted, in the most general terms, with the narrative of the

ballet. The overture curtains of the Ballets Russes were,

in effect, large paintings. Up until the 1917 spring season

of the Ballets Russes, Diaghilev had not yet used an overture

curtain. The rideau rouge opened directly on the ballet itself.

If an overture was included in the musical score, as for

example in Stravinsky's Le Sacre du Printemps, it was played

before the rideau rouge and with the house lights dimmed.

Although Picasso's commission by Diaghilev in the fall of 1916 included the creation of an overture curtain, Parade was not the first ballet in the company's repertory to use an overture curtain in actual performance. Larionov's curtain for Les Contes russes, commissioned in early 1917, was the first to appear to the public--one week before the premiere of Parade on May 11. In spite of the number of artists of the "School of Paris" who contributed their designs to the Ballets Russes, the request for an overture curtain was fairly infrequent. In a sense, the oversized, representational overture curtain was transferred by these artists from the proscenium to the back of the stage. Unlike Picasso's three-dimensional set for Parade, many of the decors for the Ballets Russes productions of the 1920's consisted of a large, painted canvas flat placed to the rear of the stage--the backcloth. These were the gargantuan "easel paintings" which many contemporary critics complained drew attention away from the choreography.[2] Bakst's overture curtain for La Boutique fantasque (1919), Benois's for the 1925 revival of Petrouschka, and Goncharova's for the 1926 revival of Firebird were the few distinguished overture curtains shown by Diaghilev during the later phase of Ballets Russes. It was Picasso who popularized the large, representational curtain and who was, almost without exception, asked to create an overture curtain when his collaboration was desired by Diaghilev. Actually, only one other overture curtain by Picasso, designed especially for the 1919 production of Le Tricorne, was executed for Diaghilev. Picasso created several plans for an overture curtain for Pulcinella

(1920), but none of them were accepted by Diaghilev for the final scenic design. Mercure (1924) used an overture curtain, but it was not originally conceived for a Ballets Russes production.[3] The overture curtain for Diaghilev's Le Train bleu was a blowup of an earlier painting by Picasso, but its transfer to a large scale curtain was not executed by him.

The Style of the Overture Curtain

Picasso's curtain for Parade was revealed during Satie's short Prélude du Rideau Rouge (Fig. 51).[4] It was singularly immense in contrast to other curtains done for the Ballets Russes by other artists and by Picasso himself. It measured 10.60 meters in height and 17.25 meters in length and was conceived specifically to fill the entire space of the proscenium arch of the Théâtre du Châtelet. Only the curtain for Le Tricorne, which was first seen at the Alhambra in London, approximated the scale of the curtain for Parade. When Massine was first asked about Parade's overture curtain in an interview with this writer, his first words were, "Si grand, ce rideau!"[5] A photograph of Picasso and several assistants, seated on the curtain during its execution in a studio on the Butte Chaumont in Paris, gives a good indication of the immense size of what, in essence, amounted to the largest painting Picasso ever created (Fig. 52). Picasso painted the curtain in tempera, which was the usual medium for a theatrical canvas flat. Although Picasso used the assistance of several artists to fill in the less compositionally important areas of the curtain, the original program

for _Parade_ claimed that "Le rideau a été brossé par Picasso
lui-même."[6]

Picasso's overture curtain depicts the gathering of
variously costumed figures in a stage setting: eight personages
and four animals. Flanking the scene are a series of tied-back
theatrical curtains. To the rear of this stage space is a
landscape. The scene itself is composed in two sections.
To the right, seated and standing around a table which is
placed on a small tapis, are six figures and a lying dog. The
attention of four of the figures is drawn to a more formalized
action at the left of the stage area. Placed behind a banded
ball patterned with stars is a mare, fitted out with a pair
of strapped-on wings, who suckles her colt. Standing on the
back of the white mare is a diminutive female figure who, in
a short dress with wings, offers assistance to a small monkey
who is mounting a striped ladder. In general terms, this is
the composition of Picasso's curtain.

In examining and situating the style of the overture
curtain, it is natural to turn back to earlier representational
and pre-Cubist moments in Picasso's _oeuvre_, especially to
the Circus Period in light of the types Picasso has chosen
for his ensemble. Picasso's line in the overture curtain
was crisp and delineated figures which were naturalistic and
devoid of the mannerist attenuations of some of the Blue
Period and earlier canvases. And yet, a direct correlation
of the figure style in this curtain with the generally more
naturalistic figures of the Circus Period is not entirely
satisfying. In spite of the apparent lack of a Cubist look

to the curtain, its figure style, like that of Picasso's
recent new realistic mode of 1914, was created not against
but through a Cubist sensibility. What qualified a "representational style" in the overture curtain was the curious flatness
of the figures. The simplified drawing, the summary modeling,
and the block-coloring of form align Picasso's style with
that of Henri Rousseau to the extent that the curtain may be
stylistically categorized as "primitivizing," and "naive."
Still, the apparent and intentional spatial ambiguities of
Picasso's composition do establish a particular Cubist allegiance, which for most matters may be dismissed in formal
discussions of Rousseau's style.

First and most strikingly, in terms of the spatial
eccentricities of the curtain, the composition of the two
figure groups tends to warp spatially into a single plane.
The positioning of this group into an actual space would
displace space in depth for at least fifteen feet—from
the banded ball back to the tricolored ladder. The hovering
quality of the group is attributable to the lack of shadows
cast by the mare and her colt, the ball, and the lying dog.
The vertical stacking of form in the table group is encouraged
by the way in which the table is drawn. Its surface is banked
more steeply than it would appear in natural vision. But the
steeping is a twisted affair. Like a Cézannesque tablecloth,
the seated Harlequin figure to our side of the table interrupts
the logical, spatial continuity of the table, and, consequently,
the left side of the table is at odds with the right side.
Another ploy Picasso used to collapse the space of his figure

composition was to bank the drawing of the tapis, on which
the right-hand group was placed, and to omit any interior
modeling so that the tapis appeared evenly scrubbed in its
brownish coloring. Two passages to the rear of the scene
further add to the sense of a forward cramping of space.
A diagonally positioned rectangle to the right of the composition behind the standing and/or kneeling woman with a bonnet
not only blocks space to the rear, but it conjoins itself
to the woman in a way so as to suggest a portrait canvas, the
effect of which further compresses the spaces of this vicinity.
To the other side of the group, the upward movement of the
ladder is enhanced by the nature of the ground on which it
is placed. Shortly behind the legs of the white mare, the
orthogonals of the stage floor are blurred so as to create
something of a flap which has been folded up from the stage
planks. Like the rectangular plane to the right, the area
of the ladder spatially arrests a continuous depth.

The front legs and wings of the white mare are fore-
shortened, yet the neck is abruptly wrenched into an apparent
profile. But, the Harlequin figure to our side of the table,
who turns his body and head to direct his attention to the
white mare, displays in his position the most aggravated
violation of foreshortening. The unmodeled, flat-diamond
pattern of his costume thwarts all attempts to locate his
figure in one static position. The lack of modeling and of
any apparent indication of neck musculature contributes to
a startling effect--two different body positions given
simultaneously. First, with his back to us, the Harlequin

may be casting his glance with his head turned over his left
shoulder with either his left leg slung over his right leg or
vice versa. Or, he may be seated, chest forward, with his
head turned across his right shoulder. In this case, his
legs may again be crossed in one of two ways. In both positions, whether the torso is seen from the front or from the
back, the reading of the left leg thrown over the right is
somewhat the stronger impression due to the suggestion of
a calf line which optically creates an overlapping of two
planes.

Leo Steinberg argues that the earlier phases of Analytic and Synthetic Cubism offered a mysterious gathering of
reminiscences and selected aspects of the object, not a
simultaneous presentation of all perspectives. It was only
towards the end of World War I that Picasso seriously addressed
himself to an "embracing of all aspects" of the object, a goal
which resulted pictorially in what might be termed a true
simultaneity of perspectives on a flat surface. Picasso's
concern for simultaneity, according to Steinberg, was first
stated in his invention of the face with dual aspects--a
frontal view which accommodated its own profile.[7] The Harlequin
(1915) and the French Manager in Parade were early examples
of this device. What may be added to these observations
was Picasso's attention, in the figure of the Parade Harlequin,
to a similar strategy, which Steinberg only sees operative
in the working out of the 1950 Femmes d'Alger series: the
quest for a corporeal simultaneity of the entire body. The
Mannerist twist of the Harlequin's body is so ambiguous that

it affords the spectator its entirety from one point of view.

The manner in which the flattened spatial effect of
the figure composition played in concert with the remainder
of the curtain's composition--the stage setting--derived
from Cubist collage. Perhaps "in concert" is an inaccurate
expression. With the subtle adjustment of flattened planes
established in the figure group, Picasso then placed that
group on a ground which countered its spatial system. Supporting the flattened assembly of people and animals is a
stage floor, whose planks are arranged in orthogonals that
converge at a vanishing area and whose configuration suggests
spatial depth. Furthermore, the landscape to the rear and
the overlapping sets of theatrical draperies contribute to
an ample illusionistic space. The scheme Picasso used in
the overture curtain to sabotage the spatial integrity of
the image--the juxtaposition of divergent styles--was a hallmark of Cubist collage. Spatial irritations were also a feature of Picasso's "representational" style, which ran from
1914 through the mid-twenties in both drawings and paintings.
The 1923 Pipes of Pan (Fig. 53) is a subtle essay in the
complication of an illusionistic system, where modeled passages
are juxtaposed with unmodeled areas and unmodulated rear
planes.[8] Although Picasso had first explored this idea in
drawings--notably, the 1915 Jacob and Vollard portraits--the
Parade overture curtain was the first painting to articulate
the artist's new and important variation in Cubist collage.

The original color of the overture curtain is difficult
to determine because of deterioration. Colors have faded

and the fabric is quite worn.[9] For the 1921 revival of _Parade_,
the colors had lost enough of their saturation that Diaghilev
asked Picasso to touch it up. Picasso refused, preferring
the curtain in its muted state.[10] The color choice of the
overture curtain, which will be assumed to have been originally
bolder, is characterized by the dominant use of red, white,
and blue. This particular color combination is stated empha-
tically in the French tri-color pattern of the ladder and
the rims of the drum. Embracing the central figure composition from the sides and above are the broad expanses of red
stage curtains. Red is also used in the diamond pattern of
the Harlequin's costume to accentuate the compositional
importance of the Harlequin. White is liberally employed to
fill the contours of the mare, the colt, and the winged female figure. Finally, blue marks the perimeter of the figure
scene which is presented within the broad framing device of
the red drapery; it colors the navy blouse of the seated male
to the far right, the starred ball to the left, and the
mountains and sky of the landscape in the background. Against
the major compositional use of red, white, and blue are played
in a more subordinate role the hues of beige, dark lavender,
gray, and lime green.

The Iconography of the Overture Curtain

Picasso's overture curtain did not depict a specific
moment from Cocteau's ballet, nor did it present any of the
personages who figured in the scenario. Likewise, in the
three other overture curtains Picasso designed for the Ballets
Russes—those for _Le Tricorne_, _Pulcinella_, and _Le Train bleu_—

no reference was made to the narrative or characters.[11] The
function of Picasso's overture curtains has thus been viewed
by previous commentators to be one which evoked a mood and
atmosphere appropriate for the ballet, without making any
direct comment upon the ballet's content. This critical
attitude implies that the overture curtains worked in exact
parallel to the musical overture--setting a mood of anticipation for the following dramatic action. If this were the
case, the conjoining of Parade's overture curtain to Cocteau's
scenario becomes awkward. The relaxed setting of the overture curtain, according to one interpretation, contains a
groups of forains finishing a meal and dawdling between acts.[12]
If this activity evokes a leisurely tone, it also expressively
opposes the rapid pace and exuberance of the ballet's action.
The curtain hardly establishes a compatible mood for Cocteau's narrative. Concerning the content of Picasso's overture
curtain, Douglas Cooper in Picasso Theater--the most extensive
critical evaluation of Picasso's scenic oeuvre to date--
writes the following:

> The prelude to the ballet, seen while the overture was
> being played, was a large drop-curtain decorated with
> one of the tenderest and most romantically evocative
> of all Picasso's circus compositions...This [the over-
> ture curtain] is popular imagery at its most decorative
> and enchanting, and the sophisticatedly naive style of
> painting emphasizes the point.[14]

Cooper's comments are representative of all critical evaluations of Parade's overture curtain. This perspective considers
the overture curtain--and the other curtains--to be essentially
decorative adjuncts to the ballet. What has gone entirely
unnoticed is the direct bearing Parade's curtain has on

Cocteau's scenario. Picasso's overture curtain, the largest
image he ever created, has remained exempt from any iconographical analysis whatsoever. The overture curtain means
considerably more than a decoratively neutral assemblage of
figures. To come closer to the curtain's meaning and to its
active relationship to Parade, it is necessary to examine
carefully the various elements of the composition and to be
on the alert for special signifying functions of the objects,
characters, and setting. The inquiry into possibly richer
levels of meaning should not seem contrary to the spirit
of Picasso's art, which mediated between the prosaic and
the mysterious.

The figure composition, the costumed characters, and
the quiet mood of the overture curtain have been observed to
find their sources in the paintings of Watteau.[14] A more
immediate source for the setting, characters, and atmosphere
of Picasso's curtain is found in the works of the artist's
1905 Circus Period. The Saltimbanque Family (Fig. 55) contained several motifs which were used again in Parade's
curtain: the ladder to the left, a girl balancing, the
Harlequin figure, and the horse. And, the gentle quietness
of the Circus Period images was repeated in the curtain.

The settings for the circus figures of 1905 are, for
the most part, undifferentiated locales and landscapes. The
setting for the figures in the overture curtain is not the
open air but a stage sheltered from above and from the sides
by draped, red velvet curtains. However, behind the group
of figures is a landscape, whose features are more specific

than those of the Circus Period landscapes. An expanse of green lawn is bordered by a row of shrubbery which partially conceals the single stone arch of the remains of a Roman viaduct. The insertion of antique architecture in the curtain is one of several reminders in Picasso's composition that its design was contrived during the artist's sojourn in Rome, Pompeii, and Naples. The impress of the south on Picasso is an important aspect of the overture curtain and the Roman arch most noticeably signals its presence, as well of course as the strangely inverted column whose location, however, appears to be more on the stage than in the open landscape. The range of mountains which rises in the distant background also offers a reminiscence of the south, although one which is somewhat ambiguous. Picasso would not have seen mountains in Rome but in Naples. And, the dominant feature of these mountains, seen from both Naples and Pompeii, would have been Mt. Vesuvius. The highest peak in Picasso's landscape does suggest the silhouette of Mt. Vesuvius, a reading supported by the two white clouds above which teasingly may be either innocent cumulus formations or smoke rising from the mouth of Vesuvius' crater. The details, then, of the landscape establish the fact that the setting is neither French nor nonspecific but Mediterranean.

The Harlequin Group

The figures on the stage break easily into two groups: those characters standing and seated around the table to the right (Fig. 57); and, the group dominated by the winged horse

to the left (Fig. 58). Several of the individuals involved
in the meal at the table are familiar figures from Picasso's
Circus Period: notably, the two Harlequins on the far and
near side of the table. The partly kneeling and standing
woman to the far right of this group is not in the costume
of a circus performer, but she is, nevertheless, associated
with the major canvas from the Circus Period, The Family of
Saltimbanques in the National Gallery of Art, Washington,
D.C. (Fig. 56). Although she is without a shawl and her hair
has been let down, the woman in the overture curtain is identified with the seated woman in the lower right-hand corner
of the earlier composition by the Majorcan hat she wears.
The other figures in this group are not affiliated with the
Circus Period directly. The "Majorcan woman" of the curtain
stands beside a seated man, who wears the uniform of a Neapolitan sailor. The woman on the far side of the table,
who nestles her head on the shoulder of the Harlequin, carries
no immediately specific identity other than female figure.
Standing and seated behind the left-hand side of the table
are a blackamoor and another male figure who strums the
guitar and wears the costume of a toreador. These two last
figures appear to be in attendance on the table's company:
the one a servant, the other a provider of music.

Who are these people gathered around the table? The
general impression, encouraged by the two Harlequins, is that
they are forains, performers affiliated with traveling fairs.
This impression is substantiated by other elements in the
tableau: the ladder, drum, the ball, and the tapis, or acro-

bats' performing mat, on which the right-hand group is placed.
Still, the Blackamoor, the Toreador, and the Sailor resist
specific placement within a fair environment other than the
simple identity of costumed performer. Nevertheless, if the
group as a whole can be associated with theatrical performance,
can the meanings of these figures be extended beyond the
simple category of "performers?"

The Harlequin figure had been prominent in Picasso's
earlier art. Even before appearing so frequently in the
paintings and drawings of the Circus Period, Picasso had painted
the Harlequin as early as 1901 in The Jugglers. Picasso's
Harlequins are always identifiable by the diamond pattern
of their costumes. Theodore Reff points out, in an article
on Picasso's circus types, that by the early twentieth century
the distinction between the Harlequin character of the commedia
dell'arte, the Saltimbanque or lowest-class acrobat in the
European fair, and the Court Fool had become blurred.[15] The
costume of the Harlequin might clothe the acrobat or the
clown, because the three earlier characters of the fair had
become assimilated into the clowns and acrobats of the modern
circus.

Picasso identified his Harlequins with the acrobats
and jugglers, specifically the Saltimbanques. A tendency of
Picasso to identify himself overtly with the Harlequin is
revealed in several self-portraits in Harlequin costume painted
between 1900 and 1905. Picasso's fascination with the Harlequin-acrobat appears to have been his association of the
figure with his own activities; the categories of performer

and outsider, which applied to the Saltimbanques, could also accommodate the modern artist. In this metaphor, Reff sees Picasso's first, fully realized alter ego. The Harlequin figure, however, is not always a self-portrait of the artist, although once the identification is made in a self-portrait, it is assumed that the artist's personal association with the character still resonates even in those works in which the features of the Harlequin do not match those of Picasso. The Harlequin in the red-diamond costume to our side of the table establishes a focal point by his isolation from the other characters and by the uninterrupted contour of his full-figure silhouette. Is this figure a self-portrait of the artist? It is important for the interpretation presented here that this identification be made either by letting the Harlequin stand as a generalized emblem of the artist or, more convincingly, by claiming it a self-portrait.

The argument for the _Parade_ Harlequin representing a self-portrait of the artist is not as easy as it is for other Harlequins, whose features are unequivocally those of Picasso. And yet, there are physical features of this Harlequin which do strongly suggest Picasso's: the squat proportions of the torso and the broad shoulders. The profile, which should offer the most convincing evidence, can be compared for argument with a photograph of the artist taken in 1917 and with a self-portrait drawing (Figs. 2 and 59). The major feature of the Harlequin which is not Picasso's is the nose, which is bolder and whose ridge is not as continuous with the brow-line as it is in Picasso's actual profile. Strong points of comparison, however, can be made between the shape of the ear, the strong jaw line, and the cut of the hair. It might be observed that the Harlequin's hair is cropped, unlike Picasso's longer hair. But, when Picasso's hair, which was parted to his left side, was slicked down close to the skull, as is seen in the 1917 photograph, its appearance was not at all dissimilar to the Parade Harlequin head. Another possible comparison can be made between the poses in the drawing and in the curtain. The figure in the drawing is not as ambiguously turned as the Harlequin, but the two do share the common features of a propped torso seen from the back and displaying a left-turned, flattened profile.

If the argument is fair that the features of the Harlequin match those of Picasso, then the compositional and color importance attached to the Harlequin is explained by its identity as a familiar alter-ego of Picasso, one which can sustain the earlier metaphor of the artist as a performer and an outsider. It will later be suggested why it would have been inappropriate for Picasso to have assigned to the Harlequin the features of an easily identifiable self-portrait.

A second Harlequin in a blue-brown diamond costume sits across the table from the Picasso Harlequin and lifts his wine glass in the gesture of a toast. His individualized features recall the man who worked closely with Picasso on Parade: Jean Cocteau. A comparison of this Harlequin with a period photograph of Cocteau allows this identity to be made (Fig. 60). The most prominent feature of Cocteau's face and the one Picasso emphasized in the Harlequin's was the nose.

And, echoed in the Harlequin are Cocteau's thin lips and the receding profile-line that runs from the upper lip down to the chin and to the jaw, which is not as squared as the Picasso-Harlequin's. In the same manner that the other Harlequin's mesomorphic body matched that of Picasso and helped establish a self-portrait, the endomorphic characteristics of the blue-brown Harlequin--narrow torso, bony shoulders, thin neck and face--suggest the portrait of the younger poet Cocteau. One might argue against the attribution by pointing out that the Harlequin's embracing of the young girl to his left runs counter to Cocteau's homosexuality. However, it is known that in emulation of Picasso's courting of Olga Koklova in Rome, Cocteau mock-courted the dancer who was first assigned by Diaghilev to play the Little American Girl--Marie Shabelska. Picasso and Cocteau double-dated, and the charade was humorously enjoyed by all.[16]

If the two Harlequins may be considered personas for Picasso and Cocteau, one solution is suggested for the identifications of the other sitters. There are four men seated at the table; Parade's collaboration consisted of four men. A portrayal of the collaborators seated around the table is an attractive interpretation, and it would accelerate the search for meaning in the overture curtain. Unfortunately, the argument is awkward. The Toreador and the Sailor would have to accommodate the identities of Satie and Massine. The only helpful clue is the guitar the Toreador is playing, a musical attribute which might suggest Satie. But little evidence supports the attributions of Satie and Massine to the Toreador and Sailor. Picasso was known to be an artist who responded quickly to his immediate environment and who incorporated topical bits and pieces into his art. The Toreador, the Sailor and the Blackamoor may be personal recollections of the past and present. The Sailor's costume is Neapolitan. The Toreador may be a biographical allusion to Picasso's Spanishness and to the seated Cubist portraits of musicians. Picasso's world during this time was not only the classical south but also the Ballets Russes, a special theatrical world with a great array of costumes backlogged in the repertory. The three men may then be a reminder of Picasso's experience with the company's productions, although no ballet in the repertory in 1917 included costumes for a Neapolitan Sailor or for a Toreador. However, the Blackamoor is associated with one ballet which was a staple of the early Ballets Russes seasons and which was performed during the itinerant 1917 season-- Schéhérazade.

Although the claim that the men at the table are Parade's collaborators is difficult to substantiate, one piece of tantalizing evidence remains. Cocteau wrote Massine in Rome in early January of 1917, introducing himself and establishing a cordial rapport before personally meeting the choreographer. In this letter, Cocteau spoke glowingly of the coming team effort and of his eagerness to meet Massine, who was the remaining link in the collaboration. At the end of the letter, Cocteau drew a square and placed around it, beginning at the top and moving counter-clockwise, the following seating: C (Cocteau); P (Picasso); S (Satie); VOUS (Massine).

The collaboration was seen to be a friendly group gathered around a table.[17]

An argument remains, though, that makes the identification of only two of the collaborators--Picasso and Cocteau-- satisfying in psychological and in historical terms. Cocteau was quickly drawn to the support of Picasso several years before Parade. He championed his work, idolized him, and identified with his artistic attitudes. For Cocteau, the first meeting with Picasso was the greatest event in his life.[18] Cocteau had enthusiastically convinced Picasso to join Parade, and it was Cocteau who traveled with Picasso to Rome in February 1917. During rehearsals in Rome, Satie was absent, preferring to remain in Arcueil and having already completed the score for Parade. Massine was extremely young at the time-- seventeen years old--and it seems natural to assume that Picasso and Cocteau were more properly contemporaries in their shared Parisian experiences and in their ages, which were respectively thirty-six and twenty-seven. With Cocteau taking the active role he did in the setting of the choreography, Picasso might have sensed during his preliminary thinking out of the curtain in Rome that the core of the collaboration was really Cocteau and himself. This particular view, if accurate, is compatible with the contention presented here that the true formative forces in the making of Parade were Picasso and Cocteau. Cocteau was intrigued by Picasso's identification with the Harlequin figure and knew about it before he met Picasso in 1914. In later writings, Cocteau used the Harlequin to refer metaphorically to Picasso. When Cocteau managed to inveigle

his first meeting with Picasso through the American composer
Edgar Varèse, the young poet contrived to present himself in
a way which would ingratiate himself with the artist. Cocteau
appeared at Picasso's doorstep dressed as a Harlequin.[19]

The Pegasus Group

Four members of the group around the table cast their
gaze to the left, although the exact focus of their glances
differs and is difficult to define precisely in each case.
The Cocteau-Harlequin and the Majorcan Woman watch the monkey
climb the ladder. The Neapolitan Sailor turns to his left
and includes in his glance the young girl on the back of the
horse and the monkey, while the Picasso-Harlequin concentrates
upon the young girl alone. What does this tableau to the
left mean? Its action is more formalized and staged than the
casually gathered group to the right. Is the activity to the
left separated dramatically from the table assembly? Does
it only cause a soft distraction away from the business of
pausing over a meal, or does it affiliate itself more intimately with the seated group? What initially appears in the
left-hand group to be a somewhat artificial gathering of
animals, a young girl, and assorted objects, only fancifully
associated with the milieu of the forains, was very much a
part of the sights and activities of the cirque and the
théâtre forain.

The dominant contrast of the entire curtain is the
large white mare, who is fitted out with a pair of wings to
suggest a Pegasus. Picasso's act of transforming a female
horse, who is suckling her colt, into a male Pegasus by

strapping a pair of wings around her whimsically confounds the identity of gender and will be important in an interpretation of the curtain's meaning. However, the mare-Pegasus combination did not issue solely from the imagination of Picasso. Horses in the cirque, as well as in equestrian competition, were trained to perform in two major categories: dressage and dressage libre. Dressage was the display of a horse's proficiency of movement with a mounted rider, bridle, and reins. Dressage libre, on the other hand, was the performance of movements made without a rider and verbally guided by a trainer using a whip. In the European circus in the nineteenth and early twentieth centuries, the trainer often strapped a pair of wings around the belly of the horse to suggest a Pegasus (Fig. 61). This device was particularly effective when the horse performed a variety of jumps (Fig. 62). There is no indication in the literature available on the European circus that a mare could not be transformed into a Pegasus for a performance. Picasso may have been intrigued with the notion of a double identity which was caused by a pair of artificial wings; and his initial choice of a mythical creature for his overture curtain may derive, in one respect, quite prosaically from the circus world.

The young girl who stands on the horse's back was also a familiar figure in the circus. Though she attends to the monkey and seems to be using the horse's back only as a prop, her activity with the monkey actually distracts her momentarily from her real métier: horseback rider. Her shortened dress drew its design from ballet costume. Practically, it was important that the horseback rider's legs be as free as possible. Everyday female sporting dress was, of course, out of the question in the nineteenth and early twentieth centuries. But, the standard female ballet costumes of the nineteenth century--the knee-length romantic skirt and the shorter, starched tutu--were ideally theatrical and decorous costumes for a female horseback rider (Fig. 63). Period photographs do not reveal a female horseback rider with wings attached to her back, which is not to say, of course, that they were not worn. But Picasso added them to the young girl's costume for more special reasons. First, the wings of her costume do unify her visually with the winged Pegasus. Secondly, the addition of wings to the costume presents another case of multiple identity. One ballet frequently performed by the Ballets Russes was Les Sylphides. Parade's debut in 1917 was included on a program with Les Sylphides. The sylphide was a water nymph whose costume consisted of the white tulle romantic skirt and wings (Fig. 64). In addition, then, to a Picasso-Harlequin, a Cocteau-Harlequin, and a Pegasus-mare, the young girl also supports two roles: horseback rider-ballet dancer.

The Saltimbanques' act often included a trained monkey. Easily trained to mimic acrobatic and comic movements, he was a favorite with the crowds (Fig. 65). The monkey's specialty was a tightrope act. In an early nineteenth-century lithograph, a monkey performs his parody of a human aerial artist on a double-rope apparatus (Fig. 66). The details in this print and in the previous photograph show how care-

fully Picasso incorporated into his art the artifacts of the
circus and fair, as well as the transcriptions by other
artists of that world. The starred acrobat's ball on which
the one monkey balances is transposed into the overture curtain.
Even the monkey's ballet tutu finds the source of its parody
in the horseback rider's costume. Richer for Picasso in its
objects and composition was the print. In fact, the borrowings
appear direct, although it is not known if Picasso saw this
particular lithograph. The monkey, the seated musician, the
tapis, the dog, the drum on its side, and the ladder were all
used by Picasso in the curtain. Especially significant is
the propped ladder to one side of the print's composition.
Incorporated earlier in the Saltimbanque Family watercolor
and placed in the Parade curtain, it later reappeared in
Minotauromachy and in a preliminary sketch for Guernica.

To get to the tautened ropes, the circus monkey
shinnied up a supporting post or was lifted to his perch
by his trainer. The Saltimbanque required a ladder if his
rope were placed high enough to impress the crowds. There
is no reason to suppose that a trained monkey might not
occasionally be led up a ladder by his trainer to begin his
act aloft. If this were the case, the horseback rider in
the curtain is performing a specific activity; she is helping
a trained monkey climb a circus ladder to his perch. The
monkey is about to walk a tightrope. What the group to the
right is watching is the commencement of a performance. The
initially puzzling omission is the perch and tightrope; the
monkey is climbing his ladder into the upper reaches of the

red-velvet curtains.

Picasso's monkey is not decoratively placed upon a
ladder. He is in the process of an act which was a familiar
sight in the contemporary circus and théâtres forains. And,
if the monkey's diminutive size does not demand the spectator's immediate attention, he is nevertheless the dramatic
center of the curtain's action. All elements are directed
towards him. The major characters at the table look up and
across to the monkey; the Pegasus, the horseback rider, and
the ladder are his assists. Picasso ironically made the
dramatic focus of his curtain one of the least significant
elements compositionally.

With the function and identities of the figures in
the Pegasus group established within the context of circus
performance, other and more fanciful meanings accrue. The
monkey appears frequently in Picasso's art, as well as his
relative the baboon. However, unlike the Harlequin and the
Minotaur, the symbolism of the monkey and baboon in Picasso's
art has never been profitably explored. John Berger in a
discussion of the 1953-54 Vallauris drawings, in which the
monkey figures prominently, parenthetically states that the
monkey represents freedom.[20] Berger's one observation provides
the extent of the criticism on the subject, which is puzzling
inasmuch as the monkey played a rich and complex role in
Picasso's imagination. And, its appearance in Parade's
overture curtain was its most ambitious performance in all
of Picasso's art.

The symbol of the simian in the west has suffered the

ascription of a goodly share of negative attributes. During

the classical period he carried the connotations of sycophant,

trickster, and ugliness.[21] His lot was not much improved

in the Middle Ages when he symbolized lasciviousness, vanity,

laziness, madness, and the vices in general. Another symbolic

function of the simian since antiquity was to represent the

Arts, specifically painting and sculpture. Until the Renais-

sance, the ape, baboon, and monkey were negative symbols for

illusionistic painting. In Platonic criticism, painting was

a second-hand imitation of an ideal realm. It was a deception.

This reputation was sustained into the Medieval period when

painting was branded a "forger of reality." As the simian

"aped" the manners of men, so did painting dare to mimic the

creativity of God.

The simian's negative symbol for the imitative arts

was inverted during the Renaissance, when the "aping" of

nature became the very essence of the startlingly illusionistic

painting of the Italian peninsula. The monkey maintained

this positive emblematic status until the 17th century in

France and Italy when the simian's behavior was viewed as

an indiscriminate copying of nature, which contrasted un-

favorably with man's intelligence and idealism. Northern

art in the 17th century and the French Rococo embraced the

simian in a more positive, if ironic, manner. The simian

metaphor took on elements of parody and travesty as a proxy

for the portrait painter and sculptor. Watteau popularized

the subject, which was part of the general vogue for the

genre of singeries. Chardin integrated another aspect into

the monkey's role in the arts by satirizing the artist's overriding preoccupation with a classical past and his slavish concern for academic theory (Fig. 67). Generally speaking, the concern for the monkey as an emblem for painting and sculpture, outside of a few isolated nineteenth-century examples, ended with the Rococo.

An examination of Picasso's art suggests that the artist played upon the notion of the simian as a symbol for the artist. Picasso's symbolic use of the simian, in many instances, did not obscure the conventional associations of the monkey and baboon, who could be presented straightforwardly in one drawing as the artist with a palette, brush, easel, and model (Fig. 68). This drawing belongs to the Vallauris series, a set of drawings Picasso executed during late 1953 and early 1954. Most of the drawings are variations upon the artist and model theme and an exploration of the sexual and emotive relationships between Picasso and woman. The model is depicted throughout the series as a beautiful, sensual creature, whereas the slot for "artist" is filled alternately by an old man, a masked man, a cupid clown, a harlequin, and monkey. The monkey's role was twofold. He can function quite clearly as the artist, or, he may pose in league with the woman and join in confronting the artist (Fig. 69). This latter function is symbolically more ambiguous, presenting opposing aspects of the artist in one image. In any event, the monkey and baboon in the Vallauris series, like the familiar Harlequin, is another, complexly realized alter ego for Picasso.

There are reasons to believe that Picasso made the association between the simian and the artist at an earlier point in his career. The Harlequin alter ego was established in the self-portraits of the Circus Period and spanned Picasso's entire career. The monkey and the baboon were introduced during the Circus Period, but their connection as alter egos to the artist was not as clearly evident as the Harlequin's. If the monkey in _Parade's_ overture curtain is to bear the role of Picasso's alter ego, it would be more assuring to have convincing examples of the monkey's metaphorical activity dated well before the Vallauris series.

Biographically, two related details help confirm the association. During her first sitting for Picasso's portrait of her, Gertrude Stein recalled that Picasso was wearing his blue _singe_, or "monkey suit."[22] She again pointed out Picasso's "monkey suit" in reference to another visit to Picasso with Alice B. Toklas. Picasso greeted them at the door in his blue _singe_, with a belt dangling behind like a tail.[23] Not that this coincidence of slang and symbol proves the argument forwarded here, but Stein did associate the monkey suit with Picasso's working hours to the point that it became an attribute of his activity as a painter. It is also known that Picasso kept a ménagerie during these years which variously consisted of a white mouse, stray cats, stray dogs, and one monkey.[24]

In the paintings of the Circus Period, the simian is usually a monkey, and his inclusion does not seem to suggest any meaning beyond the literal. The one exception is the _Saltimbanque Family with Chained Baboon_ of 1905 (Zervos, I, 131)

in which the baboon's presence strongly suggests a Holy
Family. The metaphor of the simian as artist does not seem
operative. The first major instance in Picasso's art of the
artist-signifying monkey was in the overture curtain for
Parade. There was, however, one, comical precedent. The
idea that Picasso consciously identified himself with the
monkey is fully substantiated in a drawing executed thirteen
years before Picasso's designs for Parade. In 1902, Picasso
drew a small self-portrait, signed and dated "picasso par
lui-même" (Fig. 70). Picasso with brushes tucked behind
each ear depicted himself as a monkey. The scratching gesture,
the scraggly body hair, and the exposed genitals lend the
self-portrait a certain brazen vulgarity, which accords well
with classical and medieval notions of the monkey's unclean-
liness and distastefulness.

Negative attributes were removed from the Parade monkey, yet the identification of the monkey with the artist
and with a self-portrait of Picasso is extremely important
in working out the significance of the curtain. Balancing
the two groups in the curtain's composition and singled out
for primary focus are the Harlequin and the monkey, two
creatures which served Picasso's imagination as alter egos.
Furthermore, another attribute of the monkey more closely
aligns these two symbols in their metaphoric roles. It
was pointed out above that the acrobatic Harlequin appealed
to Picasso because of the connotation of public performer.
In the Cahier romain (Fig. 101), Cocteau wrote: "For the
acrobat...look at Picasso."[25] The monkey in Parade's curtain

is, like the Harlequin, an acrobat. He is in addition to
the signifieds "artist" and "alter ego" a "performer" in a
theatrical setting. And as such, Picasso expanded the traditional metaphor and allowed the monkey to assume attributes
of the Harlequin. The monkey and the Harlequin, however, are
not entirely congruent symbols. The monkey suggestively
brings with it the special associations of Classical and
Medieval contempt, Renaissance celebration, and Baroque satire
and parody, all of which may be operative on the metaphorical
level.

The Pegasus, the ladder, the horseback rider, and the
acrobat's ball are intimately related to the monkey. They
support him--literally and figuratively. The young girl, who
extends her right hand to the monkey for support, mediates
between the prosaic circus identity of "horseback rider" and
"ballerina." The ballet allusion is made through the costume
of the girl. She is a sylphide, and the reference is not
irrelevant. Les Sylphides was first produced by Fokine
in Russia in 1908 under the title Chopiniana. Diaghilev
introduced Paris to Fokine's ballet during the first season
of Ballets Russes, renaming it Les Sylphides. The ballet
remained in the company's repertory, and it was frequently
performed until the demise of the Ballets Russes in 1929.
Picasso saw the ballet in rehearsal and in performance, and
he indicated his interest in the sylphides in a pencil and
crayon drawing done in 1917 (Fig. 71). Taking three of the
sylphides and arranging them in romantic attitudes, Picasso
evoked, in an unusual balletic variation upon the traditional

counterposed positions, the Three Graces. <u>Les Sylphides</u>
originally had a scenario which treated variously generalized
situations in the life of Chopin. In the renamed Ballets
Russes production the plot became less specific. No overt
reference was made to Chopin but rather to the one male
dancer who adopted the guise of "poet." He was surrounded
throughout the ballet by a corps de ballet of women dancers,
who, dressed as <u>sylphides</u> or wood nymphs, represented the
poet's inspiration. They were, in general, regarded as
classical <u>genii</u> or Muses. Neither designation, however,
accorded with the number of dancers in the corps--twelve to
twenty-two--whereas, an individual was only allowed one
<u>genius</u>, and the Muses numbered nine.

To the double identity of the young girl in the overture
curtain, another role may be assigned; she is a Muse, figure
of inspiration for the artist. And appropriately costumed,
the young girl performs her role. The gesture of help and
support extended to the little monkey as he makes his way up
the ladder now takes on added significance. Moreover, Picasso
provided an appropriate foundation for his Muse and Artist.
Pegasus, born of Medusa and Poseidon, was given as a gift by
Athena to the Muses. His name is associated with Apollo, the
God of the Arts, and he is traditionally the symbol of poetic
inspiration. And, posted at the foot of the Pegasus is the
acrobat's ball, which ties elegantly into the classical symbolism. The celestial globe figured with the earth and stars
was considered an attribute of poetry during the Renaissance,
an elaboration upon the globe's classical connotations of

unlimited power.

The Pegasus group is dominated by animals, the Harlequin group by humans. The horseback rider is the exception
in the group to the left, and the lying dog is the only
animal in the right-hand table gathering. The dog, however,
may join the other animals as an attribute of the Picasso-
Harlequin. Although not specifically associated with the arts
in traditional iconography, the dog's symbol for faithfulness
could be extended in this case to suggest the artist's fidelity
to his métier, to what the Harlequin witnesses in allegorical
terms to his left. The dog crouches beneath the seated
Picasso-Harlequin and physically and psychologically affiliates
himself with the artist. Picasso's probable elaboration
upon the dog's conventional symbolism is given partial confirmation by the fact that the same vulpine dog later appears
in The Three Musicians (1921) and literally stretches out
beneath the seated group of a Pierrot, a Harlequin, and a
monastic type. These figures are making music, and, once
again, the Parade dog accompanies a scene of creativity and
performance.

With the various identities of the members of the
Pegasus group understood in their circus and classical con-
texts, the left-hand tableau in the curtain may be viewed
at this point to represent in metaphorical terms the artist
surrounded by motifs of inspiration. But the configuration
of the group also lends itself to yet another complementary
and more dramatically significant meaning. What the Harlequin
group to the right is witnessing is a very special performance.

The act they toast and watch is an "Apotheosis of the Artist."

The monkey is being led up a ladder to perform his skills for an audience. The traditional symbolism of the monkey as artist is thus expanded to include "performer" and "actor." But, if the monkey is about to walk across a tight-rope for the delight of his audience, where is the rope, where is the perch? The continuation of the monkey's performance appears to be blocked by the heavy swag of drapery, a barrier which seems insurmountable. In one preliminary drawing for the overture curtain, Picasso worked out a provisional composition, which contained elements that were removed for the final version (Fig. 72). In this drawing the monkey is not climbing the ladder, but is placed on the shoulders of the horseback rider. On the ladder is a stagehand who is appending a sunburst to the overhead draperies. The rest of the composition indicates the essential design of the final version. If the elements of the Pegasus group in the final version give themselves so readily to a metaphorical interpretation, a similar analysis of the ladder, the sunburst, and the stagehand should be made.

The ladder is traditionally used, in Judeo-Christian and Classical mythologies, to represent a connecting device between the terrestrial and celestial spheres. The ladder surmounted by a star, an angel, an orb, or a sun was used in the Middle Ages to symbolize the path to a heavenly realm (Fig. 73). The apotheosis of an individual was his elevation to a divine status, or more generally speaking, his glorification. Apotheosis in antiquity involved the deification of

mortals to the rank of heroes and demi-gods. It was also a
political strategy to establish, without contest, the divine
rights of absolute rulers. Alexander the Great and Julius
Caesar were both apotheosized by their respective states.
The conceit of the apotheosis in the history of art, which
reached its apogee in the seventeenth century, was usually
less concerned with the aspect of political deification and
addressed itself to the notions of glorification and immortality.
Two examples from later French painting illustrate ways in
which an apotheosis might be represented in the arts. Mengs'
Apotheosis of Wincklemann pictures the act of Wincklemann's
Christ-like body being lifted into an Olympian realm. It
declares the poet's glorification as well as his immortality
for succeeding generations. Ingres' Apotheosis of Homer does
not deal directly with the theme of ascension but with the
glorification of the poet Homer, the begetter of the great
progeny of classical writers and artists. Ascension is,
nevertheless, implied. The glorification transpires above
the clouds on Mount Olympus. Apotheoses were also a popular
theatrical device in nineteenth-century French opera. Berlioz's
Les Troyens and Gounod's Faust both finished with spectacular
apotheoses of their major characters.

The medieval symbolism of the ladder and sunburst
for the individual's ascension into a utopian realm were ideal
accoutrements for an apotheosis. No painter since the Middle
Ages, however, had used these symbols for such an occasion.
The reason was most likely that the ladder was too rustic a
device for all the pomp and circumstance attendant upon the

panoply of apotheosis. Picasso used the ladder and sunburst
in the preliminary drawing to establish the notion of ascension
and apotheosis. The Pegasus and the horseback rider reinforce
the idea of ascension through association. Pegasus achieved
his immortality by throwing Bellerophon to earth and by
ascending ever upward to become the constellation which bears
his name. The horseback rider's alter egos of sylphide and
Muse were both winged spirits which symbolized inspiration.

Why did Picasso remove the stagehand and sunburst,
especially the latter which was so pivotal for a clarification
of the theme of apotheosis? Two moods are set in the preliminary
drawing and in the final curtain, each with its own set of
expressive options. By contrasting the two, Picasso's thinking
may be clarified. In the preliminary drawing, the Harlequin
group casts its gaze toward the Pegasus group, but they are
not witnessing a performance. Rather, they are watching
preparations for an act which has not yet begun. In the
final overture curtain the show has commenced. With the
removal of the sunburst the ascension symbolism is less apparent, but its absence, along with the removal of the stagehand, creates a sharper dramatic focus. The action in the
preliminary drawing is diffused by the addition of another
"group" to those of the Pegasus and the Harlequin: that of
the stagehand and the sunburst. The composition of the final
overture curtain, in contrast to the preliminary drawing,
gains in clarity of action, and, ironically, in ambiguity.
Further, by dismissing the stagehand and sunburst, Picasso
can play upon the conceit of a performance within a perfor-

mance; we the audience are watching the performance of another audience watching a performance. The composition of the final curtain permits an increased number of meanings which was not available in the action of the preliminary drawing. It is possible that Picasso's original intent was to set up two flanking groups, each of which could be identified with the artist, or more personally with Picasso himself. The two groups would passively watch the installation, within their own circus realm, of the stage props for an apotheosis. In the final curtain, however, Picasso drew a relationship between the two groups which did not exist in his first plan. He established a passive alter ego in the figure of the Harlequin and an active one in the guise of the monkey. The horseback rider leads the little monkey who is now crowned with the classical wreath of victory or deification to his apotheosis. By doing this, Picasso was able to extend more convincingly the monkey's traditional guise of "artist" to include the new role of acrobat. And, with the removal of the sunburst and the addition of the victory wreath, Picasso was able to maintain both the ideas of artist performing and of glorification. The final overture curtain is altogether more suggestive and effective in its ambiguity than the artist's original design in the preliminary drawing. The final solution for the overture curtain was far more in keeping with Picasso's essentially Symbolist sensibility and imagination.

With the advent of Realist painting in the middle of the nineteenth century, the depiction of an apotheosis became unmanageable for modern painters. The traditional apotheosis

thrived within a mode which made possible great flights of
fancy and the utilization of improbable props: swirling
clouds, incongruous assemblages of people and creatures, and
great operatic stage settings. Still, the idea of a tribute
to an esteemed individual is one which can function and make
its appeal outside the confines of a Baroque mode. The several
hommages of Fantin-Latour indicate that the essential gesture
of the apotheosis could still exert its appeal. Fantin-Latour's
tributes paid to Delacroix and to Manet are, in essence,
Realist versions of the apotheosis. Both canvases are homages
to significant individuals, yet they are devoid of all imaginary
props. The result is that these paintings function equally
well as group portraits, although sacrificing the formality
and exuberance of the apotheosis. The Realist "apotheoses,"
stripped of their theatrical appeal and glamour, become rather
staid and lifeless.

Cocteau's observation that Picasso drew magic from
everyday objects and events is attested by Picasso's entire
oeuvre and brilliantly demonstrated in the overture curtain
for Parade. Using everyday subject matter which would have
not been objected to by the Realists--a circus and fair
iconography--Picasso, through composition and allusion, restored
to the apotheosis, in Realist terms, all its former ritual
and ideality. He did so in terms so ambiguous that parody
is intentionally permitted to play a role: the statement of
a classical apotheosis with a circus vocabulary. For modern
sensibilities, Classical and Baroque apotheoses, even if
brilliantly conceived, are, nonetheless, too fussy and rhetorical.

Picasso returned the traditional apotheosis to modern painting;
and he did so in a way which was convincing and mysteriously
moving.[26]

The concept of the apotheosis, when used by the State,
was directed toward the perpetuation of absolute rule. As
a theatrical conceit, it was a dramatic device without ulterior
motive except effect. The apotheosis in the history of painting
was paid to individuals esteemed by a group or an individual.
What is most unorthodox in Picasso's rephrasing of the apotheosis in the Parade curtain is that on the most resonant
level of meaning the commentary made was not on the generic
category "artist," but on Picasso himself. In this respect,
the words apotheosis, tribute, and even hommage, although
they describe an aspect of the curtain in important ways, are
not ultimately satisfactory for a categorizing of the curtain
as a whole. It is difficult to find the right word which
would describe an ironic tribute to oneself with elements of
glorification, yet devoid of arrogant connotations. Picasso's
curtain was not publicly self-serving, but privately introspective. It is no more boastful than Rembrandt's or Van
Gogh's series of self-portraits. Like the self-portraits of the
two Dutch artists, Picasso created in his curtain-painting
a personal critique of self. Picasso's curtain is not an
autobiography of the artist; it contains a collection of
thoughts gathered at one point in the artist's life. In
this respect, the curtain is less a journal than an elaborate
entry into a personal diary. Like the individual canvases
of Rembrandt and Van Gogh, Picasso's overture curtain is a

self-portrait of the artist. However, in contrast to the traditional self-portrait, Picasso's was presented in a series of complex metaphors which constituted an elaborate allegory. The terms of the allegory were connotative to a high degree, but Picasso corralled the multiple associations to make a very specific statement about himself as the Artist. Still, the cryptic nature of the symbols in the overture curtain have prevented it from being recognized as a significant and major statement by the artist. Picasso's ability to situate the magical and the suggestive in the context of prosaic subject matter was best attested by the overture curtain for Parade.

The Watcher and the Watched

So far, the analysis of the curtain's meaning has been piecemeal. The various components of the curtain--the setting, the landscape, the Harlequin group, and the Pegasus group-- may now be brought together for a more comprehensive consideration of meaning. Picasso's gloss upon himself concerned the one identity which obsessed him above all others--his role as Artist. To this identity he ascribed in pictorial terms a set of attributes which described the nature of his activity and the status of that activity.

The Pegasus and Harlequin groups represent and juxtapose two psychological states: active and passive. The artist's active self is signified by the Pegasus group. The artist in action is metaphorically the monkey in performance. The artist's other self is represented by the Harlequin group,

which sits back and watches the performance: a celebration
of the creative act. The members of the latter group, although
they are relaxing and are not engaged in a performance, are,
nevertheless, performers, an identity established not only
through costume but also by their placement on an acrobat's
tapis, the traditional mat and literal arena of performance
for the Saltimbanques.[27]

The interaction of the two groups in the overture
curtain articulates a recurring and major theme in Picasso's
art: the activity of watching. Generally speaking, Picasso
established this theme with a man and a woman, and he drew
a relationship between them by assigning to each the roles
of watcher or the one being watched. Inasmuch as the one
being watched is often oblivious to the staring of the watcher,
a quality of voyeurism pervades the series. Although by no
means accounting for all the ways in which Picasso elaborated
upon this theme, there were three important variations of
the theme, which are important for an understanding of the
overture curtain.

The first category is one that has been informatively
traced and discussed by Leo Steinberg in an essay entitled
"Picasso's Sleepwatchers."[28] In this variation a man gazes
upon a sleeping woman (Fig. 74), although in a few cases the
woman observes the man. This theme was first treated by
Picasso during the Blue Period, suspended during the majority
of the Analytic and Synthetic Cubist phases, and returned
to at the beginning of Picasso's Neoclassical Period. The
sleepwatcher theme established its dominance during the 1930's

and was most ambitiously worked out in the Suite Vollard.
In the drawings and prints--the dominant media for the theme
during the entre-deux-guerres--Picasso used a classicizing
subject matter and a simple linear style. The series of
the "Sleepwatchers" is autobiographical and a personal re-
cording of the artist's feelings toward women. Picasso's
presence as the male is indicated by self-portraits, or it
is implied, more evasively, by symbolic selves: the minotaur and the faun. Steinberg sees in these images the confrontation of two different states of being: wakefulness
and sleep. The manner in which each state affects the other
in terms of aggression and passivity varies ambiguously from
picture to picture.

Another variation upon the watching theme, which may
be added to Steinberg's Sleepwatchers, is the situation in
which the woman is not asleep but involved in an activity
which is quietly observed by the male. The theme of the
spectator, where the role of the male approximates an audience
situation, was first dealt with during Picasso's Circus Period,
a fitting moment to contrive the idea. Similar in mood to
the Sleepwatcher series, Picasso juxtaposed two physically
and psychologically different modes of being and developed
relationships between a man and a woman. The male acrobat
in the 1905 Man Watching a Girl Balancing on a Ball (Fig. 75)
sits quietly, like his counterpart the Sleepwatcher, and
gazes intently upon a rephrasing of the woman's role. Here,
instead of a delicately slumbering woman, a young girl, equally
intent upon her activity, delicately balances on top of a ball.

A third articulation of the watching theme was
established in a series of works already mentioned: the
one hundred and eighty drawings which comprise the 1953-54
Vallauris Suite.   The subject matter is the relationship of
an aging Picasso to the opposite sex.   The artist as Old
Man undergoes a variety of quick changes from image to image.
He adopts the guises and disguises of cupid, clown, masks,
young man, old woman, cat, the baboon, and the monkey (Fig.
68).   Unlike the other watching variations, the two terms
of the confrontation--male and female--have been complicated
by the addition of a third member.   This third element functions as a mediating force between Picasso and the Woman and
appears variously as cat, dove, mask, old woman, other man,
and monkey (Fig. 69).   The significant characteristic of this
last series to deal with Picasso's obsessive theme of watching
is that the woman is no longer asleep or oblivious to her
watcher; she now assertively returns her watcher's gaze.

Picasso's overture curtain for Parade is a scene of
watching.   A crucial dimension of its expressive content is
the relationship between a performance and an audience established by the Harlequin and Pegasus groups.   A subtler relationship obtains between the Picasso-Harlequin, the horseback rider, and the monkey.   These three personages can be
extracted momentarily from their larger context in the curtain to represent an intimate demonstration of the watcher
and watched theme, which was examined by Picasso in his
sequence of sleepwatchers, spectators, and in the Vallauris
Suite.   The Picasso-Harlequin views a performance given by

the horseback rider and the monkey. The scene is thus con-
joined to the spectator variation of the watching theme treated
in the Circus Period. The physical equation itself matches
that of the 1905 Man Watching a Girl Balancing on a Ball (Fig.
75): a male figure watches a young girl, with arms overhead
and oblivious to her watcher, balance herself on top of a
support. In an anticipation of the added terms of the
Vallauris Suite, the relationship between man and woman is
compounded in the overture curtain by a third element--the
monkey, whose presence complicates the ways in which the
male and female relate to one another. And, as he did in
his endless variations upon the theme of watching, Picasso
places side by side not only different genders but two
psychologically disparate states of consciousness: in the
Parade curtain, passive introspection and active creativity.
The theme of the watcher in Picasso's art is one of the
artist's most highly autobiographical statements; the male
component is always associated with Picasso either through
a self-portrait or a symbolic guise. The women who figure
in this sequence may represent generic Woman or specific
personalities in the artist's life. While Picasso was in
Rome for the rehearsals of Parade, he fell in love with,
courted, and eventually married a member of Diaghilev's
corps de ballet: a young dancer named Olga Koklova. That
Olga should play a part in Picasso's scheme of watcher and
watched in the curtain should be no surprise. What documents and substantiates an identification of the horseback
rider in the overture curtain with Olga Koklova is not only

that Olga was the most important woman in Picasso's life
at the moment he was conceiving the designs for Parade, but
that the horseback rider's costume makes a specific reference.
Olga Koklova was not a ballerina; she was a member of the
corps de ballet. One role she was dancing at the time Picasso
met her, and one Picasso associated with her, was captured
in a drawing done in 1917 (Fig. 76). In it are depicted
a group of danseuses posing in their costumes for Les
Sylphides. Reclining in the immediate foreground, and the
center of attention, in spite of her costume which is identical to the others, is Olga Koklova. Olga was a sylphide and,
in her role as a new lover to Picasso and as a figurative
muse who was opening new doors for the artist, it is difficult not to see her symbolic self in the overture curtain
portrayed by the young horseback rider who assists the
monkey.

The Picasso-Harlequin's gaze across to the Pegasus
group is multi-focused. He is at once intent upon the horseback rider and her trained monkey. The confrontation Picasso
set up was not simply one between man and woman. Prior to
the Parade curtain the theme of the watcher and watched
involved two distinctly separate beings, two states opposed
in gender, mood, and activity. The inclusion of the monkey
in the Parade trio allows for an entirely new situation in
Picasso's handling of the theme--a confrontation of selves.
The relationship of the Picasso-Harlequin and the monkey
introduces a new dramatic variation on the watching theme--
one alter ego of the artist regards another alter ego of

the artist.

This innovative handling of what amounts to a double portrait of the artist suggests a particular activity. The relaxed, quiet artist looks at a symbolic self engaging in the action of his métier. A passive emblem of the artist, the Harlequin, watches a metaphorical enactment of the motions of creativity. Simultaneously, the artist acts and reflects in a state of self-criticism. The nature of Picasso's introspection concerns the ideas of inspiration, celebration, and the artist's "performance."

It is significant that Picasso chose the monkey for a personal emblem of himself, the artist. The simian, be he monkey, ape, or baboon, was an appropriate symbol for the painter and sculptor because of his imitative faculties. Medieval criticism used simian behavior to condemn illusionistic painting and sculpture. The Renaissance inverted this judgment and elevated the import of the simian's manners to a higher status—forgery became creativity. In both cases, however, the notion of imitation informed the simian's emblematic significance. In English, the expression "to ape the manners of someone" means to pattern oneself after another's style, the connotation being pejorative. Picasso's choice of the monkey and not the baboon or ape may have been determined by the fact that in French the equivalent of "to ape" is the infinitive singer, drawn from the substantive singe, or monkey. Picasso blended Medieval and Renaissance connotations in the figure of the monkey to make observations on his own activities. The little monkey is placed

within the context of an apotheosis. Consequently, from
one point of view the Picasso-Harlequin witnesses the celebration of the artist in the role of creator.

However, alongside the positive implications of a
Renaissance concept are placed the Medieval associations
of the artist as a forger of reality, a crass imitator. A
salient characteristic of Picasso's behavior was the inventory
he made of western pictorial styles. Throughout his life
Picasso often turned to preexisting modes to kindle his
imagination, not in the manner of a plagiarist or copyist
who stands subservient to his model, but in the sense of someone who turns to an alternate way of perceiving the world
and who makes of it an original point of view. Picasso did
not work in any one stylistic mode throughout his life, but
rather moved freely, often simultaneously, through several
styles: witness the two styles of the overture curtain and
the stage set. In this respect, Picasso's use of other styles
to shape his art is an example of "aping" other patterns of
behavior, and by Picasso's own admission in Parade's overture
curtain an activity which is counterfeit. For it is quite
plain that if the artist is elevated in an apotheosis, it
is after all only an artificial performance. It cannot be
a real apotheosis, only an assemblage of circus types, animals,
and theatrical props engaging in a make-believe scene. The
apotheosis in the curtain is a theatrical imitation. Even
the foundation of the ritual is fake; the very symbol of the
artist's inspiration, the Pegasus, is a fraud. Of course,
a circus "Pegasus" would not be the real article, but Picasso

underscores the sham of the spectacle by strapping the Pegasus
wings around a mare, not a stallion. A hallmark of Picasso's
handling of his theme in the curtain is its irony and sophis-
tication. It is not simply a matter of juxtaposing, for
curious effect, Medieval condemnation and Renaissance praise
of the imitative faculties of the artist. It should be
supposed that Picasso seriously esteemed his activity as
a painter, and if the articulation of this pride is ironically made it does not lessen its conviction or intensity
of feeling. What is added through parody is the artist's
own skepticism. In Picasso's world the simultaneous entertaining of opposite feelings was not impossible. Medieval
censure was made against the artist's desire to play God,
but the incorporation of the Medieval notion of the artist
as a forger by Picasso was not so simple a criticism.
Picasso admitted the sham and the artist's sleight of hand,
but not in any sense to condemn his own art, simply to
characterize very honestly, and accurately, the workings
of his imagination. After all, Picasso's scenic implementation of Cocteau's theme was a grand example of aping the
manners and style of someone else: namely, the Italian
Futurists. Picasso unabashedly used Futurist ideas, and
yet, through his elaboration and play upon them made of
Futurism something entirely his own, something which was informed by but which did not duplicate a Futurist sensibility.
That Picasso should have vetoed Cocteau's sound segments is
curious in that Cocteau's original scenario was, like
Picasso's scenic implementation, derived in large part from

Futurist theory and practice. Yet, Cocteau too went beyond
his sources to arrive at an original statement. Cocteau
in this sense was also an "aping" simian; his relationship
to his sources provides further evidence of how congruent
the sensibilities of Picasso and Cocteau were. The characteristics common to Picasso's and Cocteau's personal moldings
of Futurism were the intimately autobiographical and mystical
overlays.

In the overture curtain Picasso created a complex
variation upon his earlier theme of the watcher and watched.
It embraced, in one of his richest autobiographical images,
an ambiguous and ironic commentary on the artist's inspiration, the artist's celebration of his activity, and the
artist's self-criticism. Thirty-six years later Picasso
reconvened the key personages from the Parade curtain in the
now familiar drawing from the Vallauris sketchbook (Fig. 69).
The Harlequin-Acrobat of the curtain here is, more accurately,
a clown. He watches wistfully as a seated young woman holding
a monkey proffers a piece of fruit to him and the monkey.
The clown, monkey, and the woman sit before an easel upon
which a canvas reveals another familiar personage--the horse.
Staring across at each other, the clown and the monkey re-
establish the psychological connections of the Parade curtain.
Missing from the drawing is any evidence of apotheosis or
personal celebration, but there is no doubt that what is
signified is a commentary on inspiration and introspection.
The Vallauris drawing is the most intimately connected postscript to the Parade overture curtain. Its appearance in the

later phase of the artist's life attests to the importance
attached to the special variation of the watching theme
first worked out in the Parade curtain.

Throughout the entire set of variations on the watching theme, nuances of content and form are often reciprocal,
an indication that Picasso perceived the series not in terms
of separate subcategories but as a protean whole. In the
1908 Reclining Nude with Figures (Fig. 77) Picasso treated
the theme of the Sleepwatcher with the fragmented and angular
planes of an early Cubist vocabulary. It is significant
that for the Sleepwatcher Picasso chose an antique contrapposto
which set a precedent for the Picasso-Harlequin in the
Parade curtain. This was an instance of how the artist's
work could serve as a source for itself. With Picasso it
is difficult to speak of discrete categories or themes which
do not inflect each other. Within the watching theme itself,
Picasso confronted two different states of consciousness but
did not intend that these opposing forces should stand apart
in isolation from one another. Rather, they comment upon
each other and blend in their mutual influences. In the
Parade curtain, this phenomenon is more easily discerned
when it is recognized that what is represented is the artist
confronting himself in symbolic terms. Leo Steinberg speaks
of the relationship of the Sleepwatcher and the Sleeper in
terms which equally and eloquently speak for the psychological
complexity of the relationship between the Picasso-Harlequin,
the monkey, and the horseback rider:

At any moment Picasso's imagery may require one to
read his characters not as persons engaged in watching and being watched, but as a figuration of sleeping and waking [performing and viewing]--dependent
states that exclude and presuppose one another,
nourish and infect one another, each lacking some
richness the other has.[29]

Picasso and the Classical World

Another autobiographical dimension of the curtain is

its classicizing subject matter, style, and content. Picasso

was probably the last master painter in later western art for

whom the traditional trip to Rome exerted the spell and impact

it had on countless earlier masters. Picasso's voyage south

was not deliberately undertaken for the express purpose of

studying the antique, but, nevertheless, there was an occasion

to do so outside of the artist's immediate responsibility

to design the Parade production for Diaghilev. Picasso

visited Rome, Naples, Pompeii, and many museums.[30] Although

for the majority of twentieth-century painters the question

of a classical heritage has been entirely beside the point,

it does not seem to have been for Picasso. Antiquity was a

formative force in Picasso's art. It provided a model for

style and subject matter and a source for Picasso's private

mythologies. In doing so, it offered Picasso yet another

mode to adopt for his own purposes, giving rise to a phase

in the artist's work which has been somewhat unmanageably

labeled his Neoclassical style. But the classical past

was not just another stylistic source to be incorporated into

Picasso's art; unlike other western styles Picasso borrowed

from--Mannerism, Baroque, Rococo--the classical manner posed

a psychological confrontation. Classical art was the bedrock
of the history of western painting and sculpture. It might
be ignored, but only deliberately by the artist. Its presence
had loomed since the Renaissance as the force to be reckoned
with by the artist. For Picasso, the question was how to
relate to the classical past and how to make it his own.

Classicism is a term which suggests a broad range of
usages. Often the presence of a precise linear style has
qualified a painting for the "classicizing" label, in spite
of the absence of a classicizing subject matter or meaning.
In this way, one talks about Picasso's representational
drawing style of 1915 as "Ingriste" or "Classical," although
the subject matters are portraits of the artist's contemporaries. The "classicism" in this instance is very loosely
defined. Picasso's trip south to Rome in early February
of 1917 with Cocteau to meet with Diaghilev and his company
has been cited as the point when the Mediterranean world
and its forms and images began to reappear once again in
Picasso's art.[31] However, the full impact was not really
felt until 1921 in terms of an overt choice of classical
subject matter. In the interim between 1917 and 1921 a
linear, representational style was pursued which Picasso
had begun to explore in 1914. The grand exception to this
overview was the Parade curtain, which was an immediate and
ample response to the South.

The style of the overture curtain, like that of the
Ingrist drawings, is classicizing in its ostensible, although
subtly compromised, clarity of line and space. The land-

scape to the rear of the figure composition is Mediterranean and is equipped with a classical ruin: a Roman arch and an inverted column. The Pegasus group is clearly a classical tableau in its symbols: namely, Pegasus, Muse, celestial orb, and apotheosis. To the right, the Harlequin group appears lacking in any classical reference other than style, except, that is, for the Picasso-Harlequin figure. The figure's pose was originally antique in invention and re-called Michelangelo's Sistine ignudi. Furthermore, the position of the figure was not new to Picasso since he had included it in the Cubist Sleepwatcher painting of 1908. One source for this particular figure, which has not yet been mentioned, ties the Harlequin and Pegasus groups even more closely together. The first major instance of this figure pose in Classical art is found on the east frieze of the Parthenon among the assembly of Olympian gods and goddesses. The male personage seated in this manner is Apollo, the god of the arts and protector of the Muses (Fig. 78). That this identification fits so well into the icono-graphical puzzle the curtain presents must indicate that the reference on Picasso's part could probably not have been made unknowingly. And, it was not the first time Picasso had identified himself with a classical divinity. In the 1902 self-portrait of Picasso reclining on a beach with his back turned to us, his head in profile, and his left hand holding a palette and brushes, the figure pose is an allusion to an antique river god (Fig. 59).

The overture curtain was embroidered with a classicizing

style and subject matter, and it was replete with classical references and allusions which are critical for a complete reading of the curtain. As such, it stands alone in its classicism in Picasso's art until the early twenties. The only complication, and significant qualification, of this observation is that what the viewer of the curtain sees is not an assembly of gods and goddesses in an arcadian setting, but a somewhat artificial convocation of circus types and props in a peculiar stage setting, far removed in its prosaic associations from any classical world. The element of parody and travesty permeates Picasso's composition. The classical connotations are real enough, and yet the whole thing is, after all, a fake, a sham performance, a gathering of circus low-types aping the seriousness of an antique context. The use of the monkey in eighteenth-century art to portray the artist was satirically oriented, following the example of seventeenth-century Dutch painting.[32] Another satirical function of the monkey in eighteenth-century French painting was to represent the pompous antiquarian. Chardin popularized this emblem, which mocked the slavish attention the academic artist paid to the past. And so, the star of the show, the wreathed monkey, caps the parody in yet another allusion.

Why did Picasso lace his statement with satire and mock-seriousness? To obscure the curtain's meaning? To complicate further the already richly woven set of allusion and connotations? In part, yes, but the artist's motivation for adopting this tack was more complicated than this. John Berger, in his The Success and Failure of Picasso, views

Picasso's relationship to the antique as seriously compromised by parody and caricature.[33] What is interesting in Berger's critique of Picasso and the antique, in light of the _Parade_ curtain, which does not figure in his discussion of the problem, is that it views Picasso as an impersonator who mocked that which he adopted for his art. Picasso was a forger and performed his impersonations to prove that Picasso could do what the Masters could and to mock cultural tradition by showing that Picasso, the commoner, could discredit this tradition by showing how glibly he could imitate it. Berger grossly underestimates both Picasso's psychological and sociological positions. Picasso's overture curtain speaks very intimately about the artist's feelings and also supports Cocteau's scenario. The use of classical figures would have been inappropriate. The curtain proceeded from Picasso's immediate situation and feelings about himself, not from a classical frame of reference. The classical allusions were part of the journal entry; they did not dominate it. Picasso's response to his artistic heritage was integrated into an image which also displayed other topical concerns: the Ballets Russes, Futurism, and Olga Koklova. Picasso's experiences in early 1917 included Rome, Naples, and Pompeii; consequently, they are recollected. The classical past, costumed, as it were, for the occasion, allowed Picasso to muse about his relationship to a classical past which had exerted its pressures so roundly on earlier master painters and artists. The circus tableau in _Parade's_ overture curtain with its accompanying satirical

mood permitted Picasso to declare three positions simultaneously.
First, making fun of something either in satire or more broadly
in parody can make safe something perceived to be a possible
threat. Humor and wit can distance the subject and object
from each other and make benign any potentially deleterious
effects. On this level, Picasso maintained a psychic integrity
which allowed him to set up a comparison which if it should
collapse was, after all, one posited in jest. Secondly,
the gesture made in the curtain to celebrate the artist in
an apotheosis is prevented from becoming arrogant; a mood
of humility is asserted by the mock-seriousness of the event.
What would otherwise be a brazen gesture is softened by its
artificiality, and yet, at the same time the gesture is still
made. Finally, Picasso at once compared his art to the pres-
tige of a glorious past and remained skeptical about the
comparison. The parody of the classical allusions in the
overture curtain permitted Picasso to adopt a convincing
stance of self-criticism devoid of black and white judgments,
one voiced more honestly with attendant ambivalences. Picasso's
relationship to the classical past was defined in a contradictory manner; he simultaneously embraced it, assimilated
it, and stood apart from it.

The Setting of the Overture Curtain

In the analysis of the overture curtain thus far the
figure and animal groupings have received the primary emphasis.
The setting proper has remained neutral in the discussion,
but only procedurally, because it plays an active role in

the intended meaning of the overture curtain. With the
exception of a recently published book on Cubism, it is
curious that Picasso's overture curtain has never been photo-
graphically reproduced in its entirety.[34] Its composition
has always been cropped to reduce the curtain to the two
figure groupings alone, without any indication that the
image is partial and not a complete view of the curtain.
The stretches of draped theatrical curtain must have been
thought rhetorical and extraneous to the chief interest of
Picassos' composition, which itself appears to have been
misunderstood. For, in several instances the little monkey
at the top of the ladder is cropped off.[35] The subtle focal
point of the monkey in the curtain was not discerned; the
center of the composition was assumed to be the gathering
of figures around the table. The deletion of the monkey is
grievous in light of the iconographical argument forwarded
here; equally so is the omission of the surrounding stage
drapery. A view of the complete curtain makes it quite apparent that the figure composition is placed in a stage setting,
a situation only obscurely hinted at in cropped reproductions
of the curtain. Pulled back and decoratively tied back
with cord and tassle are two sets of rideaux à l'italienne;
that is, red-velvet theatrical curtains that are drawn apart
to reveal a stage setting, rather than a single curtain which
is raised on a scene. The first set of curtains flank the
composition frontally while the other set is pulled back
behind the figure composition.

With the full appearance of the theatrical drapery

in the overture curtain, the viewer can actively participate
in Picasso's conceit. The theme of the watcher and watched
becomes more complicated. The viewer looking at Picasso's
curtain becomes an active watcher involved himself in an
act of voyeurism. The complete pictorial composition of
Picasso's overture curtain makes one event very clear which
is otherwise obscured by cropping. The viewer constitutes
an audience which is watching a performance of a performance
with its own audience and performers. More clearly, the
viewer watches a theatrical performance which is taking place
in the overture curtain on a stage with curtains parted to
reveal the action. This theatrical performance itself can
be then divided into an audience--the Harlequin group--which
witnesses the ritual reenactment or performance of a mock
apotheosis by the Pegasus group. It is true that in the
handling of the watcher theme in other paintings, the viewer
observes the confrontation of another observer and the one
observed. But the viewer's role is not actively relevant to
the meaning of the work. This is not the case in the overture curtain where the real viewer compounds the implications
of the curtain's meaning. He watches the watcher watch;
he observes in its fullness the artist's act of introspection.
Picasso assimilated the theatrical experience into the realm
of autobiography and self-perception. The extraordinary
extension Picasso made in the meaning of the curtain was
the ramification of the viewer's active role. Picasso allows
the viewer and himself to step back and phenomenologically
perceive the very act of self-criticism. The viewer and

Picasso may reflect upon the artist reflecting upon himself.

And yet, the viewer is susceptible to a change of theatrical point of view in Picasso's scheme of things which explodes the self watching the self into an infinity of mirrored images. For it appears that the viewer's exact location as an audience member is ambiguous. Initially, it seems stabilized; he is an audience member--in a literal sense if he is attending a production of the ballet Parade--who is positioned out front in the house. The curtain represents in illusion a theatrical space beyond the footlights. Yet, it is not all so simple. In this first reading of the viewer's location, it is assumed that the Mediterranean landscape is a toile de fond, a backdrop for the figure composition. But if it is a true backdrop, this identification is confounded by the landscape's orthogonal baseline, which places the backdrop in an angled position that peculiarly interferes with the scenographic space of the stage setting. The absence of a horizontal baseline for the backdrop permits another reading of the landscape. It might be real. And if it is, what happens to the viewer's location? It then becomes possible that the stage's figurative proscenium gives onto an open landscape, the potential location for an audience. The theatrical performance on stage might be taking place in an outdoor theater, in which case the viewer is no longer out front but backstage, watching from the wings. If it is assumed that one of the viewer's positions is backstage, then he too, like the Harlequin and Pegasus groups, is susceptible to yet another audience. His own watching of a performance

within a performance is potentially watchable by another
implied agent, one who is also backstage in the wings or
one who in the landscape's audience catches a glimpse of
him backstage. Finally, the viewer who watches Picasso's
overture curtain and ponders his manifold relationships to
it may be observed by another member of the viewer's actual
audience.

Until Picasso's overture curtain for Parade, the
watching theme had been dealt with fairly simply in the
canvases of the Blue, Circus, and early Cubist periods; two
states of consciousness were juxtaposed for contrast. In
the 1917 Parade curtain, the theme is revived and given its
most complex treatment in what may be considered an allegorical self-portrait of the artist. The watching theme is transformed into a statement of self-criticism. It is permitted
an almost staggering complication by being articulated within
a theatrical setting, which allowed for visual and conceptual
plays upon performer and audience as modes of awareness.
The multiple and ambiguous identities which are assigned to
the setting and figure groups are created by Picasso's virtuoso
play upon psychologically relative theatrical points of view,
which are, moreover, stated simultaneously.

When the rideau rouge of the Châtelet rose vertically
upon Picasso's overture curtain, a paradox was immediately
posed. An overture curtain traditionally shielded the actual
performance while serving as a visual prelude, parallel
to the musical prelude provided by the orchestra. Picasso's
curtain was different. W.A. Propert, writing about Parade's

curtain after its London debut in 1919, inadvertently singled
out Picasso's intended ambiguity:

> The curtain, particularly, was remarkable for its broad,
> serene, classical air. Its only fault was that it had
> too much the look of a picture, and lacked the decora-
> tive formality that a curtain demands, as belonging to
> the proscenium rather than to the inner stage.[36]

In other words, the curtain's depiction of a theatrical setting was inappropriate. An overture curtain was a decorative,
transitional element between the _rideau rouge_ and the actual
stage space of the production. Picasso's curtain was at
once overture curtain and an actual performance being given
before the ballet proper began, if only in pictorial illusionism. The "inner stage" which Propert spoke of is further
suggested in the curtain by the rhetorical curtains tied
back to reveal the two groups of animals and characters.
This Baroque framing device was used frequently in Ballets
Russes productions as disparate in nature as _Le Pavillion
d'Armide_ and _Schéhérazade_. Tamper is perhaps the best word
to describe the way in which Picasso transposed theatrical
elements in his scenic design for _Parade_. What could have
easily been Baroque drapery framing the actual ballet was
cleverly changed into architectural stage legs. But the
conventional drapery for a ballet production was not entirely
dismissed. Here it surfaces in an unusual place--the overture curtain.

Still, if it is posited that Picasso cleverly allowed
the house curtain to rise upon a "performance," expectations
were, again, defeated. One of the few acceptable observations
on the overture curtain in the critical literature states

that the mood of the curtain was leisurely, one of between-
acts. And so, if the overture curtain does indeed offer
the viewer another performance in addition to the ballet, the
expressive state is not one of performance but of quiet inter-
mission. The leisureliness of the gathered company counters
the more active connotation of "performance." And so, if in
the overture curtain Picasso made spatial positions ambiguous,
he completed the sense of disorientation by deliberately
scrambling time and theatrical sequence. Moods of overture
and entr'acte were evoked simultaneously.

Why all the ambiguities and the shuttling of identities in the curtain? It does not suffice to say that this
aspect of the curtain displays a familiar Cubist world devoid
of absolutes. To speak of Cubism in this way may illuminate
the workings of the curtain, but it does not complete an
interpretation. And yet, an understanding of Picasso's
earlier Cubist strategies can point the investigator in the
right direction.

A formal quality of the curtain which was discussed
in the earlier stylistic analysis now demands further explica-
tion. If the figures and their props were removed from the
curtain's composition, what remains is a convincing illusionistic space derived from Renaissance schemes. Three primary
devices help fool the eye into believing that the two-dimen-
sional surface of the curtain has been punctured and figured
with a three-dimensional world: the orthogonals of the stage
planks which suggest a vanishing point; the alternate stretches
of lights and darks in the curtains which instill a tangible

volume; and finally, the bluing of the distant mountain range
in an emulation of aerial perspective. What makes the curtain
a collage is the juxtaposition next to this mode of another
mode. Placed within the illusionistic space of the theatrical
setting are the relentlessly flattened shapes and forms of
the figures, animals, and props. Traditional ways of giving
them a sense of mass and weight are dismissed. The use of
chiaroscuro is all but absent. No shadows connect the forms
solidly to the ground. In contrast to the setting, the
figures appear artificially cartoon-like. In one dramatic
respect they appear so insubstantial that they take on the
quality of a mirage, one which momentarily might disappear,
or of stage flats or cut-out props which are proper to the
theater.

Picasso accumulated in the overture curtain a series
of relationships between perceptual ambiguities and conceptual
dualities. In information theory simple or ambiguous meaning
may be established by how two things stand in relationship
to each other. A and B separately may denote two different
meanings. Placed beside each other a new series of connotations may be engendered. While the signifiers or forms remain
constant throughout the series, their signifieds or meanings
may change in each instance. For example, the dual concept
of backstage-outfront does not remain constant in the overture
curtain. Depending upon how the landscape is identified--
toile de fond or actual outdoors--the meaning of the stage
area and location is inverted. The space the viewer stands
in may change from backstage to outfront and back again.

It will be recalled that the same compounding of meanings
occurred in the relationship of the Managers to the acts.
Picasso often allowed a single shape to evoke multiple associations and identities. Ambiguity in this case was created
by the suggestive, metamorphic forms of things. The other
major strategy for the creation of ambiguity, one initiated
in Cubist collage, was the setting up of a relationship
between two terms and then allowing the interaction of connotative meanings to breed new meanings. Both strategies were
used in the creation of the overture curtain. The latter,
however, took dramatic precedence over the former. For
Picasso established a series of conceptual pairs whose elaboration constituted the foundation for the curtain's ultimate
and most profound levels of meaning. These paired items are:
watcher-watched; audience-performance; performance-intermission;
backstage-outfront; introspection-activity; conviction-
skepticism; seriousness-parody. The ambiguity of Picasso's
curtain is not obscure, it is breathtaking.

The pressing question still remains. Why the saturation of the curtain with exhaustive, almost exhausting,
ambiguities? In one respect the question has been answered:
to provide Picasso with the opportunity to examine and embrace
in its fullness the act of reflection and self-criticism.
But there is another implication of the curtain's ambiguity
which bears significantly upon Picasso's estimation of himself and of his craft. It is one which Cocteau voiced more
overtly in his scenario by establishing the Chinese Magician
as the central emblem of the parade. The English transla-

tion "magician" is somewhat inaccurate. It will be recalled
Cocteau's designation for the Chinaman was <u>Prestidigitateur</u>
<u>chinois</u>. The magician might saw a woman in half, make her
levitate, or cause her to disappear from a wardrobe. The
prestidigitator's activities were more specialized. He
performed tricks with his hands, making things appear and
disappear with a highly skillful and eye-deceiving manual
manipulation. It is with the prestidigitator that both
Picasso and Cocteau identified their art. With the wave of
the brush or pen the mundane is made marvelous. The artist
is a maker of illusions. He wields his control over the
natural world, transforms himself into multiple guises,
instills life into inanimate objects, and creates new beings.
Delighting or terrifying us, he never ceases to astonish
his audience with his sleight of hand. And, it is Picasso's
<u>legerdemain</u> which magically shifts our point of view back
and forth in the overture curtain, which causes the gathered
company to appear and to float ghost-like in a stage setting,
and which allows things to be many things. "Now you see it,
now you don't!"--the artist as magus, magician, prestidigitator
is the last attribute Picasso ascribed to himself, covertly
and silently in the workings of the universe he created in
the overture curtain, not openly in the presentation of any
specific emblem.

Conclusion

From the comments made above on the iconography of
Picasso's curtain, it has been shown that it displays an

intensely high degree of suggestiveness. This particular
quality was characteristic of Picasso's entire body of work.
If Picasso had any one aesthetic dictum it was to evoke meaning
rather than to specify it clearly. The overture curtain for
Parade is a brilliant display of this sensibility. Picasso's
symbolist imagination is one among several important reasons
why the overture curtain's meanings have been inaccessible
until now. To praise the curtain as "popular imagery at its
most decorative and enchanting" and then go on to other
matters is to limit any discussion and, subsequently, to
deny the opening up of a world of exceedingly dense information. Part of the fascination the curtain affords the viewer
is the fact that it is a puzzle of sorts. But it is not
indecipherable. Nor is the interpretation offered here a
forced one. The discerned meanings arrive naturally from
and complement previous insights into Picasso's art. Picasso
brought together and fashioned a statement which derived
from his earlier attitudes and themes and which was informed
by a literary and visual imagination steeped in western
cultural traditions.

The meanings of the overture curtain are complex. To
contemplate them fully, the viewer requires time for reflection.
This is most assuredly not allowed during the curtain's brief
minute-and-a-half exposure at the beginning of the ballet.
The short appearance of Picasso's curtain does not deny the
validity of its rich connotations, but the question may be
properly asked: how much did Picasso intend his audience
to understand during a performance of Parade? What the curtain

does convey in performance is highly effective dramatically even though the information imparted is less complete than a more leisurely reading would allow. When the house curtain is either parted or raised on Picasso's curtain, the first audience reaction is inevitably stunned awe at the incredible scale of the figures which has more in common with the size of people on a large movie screen than with the expectancies of painting. Secondly, in spite of the immensity of the curtain the mood immediately generated is one of serenity and melancholy. There is a quality about the stillness of the gathered comedians, immobile in their activity, which is best described as a wistful sadness. In one minute's time Picasso establishes an expressive state which will momentarily be abruptly and deliberately shattered when the overture curtain is flown up on the beginning of the ballet proper. What comes after the overture curtain's appearance contrasts in all ways with it. The mood of the ballet is tense and excited. The angularities of the set and costumes cancel the fluidity submitted in the curtain's design. The pacing of the dancers is increasingly accelerated and frenetic. Satie's musical score enhances the transition Picasso offers visually; during the appearance of the curtain, a muted and stately brass chorale serves as a _Prélude du rideau rouge_. It perfectly matches the atmosphere of the curtain. When the curtain raises, Satie's music also shifts in expression to the more tense ostinato of the First Manager's theme. Picasso was able to instill his curtain with the most profound resonances of meaning, while never forgetting its

primary function as a component in a theatrical production
for a large public.

Picasso's overture curtain for <u>Parade</u> relates directly
to Cocteau's scenario--as will be discussed in the last
chapter; it was not intended to stand apart as a hermetically
sealed statement disguised as a decorative drop to introduce
Cocteau's ballet. Some writers have puzzled over why all
of Picasso's overture curtains for the Ballets Russes seem
to disassociate themselves in content from the ballets they
served. This was not the case at all.[37] It is true, however,
that the <u>Parade</u> curtain can stand alone and function as a
successful work of art, unlike the costumes and set which
are incomplete without their dramatic context.

Picasso's overture curtain, which will forever remain
without a title proper, signified an "Allegory of the Artist."
More specifically, it was a statement about Picasso's own
behavior as an artist, a visual commentary in which he
ascribed to himself a set of attributes. The curtain's
meaning was implied, not expressly stated, in a series of
ambiguous metaphors which spoke of the painter's métier
and its status. In a double self portrait, Picasso assumed
two symbolic guises and appeared in the curtain as a Harlequin and as a circus monkey. The central activity of the
curtain was a variation upon Picasso's earlier theme of the
watcher and the watched. Until <u>Parade</u> this theme had been
dealt with fairly simply in the canvases of the Blue, Circus,
and early Cubist periods: two distinct beings were juxtaposed for a contrast in mood. The <u>Parade</u> curtain revived

the theme and accorded it its most complex treatment in Picasso's oeuvre. The relationship between the Picasso-Harlequin and the Picasso-monkey introduced a dramatic rephrasing of the watching theme--a confrontation of selves, one alter ego of the artist regarded another alter ego of the artist. An introspective emblem of the artist, the Harlequin, watched the monkey's metaphorical display of the creative act within the context of a mock-classical, theatrical apotheosis. The nature of the Harlequin's self-reflection concerned the ideas of inspiration, creativity, and self-celebration. The watching theme was permitted a staggering complication by being articulated within a theatrical setting, which allowed for visual and conceptual plays upon "performer" and "audience member" as modes of awareness. The multiple identities which may be assigned to the characters and setting were triggered by Picasso's virtuoso juggling of psychologically relative theatrical points of view. Picasso variously attributed to himself the roles of mimic, forger, conjurer, and performer. The autobiographical entry Picasso made in the 1917 curtain was delineated within the theatrical experience and veiled with a spirit of irony, parody, and ambivalence. Perhaps the most astounding irony was that Picasso chose to utter his intensely personal apologia on what would be physically the largest scale he ever worked. Not only is the Parade curtain the largest painting Picasso ever executed, but another tense and daring split between content and function is the fact that his intimate memoir was presented in the context of a public, theatrical arena. That a gesture so potentially brazen was inverted into reticence is remarkable.

Picasso's curtain for Parade may assume a distinguished position in the series of western paintings which have portrayed the "Artist in his Studio." Picasso's terms were unconventional, but the essential gesture was there. Spiritually, in its visual and conceptual plays upon the painter's activity, the overture curtain shares the most intriguing affinity with Velazquez's Las Meninas, which itself was an autobiographical phrasing of the "Artist's Apotheosis." If one of Picasso's most physically visible works, it also qualifies as a lost masterpiece. When Picasso chose to undertake the making of a major painting, he usually worked on a large scale and in an allegorical mode. In its ambitiousness, scale, psychological complexity, and disarming mysteriousness, the Parade curtain deserves reconsideration as one of Picasso's most significant allegorical works. It should take its place with those other great intermittent images, like The Family of Saltimbanques, Les Demoiselles d'Avignon, Young Woman before a Mirror, and Guernica, which stake out the trajectory of Picasso's art.

CHAPTER V

PARADE AS CUBIST SPECTACLE

Petite oeuvre.--Il y a des oeuvres dont toute
l'importance est en profondeur--peu importe
leur orifice.

Jean Cocteau[1]

Parade has earned innumerable epithets. Dismissed by
a dubious Parisian public as folie, scandale, and pétarde,[2]
it was conceived by Cocteau as a ballet réaliste and concep-
tualized by Apollinaire as surréaliste.[3] In view of Picasso's
contribution, it was agreed by all to be a ballet cubiste.[4]
With the exception of Fauvism and Abstraction, Parade has
critically become a repository for nearly all the names of
major early-modern movements. Although the costumes for the
Managers took their form from the earlier experiments of
collage, the technique of assembling planes which they displayed loosely affiliated them with Soviet Constructivist
sculpture. It has been shown above that from a special point
of view, that of satire, Parade made specific references to
the ideas of Italian Futurism. The pathos of Parade has
also been interpreted in its artistic negativism to have
been a manifestation of Dada.[5] For one work of art to be
the vehicle of apparently so many contemporary directions
in the arts may appear confusing. However, it is true that

Parade did comment upon and was touched by a variety of
artistic categories and that these categories can be recon-
ciled within the imaginative workings of Parade, either
through semantic juggling or through the singling out of
actual and pertinent influences. For example, both Picasso
and Cocteau actively responded to Futurism. Yet, Parade
cannot be convincingly construed in any way to be a "Futurist
ballet." Futurism may be brought fruitfully into a discussion
of Parade, but it did not provide the controlling sensibility.
The viewpoint of this dissertation is that Cubism was the
dominant shaping force behind the realization of the ballet
Parade, that its Cubism was not purely decorative but deci-
sively pivotal for the very meaning of the work. Equipped
with an understanding of Cubism, the investigator may uncover
more profound levels of meaning which have otherwise remained
obscured. Furthermore, if Parade was Cubist, a second inquiry may be made. How was an originally pictorial style
brought into a theatrical setting? The major thrust of the
dissertation is thus double-edged in posing the following
question: what was the relationship of Parade to Cubism?

Cubism as a Stylistic Problem

The first stumbling block in answering the question
of Parade's Cubism is the problem posed by the stylistic
category "Cubism." How is a Cubist style to be considered:
in terms of form alone or in terms of form and content?
These questions are not, however, easily answered. Since
its inception, Cubism has received its most convincing

criticism in discussions which have been formally oriented to the workings of style.[6] The expressive content of Cubism has been a more difficult topic. Recent vital criticism of Cubism's meanings is at once asking new questions about what Cubist paintings signify and countering earlier interpretative claims, especially those made by Cubism's first champions.[7] Added to the general revamping of critical opinion on Cubism are the rather serious doubts expressed about the ways in which theories of style effectively inhibit inquiry by limiting the number of features examined in a work of art as a result of conforming it to a prescribed category.[8] If _Parade_ is to be related to Cubism, terms are best defined, even if it must be acknowledged that decisions about scope and attributes may be limited by critical interests currently at work.

Before the terms of Cubism are suggested in a procedural definition, several questions can be posed to indicate how impossible a task it is to decide what Cubism "really was." First, how broad a range of phenomena was Cubism? How far can a basic strategy be generalized? For example, the ploy of juxtaposition--which allowed the denotative meanings of two objects when placed together to engender new connotative meanings--was Cubist. Does this make Duchamp and Magritte Cubists? What exactly is at stake in discussions of style: form, subject matter, content, media? A broad, categorical definition of Cubism which would accommodate the formal and attitudinal vagaries of all those artists designated Cubists by themselves and by others would be so

general as to be meaningless. And, if Cubism exhibited a
protean development through time, it should be asked what
phase of Cubism is under consideration: even more importantly,
whose phase? Cubist morphology, pictorially considered, is
the least problematical area. Cubist style, as form alone,
poses far fewer problems and may be acceptably identified,
if very generally, to comprise a series of interpenetrating
and flattened shapes compressed in a shallow space, which are
arranged on a plane parallel to the picture plane. Yet
this attempt to characterize Cubist form in one sentence
indicates the difficulty of even this task. It best describes
Picasso's Cubism after 1911. The variables of the particular
artist, the particular moment in that artist's career, and
his choice of subject matter and theme are the ones which
immeasurably compound the difficulties of defining a general
Cubist style. Perhaps the notion of a Cubist style functions
most successfully, critically at least, when it attends to
form alone. And yet, there has run concurrently with this
criticism an attempt to take pictorial Cubism beyond form
to considerations of world views and to its applications to
other art forms.[9]

If attitudes and meanings may be wrested from pictorial Cubism, in addition to a set of formal features, it
is the former which are brought into discussion when attempts
are made to speak of non-pictorial Cubist art forms. Quite
obviously, the morphology of a Cubist novel will be different
from that of a Cubist painting because of the different
properties of the two media. It is difficult to relate

"interpenetrating planes" with literary syntax. The concept,
however, of "multiple cognitive perspectives" is easier to
apply to non-pictorial art forms and less awkward to deal
with critically: for example, the writer might adopt the
device of three separate narrators or concentrate upon an
examination of several characters'. responses to one event.[10]

An informative example of a comparison of the expressive
effects of Cubist painting with the expressive content of
another art form is offered in a recent book, Max Jacob and
the Poetics of Cubism, by Gerald Kamber.[11] The author first
establishes a set of attributes drawn from an examination of
pictorial Cubism; then, he searches the poems of Jacob for
parallel behaviors. Having found them, Kamber concludes that
Jacob's poetry was first Cubist and, secondly, that it assumed
its shape from the influence of pictorial Cubism. Kamber's
set of Cubist attributes are not his own but borrowed from
an important article by Winthrop Judkins, "Toward a Reinterpretation of Cubism."[12] Judkins's observations which seek to
reveal the "fundamental objective of these works" are formalist
in nature but, interestingly, give themselves fairly easily
to initial considerations of meaning beyond form. The two
major attributes Judkins discerns--"a deliberate oscillation
of appearances" and "a conscious compounding of identities"--
are adept and articulate readings of Cubist painting, which
Judkins, however, limits to the Synthetic phase 1912-1916.
Kamber takes these observations and uses them in an affective
context rather than a formalist one to describe and to interpret
the poetry of Jacob. Although several points of comparison

are well made, it is disappointing that, if Kamber chooses
to work within the framework of what Cubist paintings and
Jacob's Cubist poems signify, while dropping the question of
signifiers, he ultimately fails at his task because he does
not take his criticism to a logical and skeptical conclusion:
the poetic worlds of Picasso and Jacob, however similar
their strategies may be, do not coincide. Whether this
fact does or does not deny Jacob the title Cubist poet is a
problem which Kamber skirts.

Perhaps a more serious problem in Kamber's book is
an assumption shared by nearly all writers commenting on
non-pictorial forms of Cubism; pictorial Cubism, usually
Picasso's, is cited as the prime engenderer of non-pictorial
Cubist forms, and it is to the standard of Picasso's Cubism
that they must stand up in order to be considered Cubist.
This assumption, of course, is not without problems. Although
Picasso and Braque kept to themselves during the early years
of their Cubist experiments, what they were doing was quickly
tagged and made, relatively speaking, socially visible.
It was reified into a special thing--Cubism--through critical
writings, publicity, and group organizations. Those non-
painters who have been esteemed Cubist in their imaginations--
Stein, Joyce, Woolf, Gide, Pirandello, Wilder, Jacob--were
not so self-consciously proclaimed and attached to any movement. This may account for the direction in which comparisons
and parallels are drawn. Why not, for example, decide upon
a set of attributes which describe the work of Pirandello
and then search for their counterparts in the paintings of

Picasso? Would the comparison necessarily be the same if we had moved from Picasso to Pirandello? Perhaps, but the differences would most likely be momentarily ignored. In any event, beginning with Picasso and then moving out to make observations on the relationship of the arts and the impact of pictorial Cubism upon the other arts is an arbitrary procedure and one dictated by the charisma of Picasso's activity.

If this critical problem were to be pursued, an excellent starting point would be the problematical and provocative book by Morse Peckham, Man's Rage for Chaos.[13] Peckham's hypothesis is a sophisticated application of the concept of the Zeitgeist to cultural convergence. Changes in world views are made on the scientific and philosophical levels of society and, in turn, exert new demands upon the arts. If this were the case, the label "Cubism" might serve to describe a significant impulse in the arts of the early twentieth century, but the fact that the name originally described an experiment in painting is somewhat misleading and does not suggest the true source of the impulse. A more cumbersome title, but one which more accurately pinpoints that source might be, according to Peckham's point of view, "Einsteinism."

The problems raised above naturally have implications for any discussion of a "Cubist Ballet." What shall the extent of the category Cubism be? How shall it be defined? Shall this definition be formal and/or attitudinal? Shall a list be drawn up first of pictorial Cubism's attributes

which will then be used to explore Parade for its Cubist
features? The non-pictorial form in question here is ballet
theater. The transposition of Cubism is from the canvas to
the stage. Unlike a comparison between Picasso and Gide,
the passage is made smoother and the problem exposed more
dramatically by the fact that Picasso was involved in both
terms of the equation. Of course, in the second term are
also found the names of Cocteau, Massine, Satie, and Diaghilev.
But, the distinction between generators and implementors
must obtain here. For reasons already discussed and to be
further elaborated upon, Picasso and Cocteau stood at the
center of Parade's creation. Parade's Cubism was generated
by these two men, a matter which does not necessarily preclude
a discussion of the Cubism of the other collaborators, if,
that is, it is pertinent and arguments for its display can
be convincing. Not in any way to contradict the above observation that Picasso's Cubism is usually, and perhaps speciously,
taken as the base for seeing Cubism at play in other art
forms, it behooves the investigator in an exploration of
Parade to define the transfer of Cubism from the canvas to
the stage in terms of Picasso's Cubism. It is awkward and
less revealing to proceed from a notion of a Coctelian Cubism.
Picasso's participation in Parade provides an unusual opportunity to see exactly how transferable are the strategies
of pictorial Cubism to another medium. If the strategies
are convincingly transposed within one artist's sensibility--
Picasso's--and if Cocteau's work successfully inflected or
ran parallel to Picasso's Cubism, then arguments elsewhere

for a Cubist novel, a Cubist theater, and a poetry may be
more convincing.

Picasso's Cubism

Picasso's role in the collaboration for Parade was
both that of implementor and primary shaper. The overture
curtain, the stage set and costumes dressed Cocteau's scenario
for the stage; yet, Picasso's concept of the three managers
and their demeanor on stage in relationship to the three
acts was a significant embellishment of Cocteau's original
scenario, one which lent to the narrative a disturbing dimension. And, if the participation of Massine and Satie did
not encourage any special epithets for Parade, Picasso's
involvement took on special meaning for the public; because
of Picasso, Parade became a Cubist ballet. It is from the
point of view of Picasso's Cubism that Parade's Cubism will
be discussed.

For the sake of argument, a procedural definition of
Picasso's Cubist style is mandatory, even if it is later
countered and modified. Morse Peckham demonstrates in a
recent book on obscene art that it is linguistically idle
to say what "pornography" really is.[14] Any discussion of
what Peckham calls a "categorial term" is limited by current
interests. He is not, however, deterred from exploring the
relationship between pornography and art. The various
attributes ascribed to the term "pornography" by many individuals' experience of that category, including his own,
are kept track of as the author makes his way through his

arguments. The same attitude is adopted here. "Cubism"
is a categorial term which itself has been subjected to
broad ranges of interpretation. The way in which Cubism
is perceived by this writer is the result of his experiences
with Cubist painting, with the word in art historical criticism, and, especially, the result of special interests in
the problems posed by a "Cubist ballet." Consequently, a
procedural definition is needed to allow for clarity of
discourse and, secondly, to stand ready for qualification
based upon new experience.

Picasso's "Cubist style" as it stood at the inception
of Parade shall signify style as it is usually defined--a
set of formal qualities; a choice of subject matter; and,
a semantic aspect, that is, what the forms signify from a
simple identification of objects to concepts and attitudes.
The range of the term is pictorial; Cubism describes painting--
marks made on a flat surface. The forms placed upon the flat
support are themselves flattened shapes, which in their
apparent lack of volume suggest a highly tautened and compressed space. Edges of forms, which are angular or geometric,
tend to be hard rather than brushed. On a basic level of
subject identification, these forms represent a fairly closed
series of everyday objects and individuals categorized in
the history of painting as still life and portraiture.
Semantically, the subject matters stand as visual metaphors
for a type of being-in-the-world. In this respect, Cubism
is epistemological in its concern for how the individual
knows his world. But as such, it stands in opposition to

normative, everyday attentivenesses. This daily knowing the world may be characterized as continuous, understandable, and ritualized into habit. Because of the predictability of this world, experience itself becomes a redundant source of information. The world around the individual becomes a repository for invariable and stabilized meanings; new meanings cease to be generated.

Picasso's Cubism challenges the knowable and the predictable. The mundane becomes a vehicle for shattering expectancies. Normative, everyday knowing is thrown off guard. The tendency towards the stabilization of information is thwarted. Those mundane objects, people, and events are pictorially distorted so as to assume a high level of allusiveness and to garner new and unexpected connotations. The set of meanings things display is characterized by ambiguity, paradox, and irony. In this particular presentation of the everyday, the attempt is made to prevent congealing points of view and to maintain an open-ended attentiveness to the world which is forever amendable by new experience.

Thus, Picasso's Cubism posits the relativity of experience and by extension the artificiality of systems for knowing the world. The multiple perspectives of Cubism figuratively imply a denial of absolutes. Now, the above description of Cubism's semantic aspect may have meaning apart from its being situated within the context of painting. The meaning of Cubism construed in this way could stand alone as a verbal statement in prose and result in philosophy. The individual could simply read the meaning of Cubism without seeing a Cubist canvas and respond to it as a new attitude to be adopted in his or her everyday life. This possibility conforms to Peckham's view that any semantic function or meaning in art can be found outside art. But the semantic aspect of Picasso's Cubism cannot be so easily wrenched from its formal dimension. The ultimate integrity and self-consciousness of Picasso's Cubism is that it acknowledges painting as a formal and symbolic way of representing experience, and as such, it is an artificial system of knowing the world. Consequently, a Cubist painting by Picasso which proffers epistemological ambiguities about the world must necessarily acknowledge its own inner workings as an art form. Brecht's statement that "the showing must be shown" is a basic notion that underlies Picasso's Cubism. Picasso's Cubist canvases, papiers-collés, and collages were self-referential. There were two major strategies which allowed a Cubist painting to make what Robert Rosenblum calls "an examination of the aesthetic substance"[15]: the placing of non-art materials and printing on the surface of the work and, secondly, the juxtaposition of different pictorial styles to demonstrate that each mode is a selected, limited, and artificial set of options.

Picasso's Cubist Mise en Scène

Picasso's curtain begins the ballet Parade with an image equal in significance to Cocteau's scenario, and it is the initial and primary gesture against which all other elements of Picasso's mise en scène are played and, in turn,

take meaning. With its dramatic importance submitted, the
question can be asked, "In what possible ways can this over-
sized image, which appears so reactionary in its style, relate
to Picasso's Cubism?" Several of these reasons were discussed
in Chapter Four where the curtain was momentarily allowed
to be a separate painting removed from the context of theatrical scenery. The curtain's Cubism was there seen to be not
as specious as might initially be suspected. Its "Cubism,"
however, needs to be reviewed briefly and put in another
perspective.

In its form, the curtain's affiliation with Cubist
morphology is subtle. Still, the apparent flattening of
the figures in the group composition derives from the compressed
Cubist plane, although the figures are, of course, not subjected to blatant fragmentation and distortion. The juxtaposition of the figure group's style with the more fully
realized illusionistic spaces of the stage setting creates
the effect of a collage, although it too is an admittedly
subtle manifestation. It is rather the curtain's semantic
aspect which most strongly begs for a Cubist interpretation.
Objects carry multiple identities and relate to one another
in an ambiguous Cubist dialectic. For example, the young
girl on the horse may relate to the Picasso-Harlequin in one
of the following identities: horseback rider, ballet dancer,
sylphide, classical Muse, and Olga Koklova. The conjoining
of these meanings with those afforded by the Picasso-Harlequin
results in a cross fire of connotations. In addition to the
multiple identities of things, the watcher-watched theme

and the stage setting offer a virtuoso display of Cubist
multiple perspectives. The changing perspectives of the
setting depend upon a perceptual frame of reference, whereas
the watcher theme is fragmented in a context which is more
properly psychological and personal. Moreover, Picasso's
experience of Cubism allowed him to return in the curtain
to the watcher-watched theme and to elaborate upon it in a
way impossible before the Cubist years. In the curtain,
the states of mind of the watcher and the watched are presented;
they are experienced by the viewer of the curtain simultaneously.
The artist-viewer watches, rather embraces, the acts of
active creativity and passive introspection; states of mind
normally separate in time are brought together. The watcher
watches himself being watched. Only with the earlier experiences of Cubism could Picasso have accomplished this feat.
In spite of the ostensibly non-Cubist look of the curtain,
the theme of the artist's introspection is keenly compatible
with, if not the emblem for, the self-reflexive attitude of
Cubist painting. What may seem puzzling in this analysis
is that an image, the overture curtain, which does not bear
the appearance of a Cubist canvas, is being discussed as
aggressively Cubist in its semantic aspect. Is the curtain
Cubist? Yes, but only convincingly in what the image signifies, not in its signifiers. Whether the curtain is to be
considered Cubist or not depends quite clearly on how the
categorical term Cubism is perceived.

        Picasso's overture curtain, however, was not originally
intended to be enjoyed as a painting separated from its

theatrical context. Although this may be done--and it is
the contention that a response to the curtain as a single
work of art is both valid and satisfying--the overture curtain
belongs to a ballet, and it is only in that context that its
fullest set of meanings are laid bare.

There is no ultimatum given to the scenic designer
that his overture curtain must connect carefully to the
dramatic narrative of the theater piece. An overture curtain
has traditionally been a decorative adjunct to the orchestral
overture. It has been demonstrated that this is not the
case with Picasso's curtain. Additionally, it relates in
significant ways to other scenic components of Parade. The
overture curtain is the first speaker in a Cubist dialogue
with the remaining mise en scène. Because of the theatrical
context, this dialectic will have to be discussed in a temporal
frame of reference which is different from that of painting.
In no way a decorative drop, the overture curtain begins
the ballet Parade in earnest.

A theatrical gesture occurs in Parade immediately
after the overture curtain is raised, even before the French
Manager appears from stage right. The gesture centers on
the stylistic discrepancy between the overture curtain and
the stage set (Figs. 50 and 51). In contrast to the naïve
representationalism of the overture curtain, the angular
distortions of the stage set are those of another style:
Synthetic Cubism. The only point of comparison is that the
main motifs in each--the gathering of performers and the
fair booth proscenium--are compositionally centralized. The

false stage with its painted figures and theatrical drapery
in the overture curtain gives way to the spatial realization
of the stage set. The curtain's proscenium is transformed
into the fair-booth proscenium of the set through which
real performers emerge. The shift from the flatness of the
curtain to the three-dimensionality of the set maintains,
however, the essential terms of proscenium and performers.
Still, the dominant contrast remains the difference of style
between curtain and set. The disparity was noticed at the
original performance of Parade in 1917. Two days after the
opening at the Châtelet, Abel Harmant wrote the following
in the Excelsior:

> ...the house curtain raised on a second curtain which
> the authors of Parade declare classical and in the
> style of M. Ingres. They exaggerate a bit. Neverthe-
> less, the curtain is not cubist to the same extent
> as the set which the curtain momentarily hides from
> our eyes.[16]

The style of the overture curtain was compared to the style
of Ingres and recalls the fact that Picasso's new style in
the pencil drawings of 1915 has been called his style ingriste.[17]

The juxtaposition of different styles in one painting
was a tactic Picasso had used prior to the Cubist years proper.
A confrontation of different pictorial modes was used in
the Portrait of Gertrude Stein (1906) and the Demoiselles
d'Avignon (1907). This device was again employed in the
canvases of 1911 when Picasso began to place within the
abstract forms of Cubism illusionistic and trompe-l'oeil
passages. In these works and in the following collages,
the Cubist style--flattened planes in a compressed space--

dominate. The illusionistic and real annotations are embellishments. Towards the end of the teens, Picasso played
a variation upon the juxtaposition of styles and situated
the illusionistic style ingriste in a dominant role over
Cubist notations. In a small gouache of 1919, The Open
Window (Fig. 79), a table-top Cubist still life is placed
in a room and before an open window and Mediterranean seascape which are painted in an opposing naturalistic style.

Why the confrontation of modes in Picasso's art?
And does the answer to this question help explicate Picasso's
stylistic decisions for Parade's curtain and stage set? The
jarring placement of major passages of a realistic style
next to portions of the Cubist style is a development in
Picasso's art which has been seen to belong to the early
twenties and to have been heralded in the Open Window gouache
of 1919.[18] This may be true of Picasso's paintings and
related pictorial images, but he had already used the basic
strategy quite forcefully in the juxtaposition of Parade's
curtain and stage set. That its use may have been worked
out initially in the context of Parade's designs and then
implemented in Picasso's painting is possibly attested by
a drawing executed in Rome during Parade's rehearsals (Fig.
80). To the top of the page is a sketch for an Equestrian
Manager's costume. Immediately below is a simple sketch
presaging the gouache of 1919. Picasso's concern for the
juxtaposition of modes has been observed to be his questioning
of the notions of style.[19] This questioning can further be
related to Picasso's desire to expose the artificiality of

his systems of representation and to deny the constancy of any one system. As a general statement about approach, it suffices. Still, each work of art which exhibits this concern can and should be further discussed in terms of specific content. The table-top still life in The Open Window, a conventional set up for an artist to paint, has already been, within the more literal rendition of the room, assumed into art, into artificiality. And yet, in another reading the illusionistic seascape and balcony may appear to be the artificial components while the Cubist still life declares itself more honestly because it makes no effort to fool the eye. This dialectical state of affairs is brought about because the juxtaposition of two pictorial styles triggers cross challenges of integrity. Or, more simply, both may be stated as acceptable artifices--or as simply being artifices.

In a description of the interplay between pictorial modes in The Open Window, Robert Rosenblum states that the literal passages are negated by, among other things, "the suspicion that the alluring sea and clouds beyond are nothing more than an opaque, painted backdrop."[20] (Italics mine.) Rosenblum comes unwittingly very close to the point. What he may not have been aware of is a small pencil drawing that Picasso executed in London in 1919 during his scenic preparations for Le Tricorne (Fig. 81). Done in the same year as the gouache, the pencil drawing depicts in the lower foreground a table-top Cubist still life which is juxtaposed against the summary sketching of Picasso's overture curtain for _Le Tricorne_. The still life was not included in the curtain's final rendition. Yet, its placement against the curtain was not coincidental; it suggests the momentary musing of Picasso on the problem of stylistic contrast. And, of course, the incorporation of the problem into a theatrical context had been achieved two years earlier in the ballet _Parade_.

In his choice of different styles for the overture curtain and the stage set, Picasso fixed a Cubist juxtaposition, although the contrast now occurred _sequentially_, not simultaneously. Furthermore, this ploy was used for a particular dramatic purpose to support the narrative content of the ballet. It has been observed that the lyricism of the overture curtain was a tease on the part of Picasso and a momentary appeasement of the 1917 audience members before "blowing them to the back wall"[21] with the Cubist elements of the ballet itself. The devilish humor of the gesture can be appreciated in view of the somewhat negative response to the original production, but the relationship between the curtain and the stage set was more than a political move to shock. It foiled anticipation and predictability. It was a dramatic demonstration before the audience's eyes of the artist's sleight of hand. Much like the magician with his deck of cards in one hand, who with his thumb slides one card aside to reveal the unexpected card, Picasso's overture curtain rising on the stage set was a magic trick. Actual performance reveals Picasso's curtain during the traditional harmonies of Satie's overture. When the curtain

is raised on the Cubist set for the beginning of the ballet,
Satie's music also changes modes from the counterpoint of
a traditional chorale into more freely constructed harmonic
progressions and the obsessive ostinato of the Manager's
theme. The overture curtain, supported by the music of
Satie, is, appropriately, Parade announcing itself as a
work of art, an illusion perpetrated by its makers. As
such, the relationship between the overture curtain and the
stage set evinces Cubist relativity and bears expressively
and pertinently on the ballet's theme of the artist's activity.
The overture curtain was like the magician's multicolored
silk scarf which covers his hands and which is then quickly
removed to reveal magical delights and surprises. The
surprise in Parade was the special world of the Managers,
the acts, and their angular and mysterious cityscape. Léon
Bakst, in a program note for the original production, appreciated the momentary deceit of the overture curtain and
deemed it intentionally conservative in its function. He
wrote: "A large curtain, intentionally conservative in its
design, is positioned between these flowers of the twentieth
century [the acts] and the intrigued spectator."[22]

An examination of the more ostensible Cubist elements
and relationships of the stage set, the Managers' costumes,
and the acts was undertaken in Chapter Four. The planes of
Synthetic Cubism dress the set and the costumes for the Horse
and the French and American Managers. A more telling manifestation of a Cubist awareness is found in the simultaneous
presentation of different psychological visages in the costume

for the French Manager and in the Horse's head. And, it
was pointed out that the device of picturing simultaneous
psychological states was not a postscript to earlier works,
but a significant elaboration upon the implications of Cubism,
one to be developed in Picasso's later work.

The costumes of the acts could not be considered
Cubist taken by themselves. However, if they are examined
in the context of the total scenic production, they are found
to be components in a Cubist paradigm. Their Cubist functions
are twofold. First, the colorful, volumetric presence of
the acts stands in contrast to the flat, monochrome of the
stage set. This presents a direct reversal of the situation
in the overture curtain--flat figures against a volumetric
setting. Here again is an instance of the pitting together
of different visual modes. As collage elements "attached"
to the set, the three acts occasion a further relationship
between the ballet proper and the overture curtain; they are
strays from the style of the curtain and its gathering of
performers. Secondly, Picasso originated a set of stylistic
and psychological discrepancies between the costumes and
personages of the Managers and the acts. The nature of this
particular dramatic dialogue was detailed earlier.

The most striking feature of Picasso's mise en scène
is the way in which all parts are integrated with one another.
To dismiss or redesign any element in the scenic production,
say the removal of the overture curtain, would be to violate
the grand scheme Picasso envisioned his designs to be. The
ballet Parade begins in all its seriousness with the overture

curtain. The curtain dramatically gives way to the stage set and its stylistically matching Managers. Finally the acts, which relate formally to the overture curtain, appear on the stage and submit their special relationship with the Managers. The complex way in which Picasso knitted his implementation of the production together, stylistically and expressively, was through the strategies of Cubist collage.

The Overture Curtain and the Scenario

What has been sorely misunderstood since the inception of Parade is that the overture curtain of Picasso evokes much more than a decorative mood; not only may it stand alone as an image which is highly intricate in its meanings, but it also supports and comments upon Cocteau's scenario. The curtain and the scenario are significantly compatible in their statements and, when they are taken together, produce Parade's broadest meaning. Each in its own deceptive simplicity is an intricately reflective allegory about the modern artist. Cocteau's scenario speaks about the artist's efforts to make himself known to and understood by an uncaring and contemptuous public. It describes frustration and alienation. Picasso's overture curtain celebrates in an ironic fashion the artist's homage to his métier. It also portrays and examines in metaphorical terms the act of self-criticism. An urgent dimension of both the scenario and the overture curtain is the autobiographical commentary made by the poet and the painter. Another point of similarity is that both men set their allegories within the world of theatrical performance. The central metaphor of Parade is the artist as a public performer. In the overture curtain and in the scenario this role is assigned respectively to the Harlequin and to the Chinese Magician.

If Cubism may be considered in one view as painting about painting, this dimension is extended to Parade, only in theatrical terms. Parade is concerned with performances about performances. The real audience member witnesses the allegory in the overture curtain as a performance with its own interior performance and audience. The scenario or ballet proper has as its subject matter a performance outside a théâtre forain which connects with an unseen performance within. Roger Shattuck in his book The Banquet Years, states that twentieth-century art

> ...has tended to search itself rather than exterior
> reality...what is at stake here is a theory of know-
> ledge, a theory of consciousness itself...art has
> become self-reflexive--narcissistic. It endlessly
> studies its own behaviors and considers them suitable
> subject matter.[23]

If this is a fair description of modern art--and it seems to fit most comfortably the Cubist aesthetic--then Parade should be figuratively esteemed its very signature. In a convincing proof of Cubism on the stage, Parade takes pictorial Cubism's self-awareness and transposes it to a theatrical setting.

Picasso's overture curtain and Cocteau's scenario each requests an audience to be part of its conceit. The play on the theme of the watcher and watched is only complete if the viewer is conscious about his own watching and about how it relates to the action portrayed. The curtain's

metaphor presupposes and requires a real audience to complete
its terms. Cocteau's scenario requires an audience of
passers-by who would not understand the pleas of the performers and walk away. Cocteau assigned the role of this
"audience" to the real audience in the theater. What may
have been unsettling for those members of the original audience
who did not favorably respond to Parade was the fact that
the acts played their routines directly to the audience.
The performers played to them as though the "crowd" in the
ballet's scenario were actually the real audience. The work
of art was behaving as though it were reality, not fiction.
The spectators were asked to take part in the very narrative
of the ballet. They were, perhaps to their indignation,
not watching a performance, but in one. Roger Shattuck
observes that in modern art the "frame is overrun," that
there occurs a "deliberate cross of art and life."[24] He
goes on to say that "with these distinctions broken, we
become incorporated into the work of art." Parade fits
the prescription ideally. By playing their routines to
the audience, the acts assumed another theatrical context
in addition to the category "ballet." Cocteau, writing about
the audience's outrage, stated that "...the public took
the transposition of music hall for bad music hall."[25]
To certain members of the audience, the high cultural seriousness of ballet was transgressed by a so-called ballet which
was behaving in the more vulgar vernacular of vaudeville.

In both the overture curtain and in the scenario the
artists demanded that their audience be theatricalized. A

placard was lowered, shortly before the curtain fell on
Parade, from within the small fair-booth proscenium, with
the following message emblazoned for the audience to ponder:
THE DRAMA WHICH DID NOT TAKE PLACE FOR THOSE PEOPLE WHO
STAYED OUTSIDE WAS BY JEAN COCTEAU, ERIK SATIE, PABLO PICASSO.[26]
This message to the real audience further underscored the
active role the audience members were intended to play; in
this instance they were being bawled out for not being sensitive enough to respond favorably and, by implication, being
praised for enjoying the ballet. The opening-night audience's
scornful rejection of Parade, whose performers were desperately
pleading for acceptance--within the context of the ballet's
fiction--was an ironical blending of art and life in view
of the ballet's allegory.

The overture curtain and the scenario share a variety
of aesthetic notions. Both are self-reflexive in their moods
and assign new and active roles to the viewer. The allegories
contrived in each are mutually complementary. Finally, the
dramatic strategies of each may be categorized Cubist.
Picasso's mise en scène taken as a whole should be seen as
a successful transposition of one artistic mode to another
medium. It was stated earlier that non-pictorial forms
perceived to be Cubist usually can only deal successfully
with Cubist signifieds. Pictorial Cubist signifiers are
possible to a certain extent in sculpture and in architecture;
they are impossible to transfer to literary modes. Stage
machinery is sculptural and architectural. The possibility
thus exists of bringing Cubist forms to the stage. However,

in every case, with the exception of Picasso's _Parade_, the result has been purely decorative: that is, the forms may have been Cubist, as in Survage's set for Diaghilev's production of _Mavra_, but their expressive contents displayed no true Cubist awareness. There is no difficulty in speaking of the forms of _Parade's_ scenic designs as Cubist. What may appear in isolation to be non-Cubist forms, specifically the overture curtain and the costumes for the acts, can now be seen to be the equivalent of collage elements if the scenic components are perceived as a whole and working in concert with each other. The content of Picasso's designs is also Cubist in its awareness. The crucial difference between Picasso's earlier pictorial and sculptural Cubism and the theatrical Cubism of _Parade_ is that the latter takes place through time; the visual elements impinge sequentially upon the viewer over a period of approximately fifteen minutes. The temporal structuring of a theatrical event is not the same as that of a painting.

Another aspect of Picasso's Cubism in _Parade_, one which is in part a function of Cocteau's scenario, is the disturbing mood which lurks under the witty proceedings. After World War I, Picasso's art moved into new areas of subject matter and content. This direction has been seen to have led to themes of violence, myth, and decoration at variance with the dispassionate, epistemological investigations of Picasso's earlier Cubism. Although the claim that Picasso's Cubism of 1909-1916 was emotionally neutral needs to be seriously reconsidered, it is true, nevertheless, that

Picasso's art after the war did move into new thematic directions qualified by their psychological concerns. Although Parade has not hitherto been singled out for the honor, it serves as a dramatic marker of Picasso's new concerns with the more overtly psychological and mysterious which will lead in turn to the Three Magicians (1921) and the Three Dancers (1925).

Cocteau's Cubism

If one is to speak of Cocteau's Cubism, it will have to be done in terms of a set of signifieds. These have already been broached above: the scenario's self-reflexiveness and its manipulation of the barriers between work of art and audience. Cocteau's concern with a latently magical everyday world finds its counterpart in Picasso's attitudes toward the world. It is this one point which undoubtedly drew Cocteau so close to Picasso. The two men had uncommonly similar sensibilities. If the magical manipulation of objects is cited as an attribute of Picasso's Cubism, then Cocteau too was a Cubist. In fact, it was this aspect of Picasso's scenic contribution for Parade which was elaborated upon at length by Guillaume Apollinaire in his program notes for the original production in 1917. Apollinaire's remarks are significant for the use of the word Surrealism for the first time in the history of modern art. What was its meaning for Parade? First, Apollinaire discussed a "surrealism" only in regard to the relationship between Picasso's painting and Massine's choreography. Apollinaire was not a music critic and paid scant attention to Cocteau's scenario. He devoted his comments to one aspect of Parade. To quote Apollinaire:

> From this new alliance (because up until now scenic
> design and costumes on the one hand, and choreography
> on the other, have only had an artificial bond between
> them), there has resulted in the production of Parade
> a kind of surrealism where I see the point of departure
> for a series of manifestations of this New Spirit...[27]

Another observation, referring to Picasso's efforts, is
helpful in elucidating the word Surrealism: "This realism or
this cubism, as you wish, is what has most profoundly agitated
the arts during the last ten years."[28] It is implied that
Realism and Cubism are interchangeable. Therefore, theoretically,
"Surrealism" would be a synonym for "Surcubism," a super or
intensified form of Cubism. Apollinaire went on to explain
how Picasso's Cubist method was applied to the mise en scène:
"Parade's scenic design and costumes clearly show his preoccupation with pulling from an object all the aesthetic emo-
tion it can give."[29] The artist translated reality, representing, not reproducing, the object by collecting all its
visible elements into one integrated schema. This deliberate
distortion of reality was seen by Apollinaire to be poetically
undertaken in order to instill the object with an intensely
expressive content. Cubism, in this instance, was defined
not as a cerebral investigation of perception, but as an
aesthetic means to create magic. Massine, Apollinaire pointed
out, had similar intentions in Parade when he heightened the
reality of his mundane characters, through burlesque and
caricature, in order to express "the magic of their daily
lives."[30] Elements of design and choreography were interwoven:
Massine's angular gestures matched the lines of the Cubist

cityscape; Picasso's scenery was incorporated into the costumes
of the dancing Managers. The sur-réalisme, or sur-cubisme,
conceived by Apollinaire was the formal expansion of the Cubist
method to include dance, costumes, and scenery in a new aesthetic whole.

Apollinaire may have spoken eloquently about Picasso's
Cubism on the stage, but his ignoring of Cocteau's role in
Parade, even if politically motivated, was uncritical and un-
gracious. Picasso and Cocteau were spiritually the closest
of any of the collaborators. Both men desired to rehabilitate
the commonplace and to surprise everyday objects out of their
banality through exaggeration. In 1917 Cocteau composed an
Ode à Picasso, a little known poem whose two parts entitled
"L'Homme assis" and "Les Muses" curiously and perhaps not
coincidentally suggest the two major motifs in Parade's
overture curtain. Picasso is pictured as "le dompteur de
muses" who is able to control and manipulate the Muses to
his own ends. Cocteau saw Picasso as the supreme magician,
beckoning objects to his command. The role of magician was
also the aesthetic persona Cocteau felt himself to have.
In an allusion to Picasso which finishes the ode and which
also speaks for Cocteau, the poet writes: "Nothing up his
sleeves, nothing in his pockets--you monsieur, would you
lend your hat to the Harlequin of Port-Royal."[31]

It is especially curious that Apollinaire failed to
acknowledge Cocteau's role in the setting of the choreography,
a participation freely admitted by Massine. Cocteau's suggestions made to Massine and incorporated into the ballet

qualify the poet for the additional role of co-choreographer.
It was Cocteau, and then Massine, who magically intensified
the characters through burlesque and caricature. And, it
was Cocteau's intervention in the choreography which makes
possible a discussion of how Cubism might relate to the
dancing. Furthermore, a consideration of the musical score
and Cubism can only be entertained if Cocteau's collaboration in that sphere is acknowledged. The picture emerges
again of the young poet working overtime and outside his
own responsibilities as scenarist to bring the various theatrical elements of Parade together. For the purposes of continu-
ing the examination of Parade and Cubism, Cocteau's Cubist
sensibility needs to be further explored.

Apollinaire's remark in his program notes that Massine's
choreography matched the angular lines of Picasso's stage set
was difficult to substantiate in the Joffrey production.
Apollinaire was proposing that Massine's choreography was
not only integrated with Picasso's setting but that it could
itself be termed Cubist. If this were true, and the stylized
gestures of the Chinese Magician could possibly be related
to the angularity of Cubism's geometry, it would nonetheless
remain a case of Cubism's "look" being transferred from one
medium to another; in other words, a decorative transposition.
It does not necessarily follow that Cubism's signifieds would
be present in this type of transfer. However, the choreography
of Parade does display a set of Cubist awarenesses which can
take a discussion of this sort beyond the formal.

It has already been discussed how Cocteau assisted

Massine with the choreography during preparations for Parade
in Rome. The basic structure of the Chinese Magician's routine, outlined in the Cahier romain (Fig. 93), as well as
Cocteau's series of gestures for the Little American Girl's
Steamboat Ragtime, remained intact in the Joffrey revival.
It is not known to what extent Cocteau influenced the general
shape of the dances of the Acrobats and the Managers. The
sequence of movements which Cocteau established for part of
the choreography was not the only way in which he "directed"
Massine, nor is it the most important for a Cubist reading.
Massine, in interview, acknowledged Cocteau's important
suggestions for everyday and ordinary movements, which were
then incorporated into a more conventional balletic context.
It was not uncommon in earlier productions of the Ballets
Russes for the scenic designer, and often Diaghilev, to work
directly with the choreographer.[32] Cocteau's collaboration
with Massine was undoubtedly approved by Diaghilev. The
stamping of Parade with contemporary gestures would have
been difficult for Massine, who was not yet fully acculturated
to Western Europe. And it is this aspect of Parade--everyday
gesture integrated into balletic movement--which enables
the choreography to be Cubist. However, there are certain
problems here of interpretation and of frame of reference.
On the one hand, the non-balletic movements proper in Parade--
for example, the Chinaman swallowing an egg, the Little
American Girl's ragtime steps, or the Acrobats shinnying up
a rope to their trapeze--may have been at the time unorthodox
gestures for a ballet, but they can still be categorized

within the tradition of western ballet as pantomime and character dancing. Massine, himself, has based his choreographic career upon character dancing, whose pantomimic richness stands in contrast to the "purer" gestures of the danse d'école. From the standpoint, however, of Cubist juxtaposition, a series of pirouettes suddenly followed by a Charlie Chaplin walk does bear a generic relationship to the insertion of non-art materials from the real world into the sovereign territory of oil paint in Cubist collage. It is especially tempting to see in the Little American Girl's routine a trenchant transposition of pictorial Cubism to ballet. The blend of balletic and pantomimic actions she performed in rapid succession--riding a horse, catching a train, driving a Model T Ford, peddling a bicycle, swimming, acting in a movie where a robber is driven away at gun point, snapping the shutter of a Kodak, doing a ragtime, doing a "Charlie Chaplin," getting seasick, sinking with the Titanic, and relaxing at the seashore--were disjunctive, incomplete, and cryptic gestures. Paralleling the structuring of form in pictorial Cubism, snippets of character identifying actions were strung together. The essence of the Little American Girl's character, as well as that of the Chinese Magician and the Acrobats, was suggested through Cubist reminiscences of form.

In the Cahier romain, Cocteau made a suggestion for the routine of the Acrobat which, not included in Massine's version for the Joffrey production, tantalizingly remains the most potentially subtle Cubist aspect of Cocteau's envisioned choreography. One section of a page in the Cahier romain (Fig. 92) reads: "For the acrobat, exercises at the bar."[33] Cocteau had apparently intended that the Acrobat should incorporate into his character-identifying movements the bar exercises of a ballet class. It could be imagined that in between walking a tightrope and juggling the Acrobat might momentarily pause to raise his one arm to an imaginary bar and with the other arm and feet in second position execute a grand plié. The motions, in other words, of warm-up, training, and rehearsal would have been brought into the context of the finished work of art. The mechanism of the "aesthetic substance," which is normally concealed from the viewer, is exposed: the identity of "danseur" is acknowledged within the illusion of "acrobat." The Cubist self-examination of pictorial means is transferred into the realm of dance.

Of all elements in Parade, the choreography remains the most difficult to analyze. Its discussion in terms of the ballet's Cubism must be the most hypothetical of all similar considerations of Parade's other parts. The Joffrey revival in New York in 1973 was a bracing stimulus for this writer's thinking on Parade. Nevertheless, the problems of the dancing remain. One cannot be sure to what extent the Massine version tallies with the original. In 1964 Massine mounted a revival of Parade for Maurice Béjart in Brussels, a production which he has since disavowed. A comparison of a rehearsal film of the Béjart version with the Joffrey version shows that, while basic gestures are repeated in both, the two choreographies are nonetheless different.[34] In spite of the fact that Joffrey billed the New York version "Massine's Parade,"--an indication of authorship which of course makes this writer wince--Massine, himself, was properly skeptical about all the excitement. First of all, Massine admitted that he lost his choreographic notes for the original production and that his settings for the Béjart and the Joffrey productions were redoings rather than revivals. Massine understands that historically Parade has been labeled by some to be the "first modern ballet," but he prefers himself to give that honor to Nijinsky's and Fokine's choreography for Stravinsky's Le Sacre du Printemps. With a smile on his face, Massine said that in the collaboration for Parade he was something of a greenhorn from Russia, who was surrounded in Rome by the high-powered activities of Picasso and Cocteau--men who were his senior in age and in reputation. It is easy to forget that at the time of Parade Massine was only seventeen years old. Not that age should limit potential accomplishment, but all reports indicate that Massine's contribution was actively directed by others. Consequently, the Cubist ramifications of the choreography as they are presented here are based upon what is known about the original production in Cocteau's writings and upon the Joffrey New York revival which, in turn, poses historical problems.

Not only did Cocteau obtrude, in a sense, upon the choreography, but he also made his presence felt in the musical sphere. Satie's musical score for Parade would not have

been the only aural dimension to <u>Parade</u> if Cocteau's original
scenario, which included verbal and sound segments, had been
followed. All of these sounds were jettisoned for the final
version, except a few of Cocteau's sound effects that were
begrudgingly accepted by the other collaborators. Ironically,
contemporary recordings of <u>Parade</u> are never made without the
sound effects, and in almost every instance they are credited
to the zany wit of Satie.

Upon having enlisted Satie and Picasso for the collaboration of <u>Parade</u>, Cocteau, in the fall of 1916, began
running into trouble with his ideas.[35] Satie and Picasso
developed an alliance which countered Cocteau's scenario,
particularly Cocteau's sounds and noise. In a letter to
Valentine Cross in September 1916, Cocteau wrote:

> ...Make Satie understand, if you can cut through the
> aperitif fog, that I really do count for something
> in <u>Parade</u>, and that he and Picasso are not the only
> ones involved. I consider <u>Parade</u> a kind of renova-
> tion of the theater, and not a simple "pretext" for
> music. It hurts me when he dances around Picasso
> screaming "It's you I'm following! YOU are my master!"
> and seems to be hearing for the first time, from
> Picasso's mouth, things that I have told him time
> and time again. Does he hear anything I say? Per-
> haps it's all an <u>acoustical</u> phenomenon.[36]

However annoyed Cocteau seems in this instance with Satie, the
poet was to go on and champion, in a series of critical
writings after <u>Parade's</u> debut, the importance of Satie in
heralding a new aesthetic in French music. But, in the case
of <u>Parade</u>, not only did Cocteau's sounds pose an unacceptable
interference for Satie, but Cocteau attributed meanings to
Satie's score which would have undoubtedly puzzled the composer.
Even today, the two qualities Cocteau spoke about in regard

to Satie's score are difficult to apply to musical experience,
in even the most general of terms. Rather than being examples
of penetrating musical analysis, they ballyhoo Cocteau's
concept of his own scenario. In a statement made in defense
of Parade after its debut, Cocteau wrote the following about
Satie's score:

> Little by little a sober and pristine score came into
> the world, where Satie seems to have discovered an
> unknown dimension thanks to which one can simultaneously
> hear the parade and the show inside.[37]

And, much earlier, the fall before, Cocteau spoke about Satie's
Parade in a letter to Misia Sert: "It is his drama--and the
eternal drama between the audience and the stage--in a form
as simple as a popular print."[38] The attributes Cocteau was
speaking about--simultaneity of experience and the relationship between an audience and the work of art, both attitudes
explored by Cocteau and Picasso in the mise en scène and in
the scenario--sound somewhat misplaced in a discussion of
a musical composition. Only by the most attenuated interpretations can these states of mind be read into Satie's
score.

Satie's score has, nevertheless, been discussed by
other writers as a manifestation of Cubism. These arguments
are specious at best. David Drew points out that the three
musical routines for the Chinese Magician, the Little American
Girl, and the Acrobats, constitute three cellular ideas.[39]
The musical form of Parade is then compared to Cubism. Three
cells are juxtaposed without transition, one abruptly giving
way to another. One of several musical precedents for this

form, that Drew does not mention, is the suite, which collects
a variety of forms into one work. If Satie's score adopted
this older form, and if Drew's logic is followed, then a
Partita by Bach is Cubist, which was assuredly not the intention of the composer. Over half of Satie's fifty works were
tripartite in form. In his discussion of Parade, Roger
Shattuck perceives Satie's score to be one musical idea
regarded briefly from three different directions, thereby
demonstrating in musical form the multiple perspectives of
Cubism.[40] Again, another historical precedent makes this
argument weak: the theme and variations. It is true that
Satie does not initially state a theme which is then developed,
but the traditional variations may be easily described as a
musical idea taken from different points of view. If one
adopts the Duchampian stance that anything can be called
anything through personal choice, then to challenge Drew
and Shattuck would be in part to question personal interests.
Still, it remains the opinion of this writer that the above
statements are too general to be convincing and meaningful
for a discussion of Parade as Cubist spectacle. The qualities
isolated by Drew and Shattuck are to be found virtually in
all music.

There is, though, one aspect of Parade's score which
may be incontestably discussed in terms of Cubism: the
insertion of Cocteau's sound effects. The sounds of a type-
writer, a gunshot, a lottery wheel, and a siren are materials
from the real world which are placed, untransposed, into
Satie's score. Cocteau wrote in the Cahier romain (Fig. 99):

"Picasso says, 'Don't be afraid to paste in a newspaper--
an exact gesture which is not transposed and which gives
full value to other gestures.'"[41] Instead of pasting news-
paper on the work of art, Cocteau pasted everyday sounds
into Satie's score. Cocteau was quite aware of the collage
method he was adopting. In the Coq et l'arlequin, written
two years after Parade's first production, Cocteau stated
the following:

> The score of Parade should serve as a musical base for
> suggestive noises, such as sirens, typewriters, air-
> planes, dynamos, placed in the score like what Georges
> Braque so justifiably calls "facts."[42]

Cocteau added in a footnote to this statement that "These 'noises'
play exactly the same role as the elements in trompe-l'oeil
and the papiers collés in cubist paintings."[43] The addition
of sound effects to the musical score was likened by Cocteau
to the inclusion of real elements in a Cubist collage. The
clicking of the wheel of fortune, the gunshots, and the
staccato sound of the typewriter--all used to enhance the
mime of the dancers--were strange intrusions into the world
of orchestral sounds. The exact nature of the sound effects'
allegiance to life or art remained ambivalent.

EPILOGUE

Le sérieux qui en impose. Ne jamais y croire.
Ne jamais le confondre avec la gravité.

Jean Cocteau[1]

Cocteau and Picasso brought Cubism to the stage in
Diaghilev's production of Parade. The nature of that Cubism
was not a decorative embellishment of a theater piece to lend
it a modern look. Rather, the underpinnings of the scenario
and the mise en scène, along with Cocteau's knowing touches
to the choreography and musical score, were a demonstration
in theatrical terms of both the form and content of pictorial
Cubism. There was no artificial separation between the formal
strategies of Cubism and its expressive content in Parade.
The content of the ballet was eminently suited to a Cubist
aesthetic. In fact, to separate a discussion of Parade into
its respective means and ends is impossible. It is not as
though Parade were arbitrarily implemented by Cubism in a
way which might suggest that any contemporary style would
have been equally effective. Cocteau may have created the
basis of his scenario before asking Picasso to decorate it,
but the meshing of sensibilities was so acute that Parade's
initial narrative conception and later theatrical dressing
by Picasso do not appear stylistically to have been staggered
in time. The aesthetic match of Parade's two prime movers,

205

Picasso and Cocteau, was ideal.

The central metaphor of Parade, which received parallel
statements by the scenic designer and the scenarist, was
the modern artist as public performer. The larger allegory
of the artist's self-reflection and alienation was developed
within the context of the théâtre forain. The multiple
perspectives and self-examination of aesthetic means associated
with pictorial Cubism were transferred to a stage setting
and elaborated within the theme of the theatrical experience--
the relationship of performer to audience. Cubist self-
reflexiveness was now concerned with the trappings of another
system of knowing the world: the theatrical mode.

Parade was a Cubist ballet. It also drew into its
sphere the ideas of Futurism. As a shaping force, Futurism
was extremely important, but not to the extent of making
Parade a Futurist ballet. The issue here is not a matter
of a professionally vested interest in promoting the cause
of Cubism over Futurism. The more serious problem has been
how to describe the ways in which ideas impinge upon a work
of art. The Futurist imprint on Parade cannot be ignored,
but it was incorporated into the essentially non-Futurist
ideals of Picasso and Cocteau. However, as early as 1913
the Futurists were questioning and exploring the nature of
theater; they were the first moderns to attempt in their
performances to break the theater's conventional footlight
barrier and to theatricalize the audience. The genesis of
Parade's refined rephrasing of these ideas, on the part of
Picasso and Cocteau, should be sought in the context of

Futurism.

In exploring the central issue of the dissertation--
the relationship of _Parade_ to Cubism--several new critical
observations were made, which deserve repeating for their
salience in any historical consideration of _Parade_. Diaghilev's
repertory of ballets from 1909 to 1929 was united by a concept of theater which reflected an earlier formulation of
Total Theater: a synthesis of the arts into a theatrical
whole. The impact of this idea on the productions of Diaghilev
has not been seriously noted. And, it deserves to be recognized, especially in the case of _Parade_, whose internal
workings can better be understood from the perspective of
Diaghilev's theatrical philosophy. Of all the productions
in the repertory of the Ballets Russes, _Parade_ most successfully articulated Diaghilev's ideal of ballet theater. In
a curtain speech to an audience of assembled dancers and
patrons at the dress rehearsal for Joffrey's revival of
Parade, Massine spoke of Total Theater and how the theater
should not be divorced from the sister arts of poetry,
painting, architecture, sculpture, music, and choreography.
Massine pointed to the ways in which the arts had been brought
together in Diaghilev's production of _Parade_ by the collaboration of Picasso, Satie, Cocteau, and himself.[2] It also
speaks of _Parade's_ inherent theatrical nature to point out
that Maurice Béjart, the director-choreographer who mounted
a major revival of _Parade_ in the early sixties, was drawn
to _Parade_ because of his own interests in Total Theater,
which he defines as "...a search for balance between the

various means of expression, a collaboration between complementary languages."[3]

The pivotal role of Cocteau in the creation of Parade
demands critical reevaluation. However true it may be that
Cocteau's ultimate visibility in Parade for the theater goer
may only be that of a contriver of a cleverly turned conceit,
historical perspective admits a far richer part to him. The
conceiver of Parade's theme, recruiter of its collaborators,
the co-equal of Picasso in the directing of Parade's most
significant dramatic thrust, "assistant" to both Massine and
Satie, Cocteau's sensibilities permeate the fabric of Parade's
expressive design. With many of his ideas and suggestions
vetoed by the other collaborators, Cocteau's plan for a
new theater was to a certain extent sabotaged. In his production of Les Mariés four years later, Cocteau had complete
control over the various parts of the spectacle and was able
to function as the Total Theater director he wished he could
have been for Parade. At the end of his Préface to Les
Mariés, Cocteau thanks his producers:

> In what terms can I thank MM. Rolf de Maré and Borlin?
> The first by his foresight and his generosity, the
> second by his modesty have allowed me to perfect a
> formula that I had attempted in Parade....[4]

Cocteau's Parade, alongside Jarry's Ubu Roi and Apollinaire's
Les Mammelles de Tiresias, stands at the beginning of the
French vanguard theater of this century.

Picasso's mise en scène, popularly and critically,
has been the most visible aspect of Parade's collaboration.
By no means has this dissertation pointed out for the first

time that Cubism was brought to the stage by Picasso in
Parade. What has not been noticed before is the richness,
ambitiousness, and complexity of Picasso's décor and costumes.
Parade was not a theatrical trifle for Picasso, undertaken
outside the more serious confines of painting. To judge
from Picasso's ideas and work, his participation must have
been a highly personal and private experience. When Massine
was asked in conversation about Picasso's feelings and attitudes towards his work for _Parade_, Massine replied that
Picasso would make suggestions but was "tight-lipped" about
the meanings of his creations.[5] And, the meaning of his
contribution has remained obscured for fifty-seven years.
What was almost unexpectedly uncovered in a search for _Parade's_
Cubism was the overwhelming iconographical significance of
the overture curtain. In many respects, the discovery of
this "lost masterpiece" was the key to the puzzle of _Parade's_
Cubism.

Yet another somewhat unexpected problem for a serious
analysis of _Parade_ was the political intricacies of the
theatrical collaboration, the result of which was two different
Parades: Cocteau's original plans and the final version.
Not only are the complexities of the collaboration lost to
audiences, but the question of the importance of Cocteau's
jettisoned plans may be asked. For _Parade_, the answer is
twofold: historically, the record of the team effort is
clarified; aesthetically, a knowledge of Cocteau's original
scenario helps to direct, even to demand, a more serious
response to a production deceptively simple in its request

to be taken more seriously.

The questions asked in this dissertation led to a final emphasis placed upon Cocteau and Picasso. From the critical viewpoint of Cubism, Picasso and Cocteau were primary shapers; Satie and Massine were embellishers of a pre-set structure. In this sense, this dissertation is not a critical overview, inasmuch as the choreography and the music are not investigated to the same degree as the scenic design and the scenario. This approach, in one respect, may seem curious since Parade's essential activity, even in the light of Cocteau's concern for establishing a new French theater, was ballet--or, at least, the final version of Parade took this particular theatrical focus. Had Cocteau's original scenario been followed, Parade would have been, more properly--what Les Mariés would be several years later--a ballet-comédie. However radical and surprising Cocteau's original Parade would have been--and it is a shame that it will, most likely, never be produced--its form of theatrical dancing combined with proclaimed and sung verse was a twentieth-century revival of the seventeenth-century French ballet-comédie, popularized by Molière at Versailles. Parade's original theatrical pose would have been neoclassical. Cocteau's neoclassicism--a tendency toward simplicity of statement and the use of conventional forms--was apparent as early as 1917, a fact unnoticed by his critics.

Perhaps the theatrical perspective adopted in this dissertation should be acknowledged as biased. Admittedly, Parade was not just a scenario and scenic designs. Even

an informed audience member, if queried about what he or she
had witnessed after a performance of Parade would reply, "A
ballet." The other elements of the spectacle, especially
Picasso's contributions, would be received enthusiastically,
but they would not be separated for discussion, rather they
would blend into a total performance whose central activity
was dancing. After all, the theatrical components of Parade--
scenario, design, music, and dance--were integrated into
the collective theatrical ideal of Total Theater. Massine's
choreography, which was a mixture of classical danse d'école,
character dancing, and Cocteau's gestures, was perfectly in
keeping with the mood of the scenario and the mise en scène.
The same may be said for Satie's jaunty and slightly disturbing
score. Stylized, eccentric, and witty, Massine's choreographic
setting and Satie's music are not lost in the scenic richness
of Picasso's designs, nor do they fail to convey the mystery,
charm, and pathos of Cocteau's characters.

Quite obviously, with the fullness and richness of
Parade suggested in this dissertation, certain problematical
issues of meaning arise for the average theater goer. Picasso's
designs and Cocteau's scenario make potentially sophisticated
demands on the audience. The density of the information may
appear almost overbearing for a fifteen-minute, one-act
ballet. For instance, a complaint might be registered that
if Picasso's overture curtain is so meaningful--and in hermetic
and ambiguous ways--how exactly is an audience to take it
all in when it appears briefly at the beginning of the ballet
for approximately one minute? Isn't this, as it were, stretching

Picasso's overture curtain a little too far? In rebuttal
to arguments like this, it must first be acknowledged that
any serious work of art may admit different levels of response,
from a cursory glance to an awareness approximating the
artist's own consciousness. If this apperceptual phenomenon
is sensibly granted a characteristic of any major painting,
there is no reason why a theater piece, Parade, envisioned
by its creators to mediate between the serious and the frivolous, cannot warrant potentially similar protracted looking
and thinking. After all, isn't this what Parade's very
scenario is all about? Recall that Cocteau wrote the following
about the theater:

> The secret of theatrical success is this: set a decoy
> at the door so that part of the audience can enjoy
> itself there while the others take their seats inside.[6]

How ironic and unfortunate that the category of Parade's
enterprise--a one-act ballet for the Ballets Russes--has
figuratively allowed few to enter the little sideshow since
its inception.

All too often, as Martin Duberman suggests, the historian acts like a ghost by refusing to admit that history
is a combination of basic objective data and interpretations
which derive from personal selves in the present.[7] The
present self of this dissertation may, in part, be described
as having a fondness for early modern French painting and
sculpture, an affection for ballet, and a concern that the
critical orientation of formalism has grievously overlooked
the expressive contents of "unpure forms": notably, ballet,
opera, and experimental theater. If one does turn to these

media, the appalling lack of serious documentation nearly discourages more probing investigations. The analysis of _Parade_ offerred in the previous chapters, however, is not meant to be exhaustive; it is concerned with specific theatrical dimensions. Nevertheless, it was undertaken in the spirit of expanding the terrain deemed appropriate for art-historical criticism.

NOTES--INTRODUCTION

Pages 1-10

N.B. First references will be complete. Subsequent references
will be given with shortened titles. The full reference can
be checked in the alphabetically listed bibliography.

[1]Arthur Henry Franks, Twentieth Century Ballet (London:
Burke, 1954), p.37.

[2]For the discussion here of the problems involved in
drawing critical relationships between the visual and performing arts, I was encouraged in my own research by Michael
Kirby's acknowledgment and handling of the issue in his two
books Futurist Performance (New York: E.P. Dutton, 1971) and
The Art of Time: Essays on the Avant-Garde (New York: E.P.
Dutton, 1969).

[3]See Lincoln Kirstein, Movement and Metaphor: Four
Centuries of Ballet (New York: Praeger, 1970).

[4]This characterization of a western literary theater
is taken from the distinctions Leonard C. Pronko makes between
eastern and western concepts of theater in Theater East and
West: Perspectives toward a Total Theatre (Berkeley and Los
Angeles: University of California Press, 1967).

[5]Two important exceptions to this statement are
Wylie Sypher's chapter on "The Cubist Perspective" in his
Rococo to Cubism in Art and Literature (New York: Vintage
Books, 1960), pp. 257-330; and the suggestive and articulate
comments in Robert Rosenblum's Cubism and Twentieth-Century
Art (New York: Harry N. Abrams, 1966), pp. 71, 101.

NOTES--CHAPTER I
DIAGHILEV AND THE BALLETS RUSSES

Pages 11-17

[1]National Broadcasting Company, "Conversation with Igor Stravinsky," New York, 1957.

[2]Nicolas Nabokov, "Serge Diaghilef," Atlantic Monthly 185 (March 1950): 71.

[3]Harold C. Schonberg, "Did Diaghilev Change Music History?" New York Times, March 19, 1972, sec. 4, p. 15.

[4]The following artists made contributions to Diaghilev's Ballets Russes. Choreographers: Fokine, Nijinsky, Romanov, Massine, Slavinsky, Dalbaicin, Nijinska, and Balachine. Scenic designers: Benois, Roerich, Korovine, Bakst, Golovine, Anisfield, Sovdeikine, Doboujnsky, Sert, Gontcharova, Larionov, Socrate, Jones, Balla, Picasso, Derain, Matisse, Survage, Gris, Laurencin, Braque, Laurens, Pruna, Utrillo, Ernst, Miro, Gabo, Pevsner, Yakoulov, Cocteau, Tchelitchev, Bauchant, de Chirico, and Rouault. Composers: Stravinsky, Tcherepnine, Hahn, Debussy, Ravel, Schmitt, Liadov, Satie, Respighi, Falla, and Prokofiev.

[5]Arnold Haskell, Ballet Russe: The Age of Diaghilev (London: Weidenfeld and Nicolson, 1968), p. 67.

[6]L'Ancienne Douane, Les Ballets russes de Serge Diaghilev (Strasbourg: Dernières Nouvelles de Strasbourg, 1969), p. 16.

[7]For excellent histories of the Diaghilev period, I refer the reader to the following books from which the biographical information in this dissertation is taken: Camilla Gray, The Great Experiment: Russian Art 1863-1922 (New York: Harry N. Abrams, 1962); Haskell, Ballet Russe; Boris Kochno, Diaghilev and the Ballets Russes (New York: Harper and Row, 1970); Serge Lifar, Diaghilev: An Intimate Biography (New York: G.P. Putnam's Sons, 1940).

[8]Gray, Great Experiment, p. 35.

[9]Kirstein, Movement, p. 171.

[10]Of the sixty-three ballets produced by Diaghilev between 1909 and 1929, only three were revivals of earlier ballets. The rest were original creations conceived especially

for the Ballets Russes.

[11]Lydia Sokolova, Dancing for Diaghilev (London: Murray, 1960), p. 15.

[12]The full-length ballet is an aspect of modern ballet, but only beginning in the 1920's as a revived form. Ironically, it was Diaghilev who in 1921 attempted to resurrect the full-length ballet with his production of Sleeping Beauty, although he was not able to do so successfully because French audiences were too accustomed to the one-act ballet.

[13]Kirstein, Movement, p. 210.

[14]Idem, The Book of the Dance: A Short History of Classic Theatrical Dancing (New York: G.P. Putnam's Sons, 1935), p. 349.

[15]Michel Fokine, "Letter to the Editor," London Times, July 6, 1914, sec. 2, p. 5.

[16]Benois, Roerich, Korovine, Bakst, Golovine, Sovdeikine, Doboujnsky, Sert, and Yakoulov.

[17]Rollo Myers, Erik Satie (New York: Dover, 1968), p. 28.

[18]Nathalie Gontcharova, Michel Larionov, Pierre Vorms, Les Ballets russes: Serge de Diaghilev et la décoration théâtrale (Dordogne: Belves, 1955), p. 14: "une lanterne magique pour grands enfants."

[19]Ibid., p. 21. Not until Gontcharova's designs for Le Coq d'or (1914) did Diaghilev modernize his decor.

[20]Haskell, Ballet Russe, p. 138.

[21]Kirstein, Movement, p. 182.

[22]Walter Sorell, The Dance Through the Ages (New York: Grosset and Dunlap, 1967), pp. 163-164.

[23]Angelo Philip Bertocci, From Symbolism to Baudelaire (Carbondale, Illinois: Southern Illinois University Press, 1964), p.77.

[24]Clark M. Rogers, "Appia's Theory of Acting: Eurhythmics for the Stage," in Total Theatre, ed. E. T. Kirby (New York: E.P. Dutton, 1969), p. 21.

NOTES--CHAPTER I

Pages 27-30

[25]Charles R. Lyons, "Gordon Craig's Concept of the Actor," in Total Theatre, ed: E. T. Kirby (New York: E. P. Dutton, 1969), p. 69.

[26]Before beginning his university education in St. Petersburg, Diaghilev in 1890 made a grand tour of Europe, during which he heard Wagner for the first time, adored him, and later championed his theories of music-drama in the pages of The World of Art. While in Russia, Diaghilev had the opportunity to be aware of, if not actually witnessing, the Total Theater of Alexander Tairov at the Kamerny Theater in Moscow. Tairov's productions, under the influence of Appia and Craig, were entirely orchestrated: tones of the actors' voices were pitched like instruments, movements were dance-like; and colors, lighting, and sound effects were patterned on a musical basis.

[27]André Levinson, La Danse d'aujourd'hui (Paris: Duchartre and VanBugenhoudt, 1929), p. 217.

[28]Wallace Fowlie, Mallarmé (Chicago: The University of Chicago Press, 1962), p. 123.

[29]Ibid., p. 93.

[30]Maurice Béjart, "Maurice Béjart and the Total Theater," World Theater 3 (November-December 1965): 556.

[31]Haskell, Ballet Russe, p. 52.

[32]Another aspect of the Ballets Russes which may be broadly considered religious, and one which tied the company to the idea of Total Theater as mystical experience, was the predominantly eastern bias of the themes chosen by Diaghilev for the first seasons of his new company. The exoticism of the early Ballets Russes exerted a powerful spell over audiences, where orgiastic dance was set in eastern and mythical locales distant in time and space from contemporary Christian Europe. The East never prevented the dance from playing an expressive and important part in religious services, nor did it secularize its theater. Looking to the symbolical nature of eastern drama for the confirmation of his own theories, Craig turned to an investigation of Oriental theater in 1908.

[33]During the middle of the sixteenth century in France, members of the Academy of Baïf fostered the notion of a dramatic synthesis of music, verse, and dance based on what was considered a lost Greek ideal.

NOTES--CHAPTER I

Pages 31-32

[34]Haskell, Ballet Russe, p. 34.

[35]George Amberg, Art in Modern Ballet (New York: Pantheon, 1946), p. 11.

NOTES--CHAPTER II
JEAN COCTEAU AND THE NOUVEAU THEATRE CONTEMPORAIN

Pages 33-40

[1]Oeuvres complètes de Jean Cocteau 3 (Geneva:
Marguerat, 1946): 3: "When a work seems ahead of its age,
it is really the age which has yet to catch up with the
work."

[2]Of special note are the story lines for Petrouschka,
Afternoon of a Faun, Les Biches, and Romeo and Juliet.

[3]Francis Steegmuller, Cocteau: A Biography (Boston:
Little, Brown and Company, 1970), p. 232.

[4]For two excellent sources on the French and European
fair and circus, see Jacques Garnier, Forains d'hier et
d'aujourd'hui (Orléans: Les Presses, 1968) and Henry Thétard,
La Merveilleuse histoire du cirque (Paris: Prisma, 1947).

[5]Garnier, Forains, Chapter III. The théâtre forain
comprised the following types: théâtres dramatiques et
lyriques; théâtres des spectacles de variétés, de music-
hall; théâtres de magie; théâtres de tableaux vivants et
pantomimes; and the théâtres des animaux savants.

[6]A good discussion of the sources for the types
Picasso used in the paintings of his Circus Period is found
in Theodore Reff, "Harlequins, Saltimbanques, Clowns, and
Fools," Artforum 10 (October 1971): 30-43.

[7]Ibid., p. 31.

[8]Steegmuller, Cocteau, p. 66.

[9]Ibid., p. 103.

[10]The contents of Cocteau's libretto for Parade are
suggested in Appendix 1. The list is not necessarily complete;
but until further materials surface, this appendix may serve
as a fairly accurate guide to what Cocteau would have included if he had collected his written and drawn contributions to create a libretto.

[11]The Cahier romain is a vellum bound carnet measuring
29 x 22.5 cm. Collection Edouard Dermit, Paris.

NOTES--CHAPTER II

Pages 41-44

[12]Jean Cocteau, Entre Picasso et Radiquet, ed.
André Fermigier (Paris: Hermann, 1967), p. 64: "...chantait
une phrase type, résumant les perspectives du personnage,
ouvrant un hublot sur le rêve."

[13]Ibid.: "...un trou amplificateur, imitation
théâtrale du gramaphone forain masque antique à la mode
moderne."

[14]Garnier, Forains, p. 269.

[15]Leonide Massine, interview held during rehearsals
for the City Center Joffrey Ballet's revival of Parade,
New York, September 23, 1972.

[16]Frederick Brown, An Impersonation of Angels:
A Biography of Jean Cocteau (New York: The Viking Press,
1968), p. 94.

[17]Especially similar to Cocteau's syntax and allusions
is Whitman's "Starting from Paumanok."

[18]Steegmuller, Cocteau, p. 166.

[19]Sokolova, Dancing, p. 63.

[20]Marie Shabelska, however, never danced the role
of the Little American Girl in performance. Lopokova danced
the role in the premiere production in 1917.

[21]Steegmuller, Cocteau, p. 175.

[22]"Entrez--le plus beau spectacle du monde. Entrez--
la plus belle salle du monde. Entrez--la plus belle scène
du monde. Entrez--la plus belle lumière du monde."

[23]"Si vous voulez ne plus jamais être malade...si
vous voulez avoir la toute puissance...si vous voulez avoir
une belle poitrine...si vous voulez qu'on vous aime."

[24]Douglas Cooper, Picasso Theatre (New York: Harry
N. Abrams, 1967), p. 23. Cooper's assertion that he ob-
tained this list of sound effects from Cocteau's Cahier
romain is incorrect. The list of noises Cocteau wished
inserted are not found in the notebook.

[25]Cocteau, Entre Picasso, p. 66: "J'ai composé...
un fond à certains bruits que le librettiste juge indispen-
sables à préciser l'atmosphère de ses personnages."

NOTES--CHAPTER II

Pages 45-49

[26]Cocteau, Oeuvres, 3: 30: "...fût jouée incomplète et sans son bouquet."

[27]Before Massine set the choreography with Cocteau for Parade, he had never seen an American film. Massine had to rely upon Cocteau's knowledge of both Mary Pickford and Charlie Chaplin. This information was given to me during the September interview with Massine in New York.

[28]Jean Cocteau, Les Foyers des artistes (Paris: Plon, 1947), p. 49: "...role fût d'inventer des gestes réalistes, de les souligner, de les ordonner et grâce à la science de Leonide Massine, de les hausser jusqu'au style de la danse."

[29]This sequence remained the same for the Joffrey revival.

[30]"Mon cher Massine, vous ne serez jamais moche, partez donc du moche. Vive le moche."

[31]W. S. Liebermann, "Picasso and the Ballet," Dance Index 3 (November 1946): 230.

[32]Kirstein, Movement, p. 183.

[33]Cocteau, Oeuvres, 3: 30: "...une lucarne ouverte sur ce que devrait être le théâtre contemporain."

[34]Jean Cocteau, Les Mariés de la tour Eiffel (Paris: Nouvelle revue française, 1924).

[35]Pierre Dubourg, La Dramaturgie de Jean Cocteau (Paris: Grasset, 1954), p. 25.

[36]Cocteau, Les Mariés, p. 18.

[37]Sophia Delza, "The Classic Chinese Theatre," in Total Theatre, ed: E. T. Kirby (New York: E. P. Dutton, 1969), p. 229.

[38]Pronko, Theatre, pp. 1-2.

[39]Leonard C. Pronko, "Kabuki and the Elizabethan Theatre," in Total Theatre, ed: E. T. Kirby (New York: E. P. Dutton, 1969), p. 190.

[40]Walter Sorell, "An Appreciation of Jean Cocteau," Dance Magazine 9 (February 1964): 40.

NOTES--CHAPTER II

Pages 49-53

[41]"Ne pas oublier que la parade se donne dans la rue."

[42]Dorothy Knowles, French Drama of the Inter-War Years: 1918-1939 (London: Harrap, 1967), p. 49.

[43]Cocteau, Les Mariés, pp. 13-14: "...je reha-bilite le lieu commun...à moi de le placer, de le présenter sous tel angle qu'il retrouve ses vingt ans. Un génération d'obscurité, de réalité fade, ne se rejette pas d'un coup d'épaule, Je sais que mon texte à l'air trop simple, trop LISIBLEMENT ECRIT, comme les alphabets d'école. Mais, dites, ne sommes-nous pas à l'école? Nous déchiffrons-nous pas les premiers signes?"

[44]Ibid.: "...objets et sentiments de leurs voiles et de leurs brumes, les montrer soudain, si nus et si vite que l'homme a peine à les reconnaître."

[45]Ibid., p. 22: "L'esprit de bouffonnerie est le seul qui autorise certaines audaces."

[46]"Soyons vulgaire--puisque c'est impossible."

[47]Wallace Fowlie, Jean Cocteau: The History of a Poet's Age (Bloomington: Indiana University Press, 1966), p. 14.

[48]Jean Cocteau, "Avant Parade," Excelsior, May 18, 1917, sec. 4, p. 4: "...comme une oeuvre qui cache des poésies sous la grosse enveloppe du guignol."

[49]Leonide Massine, interview, New York, September 23, 1972.

[50]E. P. Kirby, Total Theatre, p. xvi.

[51]See Jacques Rouché's introduction to his translation of Craig's De l'art du théâtre (Paris: Prisma, 1916) and Rouché's l'Art théâtrale moderne (Paris: Bloud et Gay, 1924). Cocteau knew Rouché who was the director of the Paris Opera during the late teens and early twenties when the Ballets Russes appeared there.

[52]Michael Benedikt and George E. Wellwarth, eds., Modern French Theatre: The Avant-Garde, Dada, and Surrealism-- An Anthology of Plays (New York: Dutton, 1964), p.47.

[53]Ibid., p. 48.

NOTES--CHAPTER II

Pages 54-60

[54]Francis Steegmuller, Apollinaire: <u>Poet among the Painters</u> (New York: Farrar and Straus, 1963). See Steegmuller's Appendix II.

[55]Ibid.

[56]Cocteau, <u>Oeuvres</u>, 3: 28: "Lorsque je dis de certain spectacles de cirque ou de music-hall que je les préfère à tout ce qui donne au théâtre, je ne veux pas dire que je les préfères à tout ce qui pourrait se donner au théâtre."

[57]Huntly Carter, <u>The New Spirit in the European Theatre, 1914-1924</u> (London: E. Benn, 1925), p. 49.

[58]Steegmuller, <u>Cocteau</u>, p. 166.

[59]"Travailler avec trois couleurs--trop de couleurs font de l'impressionnisme (Picasso)...Les Futuristes sont des impressionnistes d'idées...Prendre garde aux idées."

[60]Kirby, <u>Futurist Performance</u>, p. 184.

[61]Ibid.

[62]Cocteau, <u>Les Mariés</u>, p. 12: "compère et la commère, parlent, sans la moindre littérature, l'action ridicule qui se déroule, se danse, se mime au milieu."

[63]Georges Auric, "Chronique sur <u>Parade</u>," <u>La Nouvelle revue française</u> 7 (February 1921): 225: "...un gros jouet, simple comme bonjour...pourquoi chercher du crime, du mystère, de l'intention secrète dans ce divertissement qui nous a couté tant de travaille à Satie, Picasso, Massine et moi."

[64]Neal Oxenhandler, <u>Scandal and Parade: The Theater of Jean Cocteau</u> (New Brunswick: Rutgers University Press, 1957), p. 49.

[65]Steegmuller, <u>Cocteau</u>, p. 162.

[66]Ibid., p. 161.

[67]Jacques Guicharnaud, <u>Modern French Theatre from Giraudoux to Beckett</u> (New Haven: Yale University Press, 1961), p. 74.

NOTES--CHAPTER II

Pages 61-65

[68]Cocteau, Entre Picasso, p. 51: "...n'avaient
rien d'humoristique. Elles insistaient au contraire sur
le côté mystérieux, sur le prolongement des personnages,
sur le verso de notre baraque foraine. Le chinois y était
capable de torturer des missionnaires, la Petite Fille de
sombrer sur le Titanic, l'acrobat d'être en confiance avec
les astres."

[69]Cocteau, Les Mariés, pp. 16-17: "Toute oeuvre
vivante comporte sa propre parade. Cette parade seule est
vue par ceux qui n'entrent pas. Or, la surface d'une
oeuvre nouvelle heurte, intrigue, agace trop le spectateur
pour qu'il entre. Il est détourné de l'âme par le visage,
par l'expression inédite qui le distrait comme une grimace
de clown à la porte. C'est le phénomène qui trompe les
critiques les moins esclave de la routine. Ils ne se rendent
pas compte qu'ils assistent à un ouvrage qu'il faut suivre
attentivement au même titre qu'un drame du boulevard. Ils
se croient à la foire du Trône."

[70]Ibid., pp. 18-19: "Le secret du théâtre, qui
necessite le succès rapide, est de tendre un piège, grâce
auquel une partie de la salle s'amuse à la porte pour que
l'autre partie puisse prendre place à l'intérieur.
Shakespeare, Molière, C. Chaplin le font."

[71]Robert Phelps, Professional Secrets: An Autobiography of Jean Cocteau, Drawn from his Lifetime Writings
(New York: Farrar, Straus, and Giroux, 1970), p. 93.

[72]Oxenhandler, Scandal, p. 52.

[73]Cocteau, Foyers, p. 50: "Et lorsqu'on demandait
à Diaghilef pourquoi il ne le montait pas davatage il
répondait: 'C'est ma meilleure bouteille, je n'aime pas
remuer son vin.'"

NOTES--CHAPTER III
THE MISE EN SCENE: COSTUMES AND SET

Pages 66-72

[1]Cocteau, Entre Picasso, p. 123: "...before him the decor was not an actor in the drama; it was a spectator."

[2]Le Tricorne (1919), Pulcinella (1920), Cuadro Flamenco (1921), Afternoon of a Faun (1922 revival), Mercure (1924), and Le Train bleu (1924).

[3]Gontcharova, Ballet russes, p. 14.

[4]Gontcharova: Le Coq d'or (1914), Liturgie (1914)-- not produced. Larionov: Le Soleil de nuit (1915), Kikimora (1916), Histoires naturelles (1916).

[5]In conversation with Leonide Massine, New York, September 1972.

[6]Kirstein, Movement, p. 183.

[7]These facets of the choreography for the Chinese Magician were observed in the City Center Joffrey Ballet's revival production of Parade, March 23, 1973, New York City.

[8]Cocteau, Entre Picasso, p. 51.

[9]Picasso's original Acrobat's costume is stored at the Paris Opera. For the recreation of the costume for the Joffrey revival, Jean Bonnelye traveled to Paris and sketched the back of the Acrobat's costume since no photographic reproduction was available of it.

[10]It is revealing that when Joffrey's costume designers began to copy the female Acrobat's costume, they were puzzled by the gaucheness of it. Their response led to the inquiry made to Picasso through Douglas Cooper, which in turn resulted in permission to duplicate the male Acrobat's costume for the female dancer.

[11]Steegmuller, Cocteau, p. 56.

[12]Complaints were especially strong after Picasso's death in 1973 that the works of the 1960's were obsessive and weak redoings of earlier themes.

[13]Boris Kochno, Diaghilev and the Ballets Russes (New York: Harper and Row, 1970), p. 120.

[14]Sokolova, Dancing, p. 93.

[15]Steegmuller, Cocteau, p. 163.

[16]In conversation with Leonide Massine, New York, September 1972.

[17]Steegmuller, Cocteau, p. 178.

[18]Ibid.

[19]See Rosenblum, Cubism, and Max Kozloff, Cubism/Futurism (New York: Charterhouse, 1973).

[20]Roland Penrose, Picasso: His Life and Work (New York: Harper, 1958), p. 34.

[21]Kozloff, Cubism, pp. 159-160.

[22]Leo Steinberg, Other Criteria: Confrontations with Twentieth-Century Art (New York: Oxford University Press, 1972), pp. 193-195.

[23]Michael Kirby, Performance, pp. 91-119.

[24]Ibid., p. 97.

[25]Ibid., pp. 203-206.

[26]Marianne Martin, "The Ballet Parade or Cubism and Futurism," paper presented at the College Art Association meeting, New York, January 1973.

[27]Michael Kirby, Performance, p. 101.

[28]Cocteau, Entre Picasso, p. 64: "Lorsque Picasso nous montra ses esquisses, nous comprîmes l'intérêt d'opposer à trois personnages réels, comme des chromos (cartes postales rayées) collés sur une toile, des personnages inhumains, surhumains, d'une transposition plus grave, qui deviendraient en somme la fausse réalité scenique jusqu'à réduire les danseurs réels à des mésures de poupées."

[29]The crowd's silhouette would have been a cut-out stage flat placed considerably downstage near the footlights. See lower left-hand corner of Fig. 49.

NOTES--CHAPTER III

Pages 94-98

[30]Picasso was of little direct assistance to Joffrey's designers. Douglas Cooper was his spokesman in all matters.

[31]Letter dated December 10, 1972. It was kindly shown to me by Mr. William Crawford.

[32]This was confirmed in a letter from Douglas Cooper to William Crawford in which Cooper quotes Picasso as saying, "You know better than I do at this stage. So take all decisions for me because I know they will be right."

[33]"Doive former les rues en se combinant--les perspectives de rues de maisons qui buoyant à Naples, Paris, Montmartre, 3e de Clichy [sic] --place Pigalle-- etc..."

[34]"La corégraphie des Perspectives s'inspire non de ce qui bouge mais des objets immobiles, auteur desquels on bouge, surtout [sic] des maisons de la manière dont elles tournent, se combinent, se baissent, remontent et se bouailent selon la marche dans la rue."

[35]In conversation with Leonide Massine, New York, September 1972.

NOTES--CHAPTER IV
THE MISE EN SCENE: THE OVERTURE CURTAIN

Pages 99-108

[1]L'Anciènne Douane, Ballets russes, p. 17: "The
rideau rouge is rising on festivals which are upsetting
France and which are leading the crowds in ecstasy behind
the chariot of Dionysos."

[2]Levinson, La Danse, p. 163.

[3]The ballet Mercure was originally created by the
Count E. de Beaumont at the Soirées de Paris. Diaghilev
mounted it for the Ballets Russes during the 1927 season
in Paris.

[4]It would seem that Satie entitled his overture
before he knew that Picasso would be asked to create an
overture curtain. Satie was, for the most part, finished
with Parade's score by Christmas 1916; Picasso did not
begin sketching his ideas for the curtain until February-
March 1917 in Rome. In any event, Satie's overture would
have been more accurately entitled Prélude du rideau de
scène.

[5]In conversation with Leonide Massine, New York,
September 1972.

[6]Cooper, Picasso, p. 26.

[7]Steinberg, Other Criteria, pp. 192-223.

[8]For an excellent discussion of this problem, see
Rosenblum, Cubism, pp. 101-102.

[9]This description of the curtain is based upon a
personal examination of it at the Musée de l'art moderne
in Paris in October 1972.

[10]Kochno, Ballets Russes, p. 123.

[11]For example, Le Tricorne, whose narrative action
concerned the flirtations between a provincial Spanish
magistrate and a miller's wife, had for its overture curtain
a scene depicting a bullfight seen from the stands.

NOTES--CHAPTER IV

Pages 108-135

[12]Denis Milhau, Picasso et le théâtre (Toulouse: Musée des Augustins, 1965), p. 46.

[13]Cooper, Picasso, p. 24.

[14]Kirstein, Movement, p. 211. Although no specific paintings are cited, A Gathering Under the Portico (Fig. 54) is one of many examples which make this correlation apparent. In an open air setting flanked by banded columns, a group of young aristocrats is serenaded by a young man in the fancy dress of the commedia dell'arte.

[15]Reff, "Harlequins," pp. 30-43.

[16]Steegmuller, Cocteau, p. 175.

[17]This letter was kindly shown to me by Leonide Massine in New York, September 1972. It was subsequently given to Robert Joffrey as a gift.

[18]Steegmuller, Cocteau, p. 137.

[19]Ibid., p. 138.

[20]John Berger, The Success and Failure of Picasso (Baltimore: Penguin Books, 1965), p. 189.

[21]For the discussion of simian iconography in western art, I have carefully followed the arguments put forward by H. W. Janson, Apes and Ape Lore in the Middle Ages and in the Renaissance (London: The Warburg Institute, 1952), pp. 287-325.

[22]James Mellow, Charmed Circle: Gertrude Stein and Friends (New York: Praeger, 1974), p. 91.

[23]Ibid., p. 109.

[24]Ibid.

[25]"Pour acrobat...regardez de Picasso."

[26]In 1901, upon the death of his close friend Casagemas, Picasso set to work on a major canvas to be entitled Evocation. The subject matter of the painting was the apotheosis of Casagemas. The painting was never completed, but what is important for the present argument is that Picasso at an earlier date had attempted to give image to an apotheosis. A significant aspect of this painting for the Parade curtain is Casagemas's transportation to the celestial sphere on the back of a winged horse.

NOTES--CHAPTER IV

Pages 137-164

[27]Diaghilev introduced the placement of a tapis on the stage for the dancers to perform on. They were often painted with designs to match the scenery. Parade's tapis was all white.

[28]Steinberg, Other Criteria, pp. 93-114.

[29]Ibid., p. 105.

[30]Alfred H. Barr, Picasso: Fifty Years of his Art (New York: Museum of Modern Art, 1946), p. 115.

[31]Ibid.

[32]H. W. Janson, Apes and Ape Lore, p. 320.

[33]Berger, Picasso, pp. 94-98.

[34]For the full published reproduction of Picasso's overture curtain, see Paul W. Schwartz, The Cubists (London: Thames and Hudson, 1971), p. 83.

[35]See Barr, Picasso, p. 98 and Zervos II, 951.

[36]W. A. Propert, The Russian Ballet in Western Europe, 1909-1920 (London: John Lane, 1921), p. 29.

[37]Le Tricorne and Pulcinella warrant a closer inspection of the relationships which appear to exist between Picasso's mise en scène and the ballet narratives.

NOTES--CHAPTER V
PARADE AS CUBIST SPECTACLE

Pages 167-171

[1]Jean Cocteau, Cocteau's World: An Anthology of Writings, ed. Margaret Crosland (London: Peter Owen, 1972), p. 310: "There are certain small works of art whose whole importance lies in their depth; the size of their orifice is of small account."

[2]Auric, Chronique, p. 225.

[3]Cocteau, Entre Picasso, p. 70. Guillaume Apollinaire's program notes for the first performance of Parade are included in Fermigier's anthology of Cocteau's criticism, pp. 69-71.

[4]Cocteau, Entre Picasso, p. 74. Léon Bakst's short article, "Chorégraphie et Décors des Nouveaux Ballets Russes," included in the original program for the first performance of Parade, is also included in Fermigier's anthology.

[5]David Drew, "Modern French Music," in European Music in the Twentieth Century, ed: Howard Hartog (New York: Praeger, 1957), p. 251.

[6]See Ellen Johnson, "On the Role of the Object in Analytic Cubism," Allen Memorial Art Museum Bulletin 13 (N.D.): 11-25, and Winthrop Judkins, "Toward a Reinterpretation of Cubism," Art Bulletin 30 (December 1948): 270-278. The most articulate formal description of Cubism is found in Rosenblum, Cubism.

[7]See Leo Steinberg's chapters on Picasso in Other Criteria and Max Kozloff, Cubism/Futurism.

[8]See the discussions on style in Jack Burnham, Structure of Art (New York: George Braziller, 1971), pp. 32-58, and in Morse Peckham, Man's Rage for Chaos: Biology, Behavior, and the Arts (New York: Schocken, 1965), pp. 41-73.

[9]See Wylie Sypher, Rococo to Cubism in Art and Literature (New York: Vintage, 1960), pp. 257-330.

[10]This is specifically the method used in André Gide's Les Faux-Monnayeurs, Virginia Woolf's Mrs. Dalloway, and Lawrence Durrell's Alexandria Quartet.

NOTES--CHAPTER V

Pages 171-191

[11]Gerald Kamber, Max Jacob and the Poetics of Cubism (Baltimore: John Hopkins Press, 1971).

[12]Judkins, "Reinterpretation," p. 275.

[13]Peckham, Man's Rage.

[14]Idem, Art and Pornography: An Experiment in Explanation (New York: Harper and Row, 1969), p. 46.

[15]Rosenblum, Cubism, p. 71.

[16]Abel Hermant, "Les Ballets russes," Excelsior, Mary 20, 1917, p. 13: "...le rideau s'est relevé un quart d'heure après sur un second rideau, que les auteurs de Parade déclarent encore classique et du style de M. Ingres. Ils exagèrent un peu. Néanmoins, ce rideau n'est pas cubist au même degré que le décor qu'il cache un moment à nos yeux."

[17]Barr, Picasso, p. 94.

[18]Rosenblum, Cubism, p. 101.

[19]Ibid.

[20]Ibid.

[21]Lieberman, "Picasso," p. 232.

[22]Cocteau, Entre Picasso, p. 74: "Un grand rideau, 'passéiste' à dessein, tranche entre ces fleurs du vingtième siècle et le spectateur intrigué."

[23]Shattuck, Banquet Years, pp. 326-327.

[24]Ibid., p. 327.

[25]Cocteau, Entre Picasso, p. 32: "...le public prenait la transposition du music-hall pour du mauvais music-hall."

[26]Brown, Impersonation, p. 144. Inasmuch as Brown does not cite his source for the placard which was lowered, it is difficult to authenticate its presence in the first performance. It was not used in the Robert Joffrey revival of Parade in 1973.

NOTES--CHAPTER V

Pages 194-204

[27]Cocteau, _Entre Picasso_, p. 69: "De cette alliance nouvelle, car jusqu'ici les décors et les costumes, d'une part, la chorégraphie d'autre part, n'avaient entre eux qu'un lien factive, il est resulté, dans _Parade_, une sorte de sur-réalisme où je voie le point de départ d'une série de manifestations de cet Esprit Nouveau..."

[28]Ibid., p. 70: "Ce réalisme ou ce cubisme, comme on voudra, est ce qui a le plus profondément agité les arts durant les dix dernières années."

[29]Ibid.: "Les décors et les costumes de _Parade_ montrent clairement sa préoccupation de tirer d'un objet tout ce qu'il peut donner d'émotion esthétique."

[30]Ibid., p. 71: "...la magie de leur vie quotidienne."

[31]Cocteau, _Entre Picasso_, pp. 188-191: "Rien dans les manches, rien dans les poches, un monsieur voudrait-il prêter son chapeau à l'arlequin de Port-Royal."

[32]For example, Larionov worked closely with the choreographers on the productions for which he created the mise en scène.

[33]"Pour l'acrobat, exercices de barre."

[34]The film of Massine's version of _Parade_ for Maurice Béjart is found in the Dance Collection of Lincoln Center, New York.

[35]Steegmuller, _Cocteau_, p. 166.

[36]Ibid., p. 167.

[37]Cocteau, _Entre Picasso_, p. 64: "Peu à peu vint au monde une partition sobre, nette, où Satie semble avoir découvert une dimension inconnue grâce à laquelle on écoute simultanément la parade et le spectacle intérieur."

[38]Steegmuller, _Cocteau_, p. 171.

[39]Drew, "French Music," p. 250.

[40]Shattuck, _Banquet Years_, p. 157.

[41]"Picasso dit Ne pas avoir peur de coller un journal-- un geste exact qui ne se transpose pas et donne toute la valeur aux autres gestes."

NOTES--CHAPTER V

Page 204

[42]Cocteau, _Entre Picasso_, p. 54: "La partition de _Parade_ devait servir de fond musical à des bruits suggestifs, tels que sirènes, machines à écrire, aéro-planes, dynamos, mis là comme ce que Georges Braque appelle si justement des faits."

[43]Ibid.: "Ces 'bruits' jouent exactement le rôle des éléments en trompe-l'oeil et des papiers collés dans les tableaux cubists."

NOTES--EPILOGUE

Pages 205-213

[1]Cocteau, Cocteau's World, p. 476: "Seriousness that asserts itself. Never believe in it. Never confuse it with gravity."

[2]Leonide Massine, City Center Theater, New York, March 23, 1973.

[3]Maurice Béjart, "Maurice Béjart and the Total Theater," World Theater 3 (November-December 1965): 560.

[4]Cocteau, Les Mariés, p. 28: "En quels termes remerciérai-je MM. Rolf de Maré et Borlin? Le premier par sa clairvoyance et sa largesse, le second, par sa modestie m'ont permis de mettre au point une formule que j'avais essayé dans Parade."

[5]In conversation with Leonide Massine, New York, September 1972.

[6]Cocteau, Les Mariés, pp. 18-19. See Chapter II, n. 64.

[7]Martin Duberman, "The Historian as Ghost," New York Times, July 8, 1973, sec. 4, p. 13.

APPENDIX 1

JEAN COCTEAU'S "LIBRETTO" FOR PARADE

1. Material given to Erik Satie between April 1 and May
   6, 1916.

   a) An empty notebook whose cover was inscribed with
       the Larousse definition of parade: "A burlesque
       scene played outside a sideshow booth to entice
       spectators inside."

   b) Three sheets of onionskin which listed free-associa-
       tions that were meant to "expand" the characters of
       the Chinese Magician, the Little American Girl, and
       the Acrobat. Frederick Brown in An Impersonation of
       Angels (New York: The Viking Press, 1968), pp. 128-
       129, provides an English translation of the sheet
       devoted to the Little American Girl. Brown's transla-
       tion is the only published page of the three sheets.

                  The Little American Girl

              The Titanic--"Nearer My God to Thee"--
       elevators--the sirens of Boulogne--submarine
       cables--ship-to-shore cables--Brest--tar--
       varnish--steamship apparatus--The New York Herald--
       dynamos--airplanes--short circuits--palatial
       cinemas--the sheriff's daughter--Walt Whitman--
       the silence of stampedes--cowboys with leather
       and goat-skin chaps--the telegraph operator
       from Los Angeles who marries the detective in
       the end--the 144 express--the Sioux--the cordillera

of the Andes--Negroes picking maize--jail--the
reverberation--beautiful Madame Astor--the
declarations of President Wilson--torpedo
boats--mines--the tango--Vidal Lablanche--
mercury globes--projectors--arc lamps--gramo-
phones--typewriters--the Eiffel Tower--the
Brooklyn Bridge--huge automobiles of enamel
and nickel--Pullman cars which cross the vir-
gin forest--bars--saloons--ice-cream parlors--
roadside taverns--Nick Carter--Helene Boodge--
the Hudson and its docks--the Carolinas--my
room on the seventeenth floor--panhandlers--
posters--advertising--Charlie Chaplin--Chris-
topher Columbus--metal landscapes--the list
of the victims of the Lusitania--women wearing
evening gowns in the morning--the isle of
Mauritius--Paul et Virginie.

c) A musical libretto for two voices using images from

the three sheets of onionskin. The words curve down

the page in serpentine. Satie received this "score"

with a covering note.

2. The "January Notebook." In January 1917, Cocteau sent

Massine, who was in Rome with Diaghilev, a small notebook

which was filled with words, sounds and phrases designed

to "extend" the character of the Chinaman.

3. A small notebook with drawings and comments pertaining to

Parade, Collection Boris Kochno, Paris.

4. Le Cahier romain, private collection, Edouard Dermit,

Paris. Drawings, aphorisms, and stage directions were

placed in this notebook, a gift from Massine, during

Cocteau's stay in Rome (Figs. 82-115).

5. Assorted sketches on loose pages, Collection Edouard

Dermit, Paris (Figs. 116-127).

APPENDIX 2

PICASSO'S STAGE SET FOR PARADE

The following two diagrams illustrate the three-
dimensional layout of Picasso's stage set for the original
production of Parade as it was reconstructed for the Robert
Joffrey revival. Since the only guide in the recreation of
the set was a single, black-and-white photograph taken of
the 1917 production, one which has prompted many writers
to refer to Picasso's set as a backdrop, Robert Joffrey's
designer, Mr. Edward Burbridge, had to rely upon the memories
of those who saw the original Ballets Russes production.
The two most important individuals consulted were Leonide
Massine and, of course, Pablo Picasso, through the cooperation
of Mr. Douglas Cooper.

The reconstructed set for the Joffrey production
consisted of the following elements:

1. One backdrop

2. One flat: proscenium with curtains

3. Eight legs: six architectural panels and two
   tree trunks

4. Two railings

5. One bush

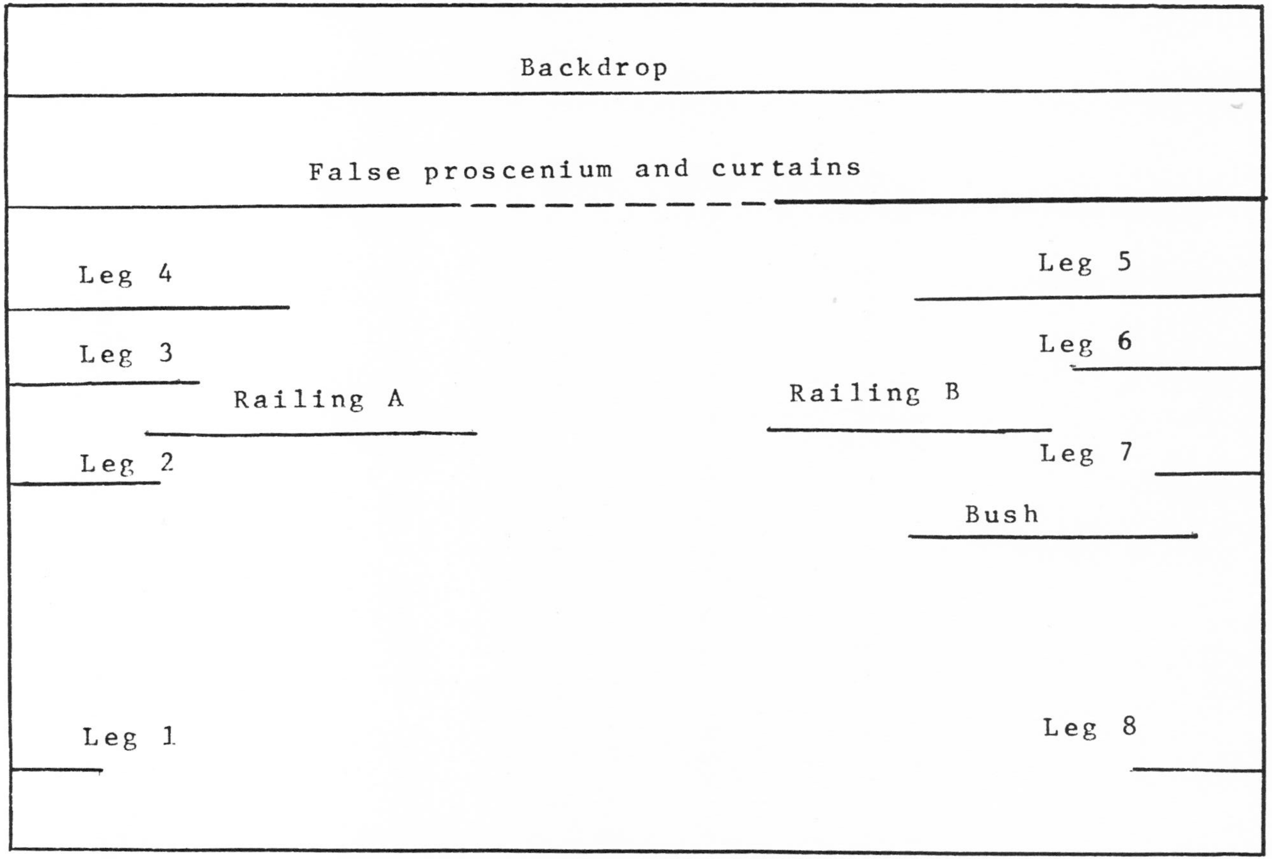

Backdrop

False proscenium and curtains

Leg 4

Leg 3

Leg 5

Leg 6

Railing A

Railing B

Leg 2

Leg 7

Bush

Leg 1

Leg 8

Fig. 50.--Picasso, The set for Parade.
(Diagram of the legs and flats.)

Fig. 50.--Picasso, The set for Parade.

BIBLIOGRAPHY

Alexandre, Arsène. The Decorative Art of Léon Bakst. London:
The Fine Arts Society, 1913.

Amberg, George. Art in Modern Ballet. New York: Pantheon,
1946.

L'Ancienne Douane. Les Ballets Russes de Serge de Diaghilev,
1909-1929. Strasbourg: Dernières Nouvelles de Strasbourg, 1969.

Anthony, Gordon. Massine. Paris: Gallimard, 1939.

Apollinaire, Guillaume. Chroniques d'art. Edited by L.-C.
Breunig. Paris: Gallimard, 1960.

Auric, Georges. "Une Oeuvre Nouvelle de Satie," Littérature
4 (April 1919): 225.

_____. "Chronique sur Parade," La Nouvelle revue française
7 (February 1921): 224-227.

Baker, Robb. "Joffrey's Parade: A Controversial Collaboration-
56 Years Later," Dance Magazine 19 (March 1973): 40-43.

Barr, Alfred H. Picasso: Fifty Years of his Art. New York:
Museum of Modern Art, 1946.

Beaumont, Cyril W. Five Centuries of Ballet Design. New
York: The Studio Publications, 1936.

_____. Complete Book of Ballets. New York: Grosset and
Dunlap, 1938.

_____. The Diaghilev Ballet in London. London: Putnam,
1940.

_____. A Short History of Ballet. London: C.W. Beaumont,
1947.

Béjart, Maurice. "Maurice Béjart and the Total Theater,"
World Theater 3 (November-December 1965): 556-563.

Bell, Clive. "The New Ballet," The New Republic 5 (July
30, 1919): 414-416.

Benedikt, Michael, and Wellwarth, George E., eds. Modern
   French Theatre: The Avant-Garde, Dada, and Surrealism--
   An Anthology of Plays. New York: Dutton, 1964.

Berger, John. The Success and Failure of Picasso. Baltimore:
   Penguin Books, 1965.

Bertocci, Angelo Philip. From Symbolism to Baudelaire.
   Carbondale, Illinois: Southern Illinois University
   Press, 1964.

Blunt, Anthony, and Pool, Phoebe. Picasso, the Formative
   Years: A Study of his Sources. London: Studio Books,
   1962.

Boeck, Wilhelm, and Sabartés, Jaime. Picasso. New York:
   Harry N. Abrams, 1955.

Brown, Frederick. An Impersonation of Angels: A Biography
   of Jean Cocteau. New York: The Viking Press, 1968.

Buckle, Richard. In Search of Diaghilev. London: Sidgwick
   and Jackson, 1955.

Burnham, Jack. The Structure of Art. New York: George
   Braziller, 1971.

Camesasca, Ettore. The Complete Paintings of Watteau.
   London: Weidenfeld and Nicolson, 1971.

Carter, Huntly. "Newest Tendencies in the Paris Theatre,"
   Theatre Arts Magazine 3 (December 1917): 35-43.

_____. The New Spirit in the European Theatre, 1914-1924.
   London: E. Benn, 1925.

Cassou, Jean. "Le Rideau de Parade de Picasso au Musée
   de l'art moderne," La Revue des arts 7 (January 1957):
   15-18.

Cirlot, Juan Eduardo. Birth and Genius of Picasso. New York:
   Praeger, 1972.

Clough, Rosa. Futurism. New York: Philosophical Library, 1961.

Cocteau, Jean. "Avant Parade." Excelsior, May 18, 1917,
   sec. 4, p. 4.

_____. "Parade," Vanity Fair 5 (September 1917): 17-19.

_____. "Petits souvenirs de théâtre," Das Querschnitt
   4 (December 1922): 23-26.

_____. "Allocution prononcée par Cocteau au Boeuf sur
   le toit avant la farce." Original manuscript,

Bibliothèque Jacques Doucet, Paris.

_____. Les Mariés de la tour Eiffel. Paris: Nouvelle revue française, 1924.

_____. Oeuvres complètes de Jean Cocteau. 10 vols. Geneva: Marguerat, 1946.

_____. Les Foyers des artistes. Paris: Plon, 1947.

_____. Nouveau théâtre de poche. Monaco: Editions du Rocher, 1960.

_____. The Journals of Jean Cocteau. Edited by Wallace Fowlie. New York: Praeger, 1965.

_____. Le Cap de Bonne-Espérance. Paris: Gallimard, 1967.

_____. Jean Cocteau entre Picasso et Radiquet. Edited by André Fermigier. Paris: Hermann, 1967.

_____. Cocteau's World: An Anthology of Writings by Jean Cocteau. Edited by Margaret Crosland. London: Peter Owen, 1972.

Cooper, Douglas. Picasso Theatre. New York: Harry N. Abrams, 1967.

_____. The Cubist Epoch. London: Phaidon, 1970.

Cooper, Martin. French Music from the Death of Berlioz to the Death of Fauré. London: Oxford University Press, 1961.

Craig, Edward Gordon. De l'art du théâtre. Paris: Prisma, 1916.

_____. "The Actor and the Übermarionette." In Total Theater, pp. 33-57. Edited by E. T. Kirby. New York: E. P. Dutton, 1969.

Crespelle, Jean-Paul. La Folle époque: des ballets russes au surréalisme. Paris: Hachette, 1968.

Delza, Sophia. "The Classic Chinese Theatre." In Total Theater, pp. 224-242. Edited by E. T. Kirby. New York: E. P. Dutton, 1969.

Drew, David. "Modern French Music." In European Music in the Twentieth Century, pp. 232-295. Edited by Howard Hartog. New York: Praeger, 1957.

Duberman, Martin. "The Historian as Ghost." New York Times, July 8, 1973, sec. 4, p. 13.

Dubourg, Pierre. La Dramaturgie de Jean Cocteau. Paris:
B. Grasset, 1954.

Fokine, Michel. "Letter to the Editor." London Times,
July 6, 1914, sec. 2, p. 5.

Fowlie, Wallace. Mallarmé. Chicago: The University of
Chicago Press, 1962.

_____. Jean Cocteau: The History of a Poet's Age.
Bloomington: Indiana University Press, 1966.

Franks, Arthur Henry. Twentieth Century Ballet. London:
Burke, 1954.

Fry, Edward. Cubism. New York: McGraw-Hill, 1966.

Fuerst, Walter René, and Hume, Samuel J. Twentieth Century
Stage Decoration. 2 vols. New York: Dover, 1967.

Gadan, Francis; Maillard, Robert; Cohen, Selma. Dictionary
of Modern Ballet. New York: Tudor Publishing Co., 1959.

Garnier, Jacques. Forains d'hier et d'aujourd'hui. Orléans:
Les Presses, 1968.

Geiser, Bernhard. Picasso: peintre-graveur. Berne:
Bernhard Geiser, 1933.

Gilliam, Florence, "The Russian Ballet of 1923," Theatre
Arts Magazine 10 (March 1924): 191-194.

Golding, John. Cubism: A History and An Analysis, 1907-1914.
Boston: Boston Book and Art Shop, 1968.

Gontcharova, Nathalie; Larionov, Michel; Vorms, Pierre.
Les Ballets russes: Serge de Diaghilew et la décoration
théâtrale. Dordogne: Belves, 1955.

Gray, Camilla. The Great Experiment: Russian Art 1863-1922.
New York: Harry N. Abrams, 1962.

Grigoriev, S. L. The Diaghilef Ballet, 1909-1929. London:
Constable, 1953.

Guicharnaud, Jacques. Modern French Theatre from Giraudoux
to Beckett. New Haven: Yale University Press, 1961.

Haskell, Arnold. Ballet Russe: The Age of Diaghilev. London:
Weidenfeld and Nicolson, 1968.

_____. The Russian Genius in Ballet. Oxford, New York:
Pergamon Press, 1963.

Hermant, Abel. "Les Ballets russes." Excelsior, May 20, 1917, p. 13.

Jacobson, Robert. "The Musical Cocteau," New York Philharmonic Hall Program 15 (February 10, 1967): 36-37.

Janson, H. W. Apes and Ape Lore in the Middle Ages and in the Renaissance. London: The Warburg Institute, 1952.

Johnson, Ellen. "On the Role of the Object in Analytic Cubism," Allen Memorial Art Museum Bulletin 3 (N.D.): 11-25.

Judkins, Winthrop. "Toward a Reinterpretation of Cubism," Art Bulletin 30 (December 1948): 270-278.

Kamber, Gerald. Max Jacob and the Poetics of Cubism. Baltimore: John Hopkins Press, 1971.

Kerensky, Oleg. The World of Ballet. New York: Coward McCann, 1970.

Kernodle, George R. "Wagner, Appia and the Idea of Musical Design." In Total Theatre, pp. 9-19. Edited by E. T. Kirby. New York: E. P. Dutton, 1969.

Kihm, Jean-Jacques. Cocteau. Paris: Gallimard, 1960.

Kirby, E. T., ed. Total Theatre: A Critical Anthology. New York: E. P. Dutton, 1969.

Kirby, Michael. The Art of Time. New York: E. P. Dutton, 1969.

_____. Futurist Performance. New York: E. P. Dutton, 1971.

Kirstein, Lincoln. "The Diaghilev Period," The Hound and Horn 5 (Summer 1930): 468-501.

_____. The Book of the Dance: A Short History of Classic Theatrical Dancing. New York: G. P. Putnam's Sons, 1935.

_____. Movement and Metaphor: Four Centuries of Ballet. New York: Praeger, 1970.

Kisselgoff, Anna. "So Talked About But Never Seen." New York Times, March 19, 1972, sec. 2, p. 15.

Knapp, Bettina L. Jean Cocteau. New York: Twayne Publishers, 1970.

Knowles, Dorothy. French Drama of the Inter-War Years, 1918-1939. London: Harrap, 1967.

Kochno, Boris. Le Ballet. Paris: Hachette, 1954.

_____. Diaghilev and the Ballets Russes. New York: Harper and Row, 1970.

Kozloff, Max. Cubism/Futurism. New York: Charterhouse, 1973.

Lecaldano, Paolo. The Complete Paintings of Picasso: Blue and Rose Periods. London: Weidenfeld and Nicolson, 1971.

Levinson, André. La Danse d'aujourd'hui. Paris: Duchartre and VanBugenhoudt, 1929.

Lieberman, W.S. "Picasso and the Ballet," Dance Index 3 (November 1946): 230-240.

Lifar, Serge. Diaghilev: An Intimate Biography. New York: G. P. Putnam's Sons, 1940.

_____. A History of the Russian Ballet. New York: Roy Publishers, 1957.

Lyons, Charles R. "Gordon Craig's Concept of the Actor." In Total Theatre, pp. 58-77. Edited by E. T. Kirby, New York: E. P. Dutton, 1969.

Marinetti, F. T. Teatro. Edited by Giovanni Calendoli. Rome: V. Bianco, 1960.

Martin, Marianne. Futurist Art and Theory 1905-1915. Oxford: Clarendon Press, 1968.

Massine, Leonide. My Life in Ballet. London: Macmillan, 1968.

Mellow, James. Charmed Circle: Gertrude Stein and Friends. New York: Praeger, 1974.

Milhau, Denis. Picasso et le théâtre. Toulouse: Musée des Augustins, 1965.

Myers, Rollo. Erik Satie. New York: Dover, 1968.

Nabokov, Nicolas. "Serge Diaghilef," Atlantic Monthly 185 (March 1950): 68-72.

Oxenhandler, Neal. Scandal and Parade: The Theater of Jean Cocteau. New Brunswick: Rutgers University Press, 1957.

Peckham, Morse. Man's Rage for Chaos: Biology, Behavior, and the Arts. New York: Schocken, 1965.

_____. Art and Pornography: An Experiment in Explanation. New York: Harper and Row, 1969.

Penrose, Roland. _Picasso: His Life and Work_. New York: Harper, 1958.

Phelps, Robert. _Professional Secrets: An Autobiography of Jean Cocteau, Drawn from his lifetime writings_. New York: Farrar, Straus, and Giroux, 1970.

Pronko, Leonard C. _Avant-Garde: The Experimental Theatre in France_. Berkeley: University of California Press, 1962.

_____. _Theatre East and West: Perspectives Toward a Total Theatre_. Berkeley and Los Angeles: University of California Press, 1967.

_____. "Kabuki and the Elizabethan Theatre." In _Total Theatre_, pp. 187-196. Edited by E. T. Kirby. New York: E. P. Dutton, 1969.

Propert, W. A. _The Russian Ballet in Western Europe, 1909-1920_. London: John Lane, 1921.

Radiguet, Raymond. "_Parade_." _Le Gaulois_, December 25, 1920, p. 4.

Reff, Theodore. "Harlequins, Saltimbanques, Clowns, and Fools," _Artforum_ 10 (October 1971): 30-43.

Reyna, Ferdinando. _A Concise History of Ballet_. New York: Grosset and Dunlap, 1965.

Rischbieter, Henning, and Storch, Wolfgang. _Art and the Stage in the 20th Century: Painters' and Sculptors' work for the Theatre_. Greenwich, Conn.: New York Graphic Society, 1968.

Rogers, Clark M. "Appia's Theory of Acting: Eurhythmics for the Stage." In _Total Theatre_, pp. 20-28. Edited by E. T. Kirby. New York: E. P. Dutton, 1969.

Rosenblum, Robert. _Cubism and Twentieth-Century Art_. New York: Harry N. Abrams, 1966.

Rouché, Jacques. _L'Art théâtral moderne_. Paris: Bloud and Gay, 1924.

Sabartés, Jaime. _Picasso: documents iconographiques_. Geneva: Pierre Cailler, 1954.

Schonberg, Harold, C. "Did Diaghilev Change Music History?" _New York Times_, March 19, 1972, sec. 2, p. 15.

Schwartz, Paul W. _The Cubists_. London: Thames and Hudson, 1971.

Shattuck, Roger. <u>The Banquet Years: The Origins of the Avant-Garde in France 1885 to World War I</u>. New York: Vintage Books, 1968.

Sokolova, Lydia. <u>Dancing for Diaghilev</u>. London: Murray, 1960.

Sorell, Walter. "An Appreciation of Jean Cocteau," <u>Dance Magazine</u> 9 (February 1964): 38-41.

_____. <u>The Dance through the Ages</u>. New York: Grosset and Dunlap, 1967.

Steegmuller, Francis. <u>Apollinaire: Poet among the Painters</u>. New York: Farrar and Straus, 1963.

_____. <u>Cocteau: A Biography</u>. Boston: Little, Brown, and Co., 1970.

Steinberg, Leo. <u>Other Criteria: Confrontations with Twentieth-Century Art</u>. New York: Oxford University Press, 1972.

Sypher, Wylie. <u>Rococo to Cubism in Art and Literature</u>. New York: Vintage Books, 1960.

Taylor, Joshua. <u>Futurism</u>. New York: Doubleday, 1961.

Thétard, Henry. <u>La Merveilleuse histoire du cirque</u>. Paris: Prisma, 1947.

Zervos, Christian. <u>Pablo Picasso</u>. 27 vols. Paris: Cahiers d'art, 1932-1973.

Fig. 1.--Picasso, <u>Jean Cocteau</u>, 1916.

Fig. 2.--Picasso in Rome, 1917.

Fig. 3.--Picasso, Leonide Massine, 1919.

Fig. 4.--Picasso, Erik Satie, 1920.

Fig. 5.--Diaghilev, Ansermet, Stravinsky, and Prokofiev in London, 1921.

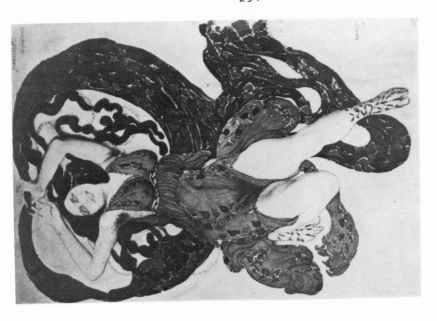

Fig. 7.--Bakst, Costume sketch for Narcisse, 1911.

Fig. 6.--Bakst, Set design for Schéhérazade, 1910.

Fig. 8.--A French <u>Théâtre forain</u>.

Fig. 9.--A French <u>Théâtre forain</u>.

256

Fig. 10.--Dancers performing
in a parade.

Fig. 11.--An Italian Théâtre forain.

Fig. 12.--Cocteau, Poster
for the Ballets Russes.

Fig. 13.--Stage set for
Ibsen's The Doll House.

Fig. 14.--A battery of intonarumori.

Fig. 16.--Balla,
A vocal-sound script.

Fig. 15.--Carrà, Manifesto
for Intervention, 1914.

Fig. 17.--Picasso, Final design
for the costume of the Chinese Magician.

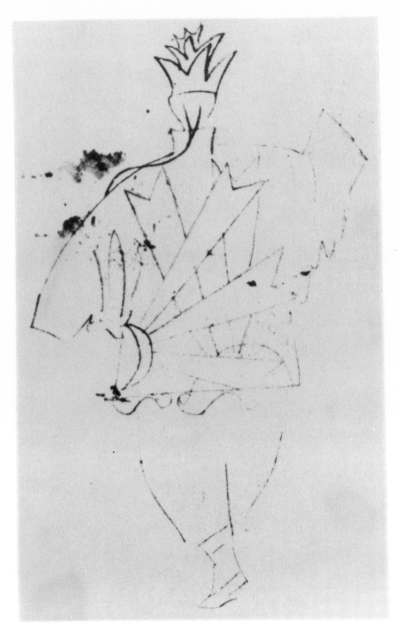

Fig. 18.--Picasso, Costume sketch
for the Chinese Magician.

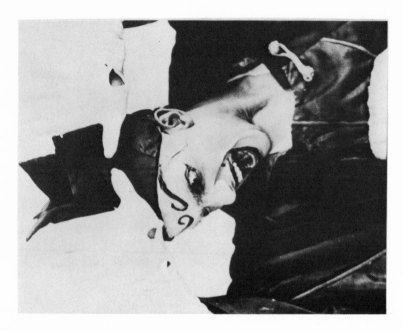

Fig. 20.--Massine
as the Chinese Magician.

Fig. 19.--Massine
as the Chinese Magician

Fig. 21.--Picasso, Final design
for the Acrobat.

Fig. 22.--Zverev as the Acrobat.

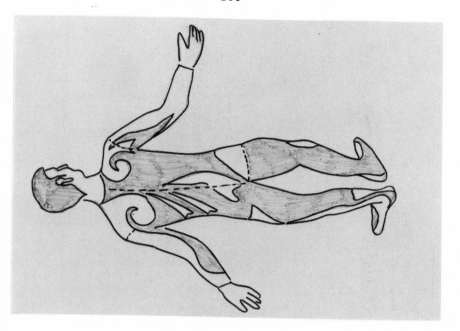

Fig. 24.--Costume sketch
for the Acrobat.

Fig. 23.--Costume sketch
for the Acrobat.

Fig. 25.--Costumes for the
male and female Acrobats.

Fig. 26.--Chabelska as the
Little American Girl.

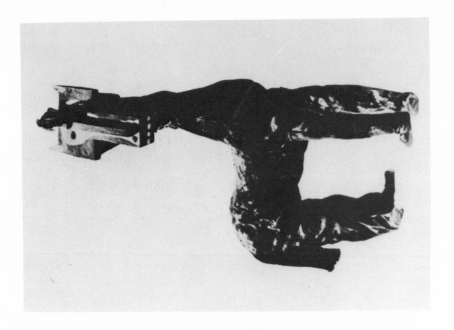

Fig. 28.--The Horse

Fig. 27.--The Horse

269

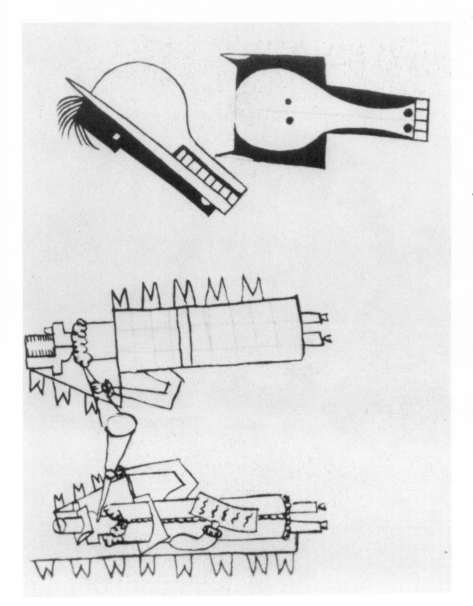

Fig. 29.--Picasso, Sketch for a Manager's costume and for the Horse's head.

Fig. 30.--Picasso, Sketch for
a Manager's costume.

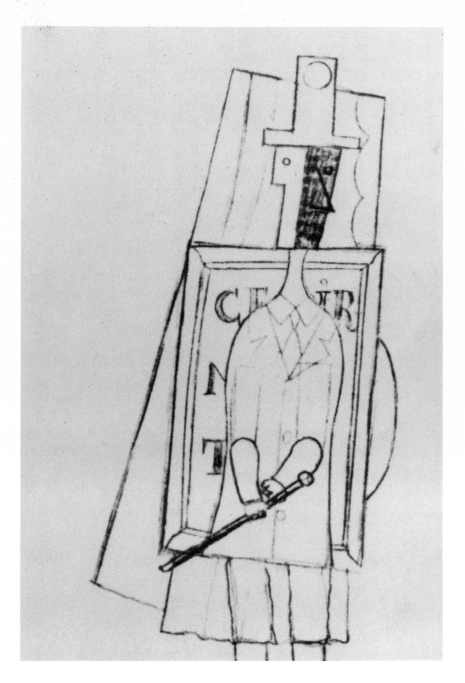

Fig. 31.--Picasso, Sketch for
a Manager's costume.

Fig. 32.--Picasso, Sketch for
a Manager's costume.

Fig. 33.--Woizikowsky as the French Manager.

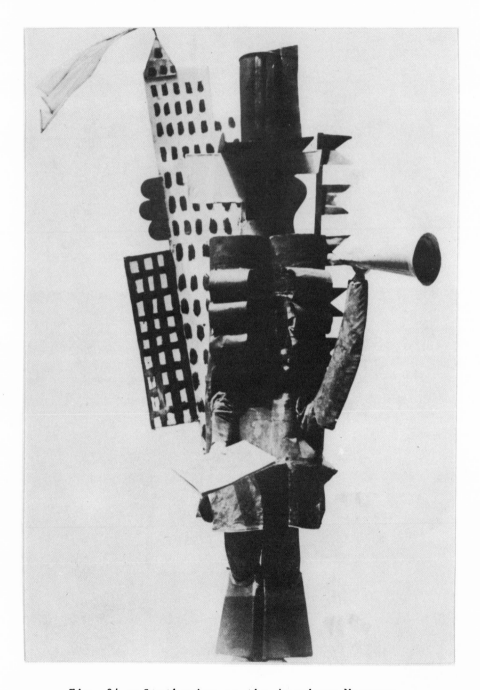

Fig. 34.--Statkewicz as the American Manager.

Fig. 35.--Picasso, <u>Guitar</u>, 1912.

Fig. 36.--Picasso, <u>Harlequin</u>, 1913.

Fig. 37.--Picasso, <u>Harlequin</u>, 1915.

Fig. 38.--Gris, <u>Torero</u> (Harlequin), 1917.

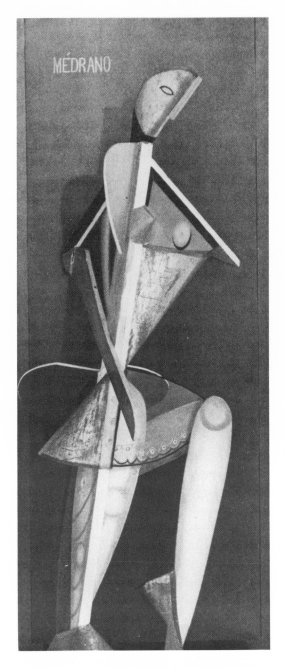

Fig. 39.--Archipenko, <u>Médrano</u>, 1914.

Fig. 40.--Baranoff-Rossine, <u>Symphony 1</u>, 1913.

Fig. 42.--Boccioni,
Head→House→Light, 1912.

Fig. 41.--Boccioni, Materia, 1912.

Fig. 44.--Picasso,
L'Italienne, 1917.

Fig. 43.--Gleizes,
Man on a Balcony, 1912.

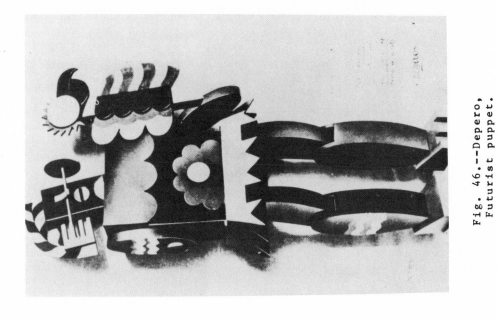

Fig. 46.--Depero,
Futurist puppet.

Fig. 45.--Depero,
Futurist costume designs.

Fig. 47.--Picasso, Preliminary sketch for the set of Parade.

Fig. 48.--Picasso, Preliminary sketch for the set of Parade.

Fig. 49.--Picasso, Costume and
set sketches for <u>Parade</u>.

Fig. 50.--Picasso, The set for _Parade_.

Fig. 51.--Picasso, The overture curtain for
Parade.

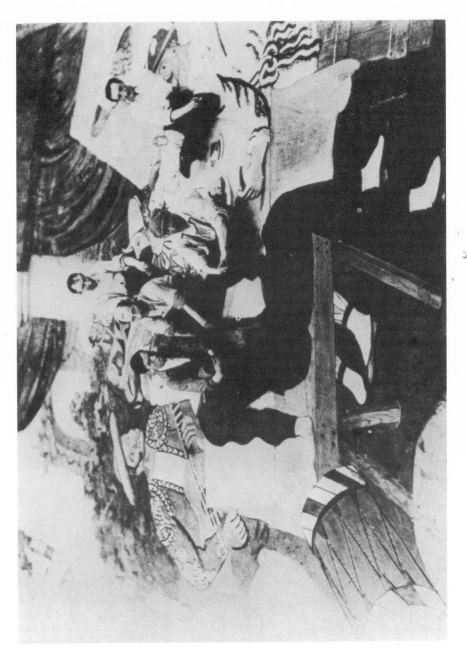

Fig. 52.--Picasso and his assistants
seated on the overture curtain.

Fig. 53.--Picasso, <u>The Pipes of Pan</u>, 1923.

Fig. 54.--Watteau, Gathering under a Portico, 1718.

Fig. 55.--Picasso, A Saltimbanque Family, 1905.

Fig. 56.--Picasso, The Family of Saltimbanques, 1905.

Fig. 57.--Picasso, The overture curtain (detail).

Fig. 58.--Picasso, The overture curtain (detail).

Fig. 59.--Picasso, Self Portrait, 1903.

Fig. 60.--Jean Cocteau, 1918.

Fig. 61.--Winged circus horse.

Fig. 62.--Winged circus horse.

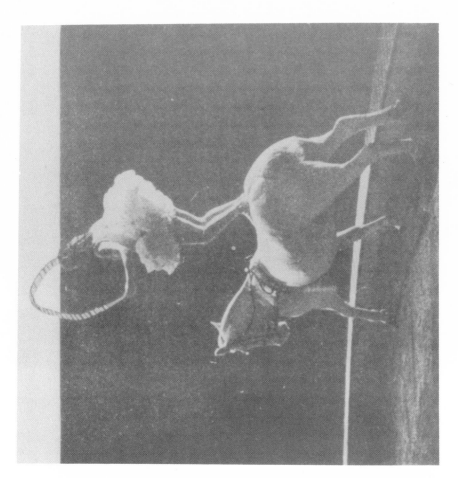

Fig. 63.--Circus horseback rider.

Fig. 64.--A ballet dancer
as a <u>sylphide</u>.

Fig. 65.--A circus monkey.

Fig. 66.--Vernet, Scene from a Village Fair.

Fig. 67.--Chardin, <u>The Monkey Painter</u>, 1739-40.

Fig. 68.--Picasso, Drawing from the Vallauris Suite, 1954.

305

Fig. 69.--Picasso, Drawing from the Vallauris Suite, 1954.

Fig. 70.--Picasso, <u>Self Portrait</u>, 1903.

Fig. 71.--Picasso, <u>Three Ballerinas</u>, 1917.

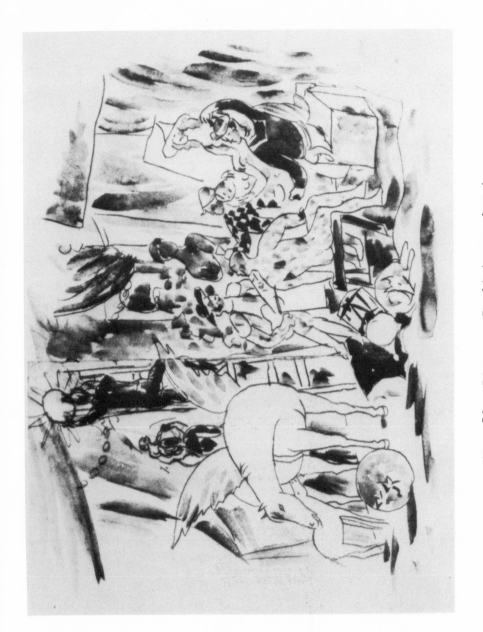

Fig. 72.--Picasso, Preliminary sketch for the overture curtain.

Fig. 73.--Ladder and celestial emblem.

Fig. 74.--Picasso, <u>Contemplation</u>, 1904.

Fig. 75.--Picasso, <u>Girl Balancing on a Ball</u>, 1905.

Fig. 76.--Picasso, Dancers gathered around Olga Koklova, 1919-20.

Fig. 77.--Picasso, Reclining Nude with Figures, 1908.

Fig. 78.--Section of the East Frieze of the Parthenon.

Fig. 79.--Picasso, <u>The Window</u>, 1919.

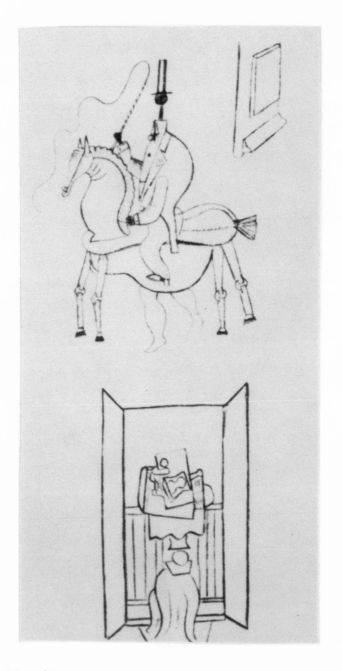

Fig. 80.--Picasso, Sketch for a Manager's costume
and for a still life, 1917.

Fig. 81.--Picasso, Still life in front of
the overture curtain for Le Tricorne, 1919.

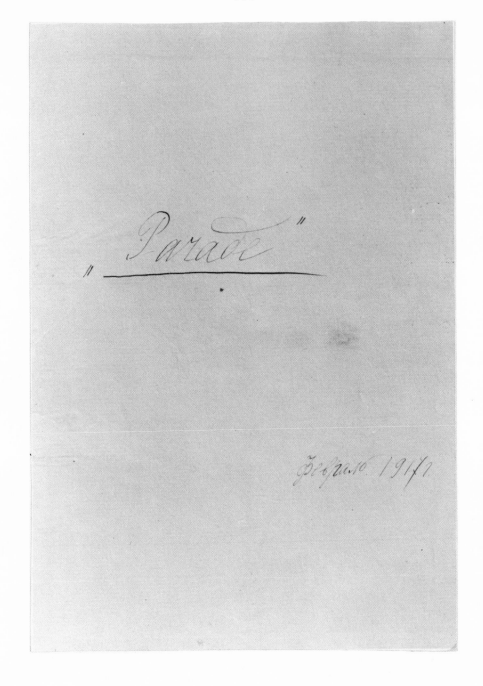

Fig. 82.--Cocteau, Le Cahier romain, 1917.

Fig. 83.--Cocteau, <u>Le Cahier romain</u>, 1917.

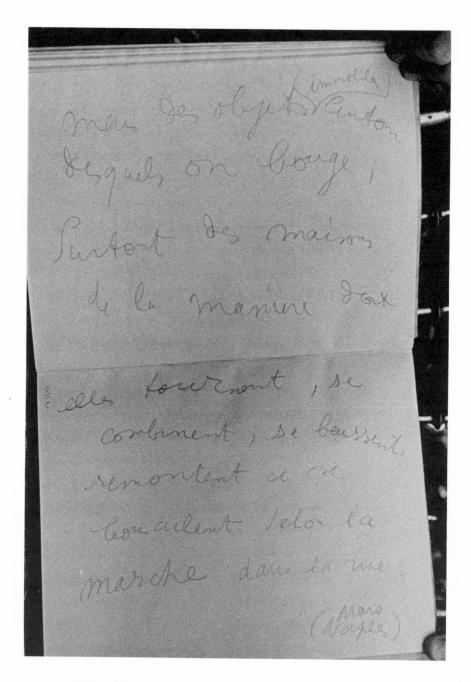

Fig. 84.--Cocteau, <u>Le Cahier romain</u>, 1917.

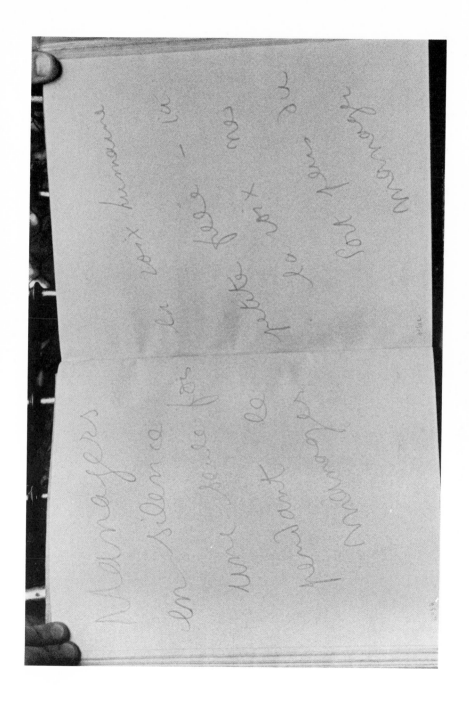

Fig. 85.--Cocteau, Le Cahier romain, 1917.

Fig. 86.--Cocteau, Le Cahier romain, 1917.

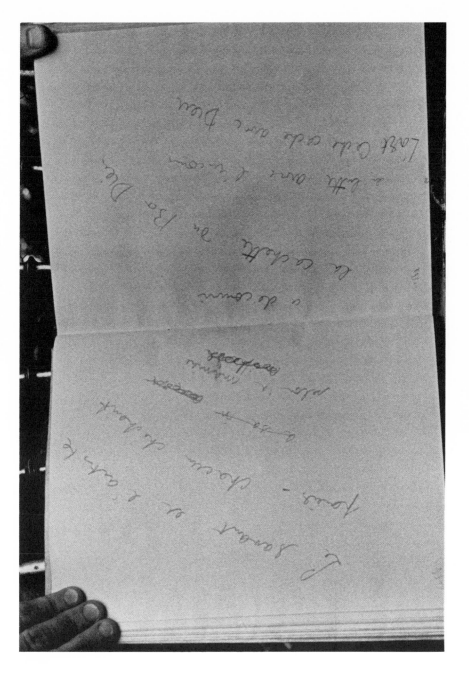

Fig. 87.--Cocteau, <u>Le Cahier romain</u>, 1917.

324

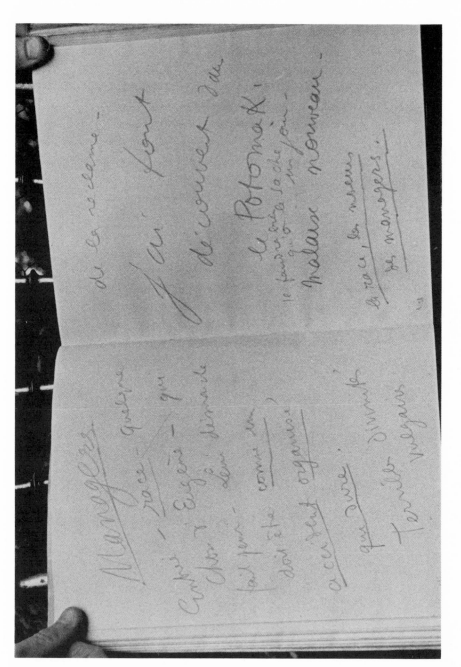

Fig. 88.--Cocteau, Le Cahier romain, 1917.

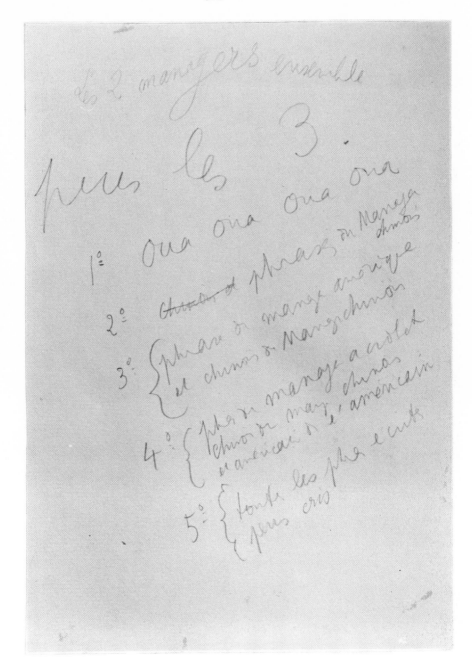

Fig. 89.--Cocteau, <u>Le Cahier romain</u>, 1917.

326

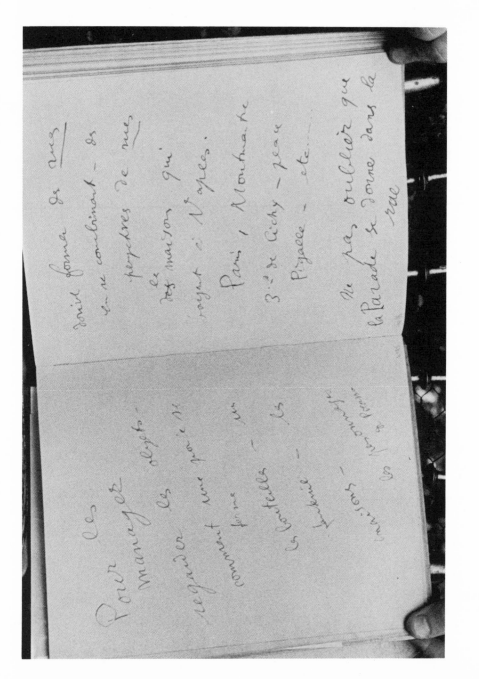

Fig. 90.--Cocteau, Le Cahier romain, 1917.

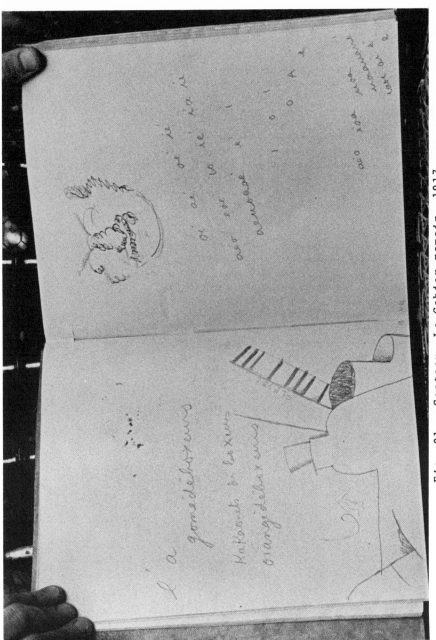

Fig. 91.--Cocteau, *Le Cahier romain*, 1917.

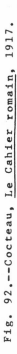

Fig. 92.--Cocteau, <u>Le Cahier romain</u>, 1917.

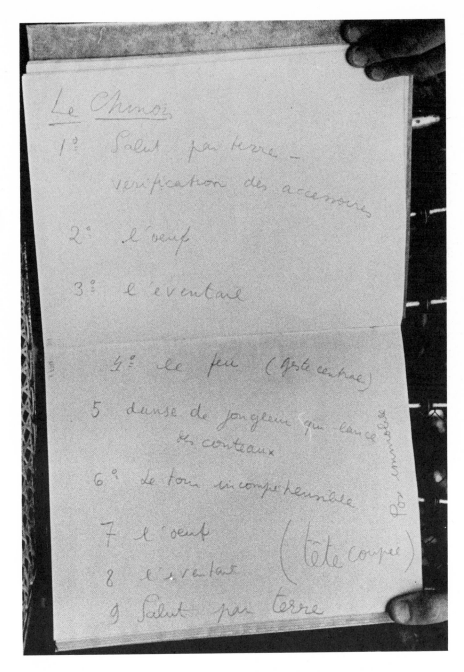

Fig. 93.--Cocteau, <u>Le Cahier romain</u>, 1917.

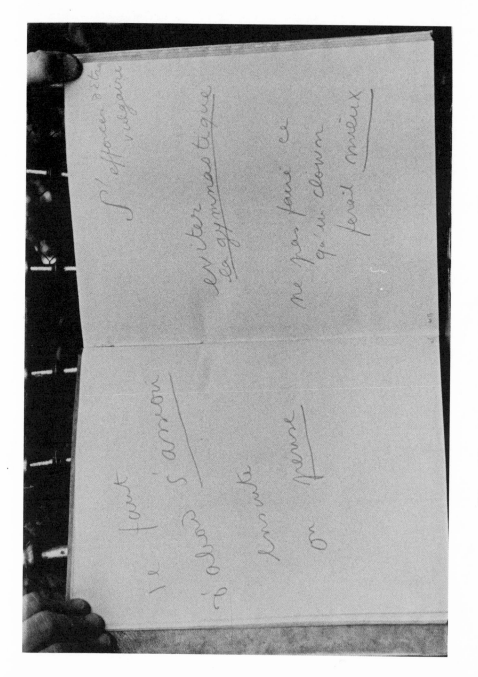

Fig. 94.--Cocteau, Le Cahier romain, 1917.

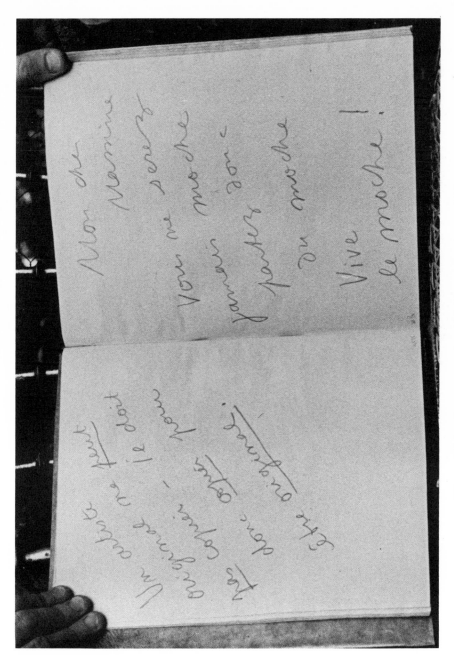

Fig. 95.--Cocteau, Le Cahier romain, 1917.

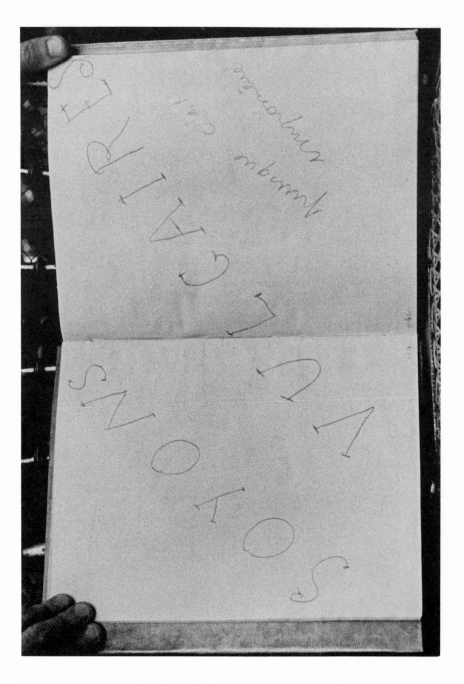

Fig. 96.--Cocteau, Le Cahier romain, 1917.

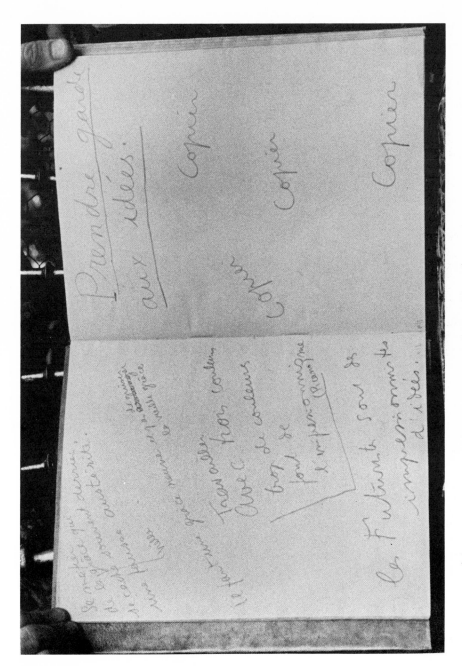

Fig. 97.--Cocteau, <u>Le Cahier romain</u>, 1917.

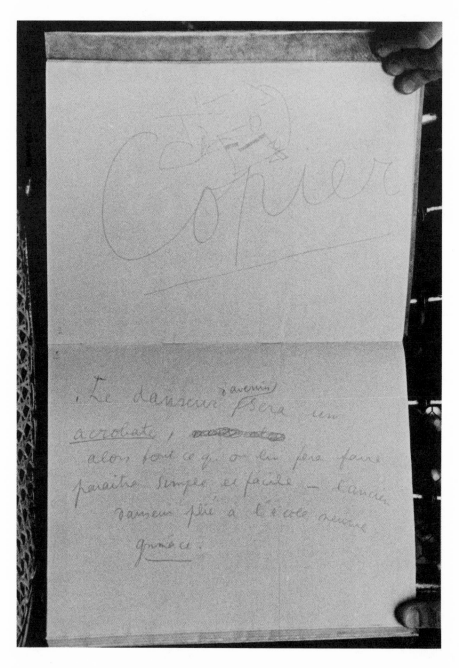

Fig. 98.--Cocteau, <u>Le Cahier romain</u>, 1917.

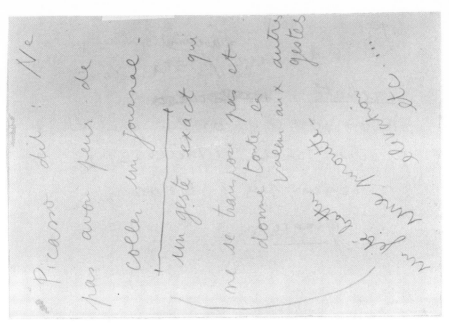

Fig. 99.--Cocteau, <u>Le Cahier romain</u>, 1917.

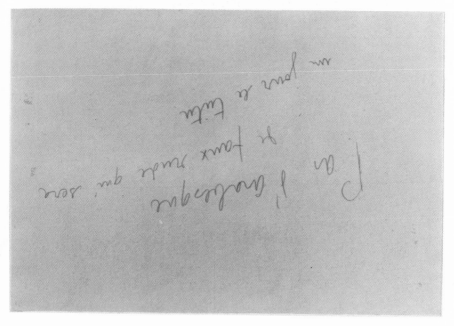

Fig. 100.--Cocteau, Le Cahier romain, 1917.

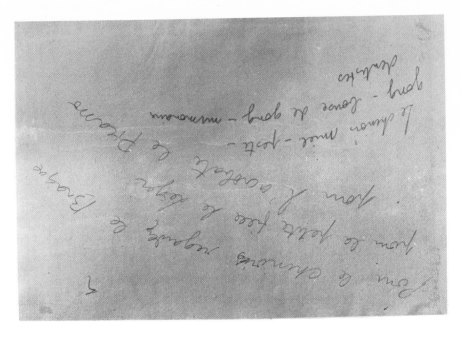

Fig. 101.--Cocteau, Le Cahier romain, 1917.

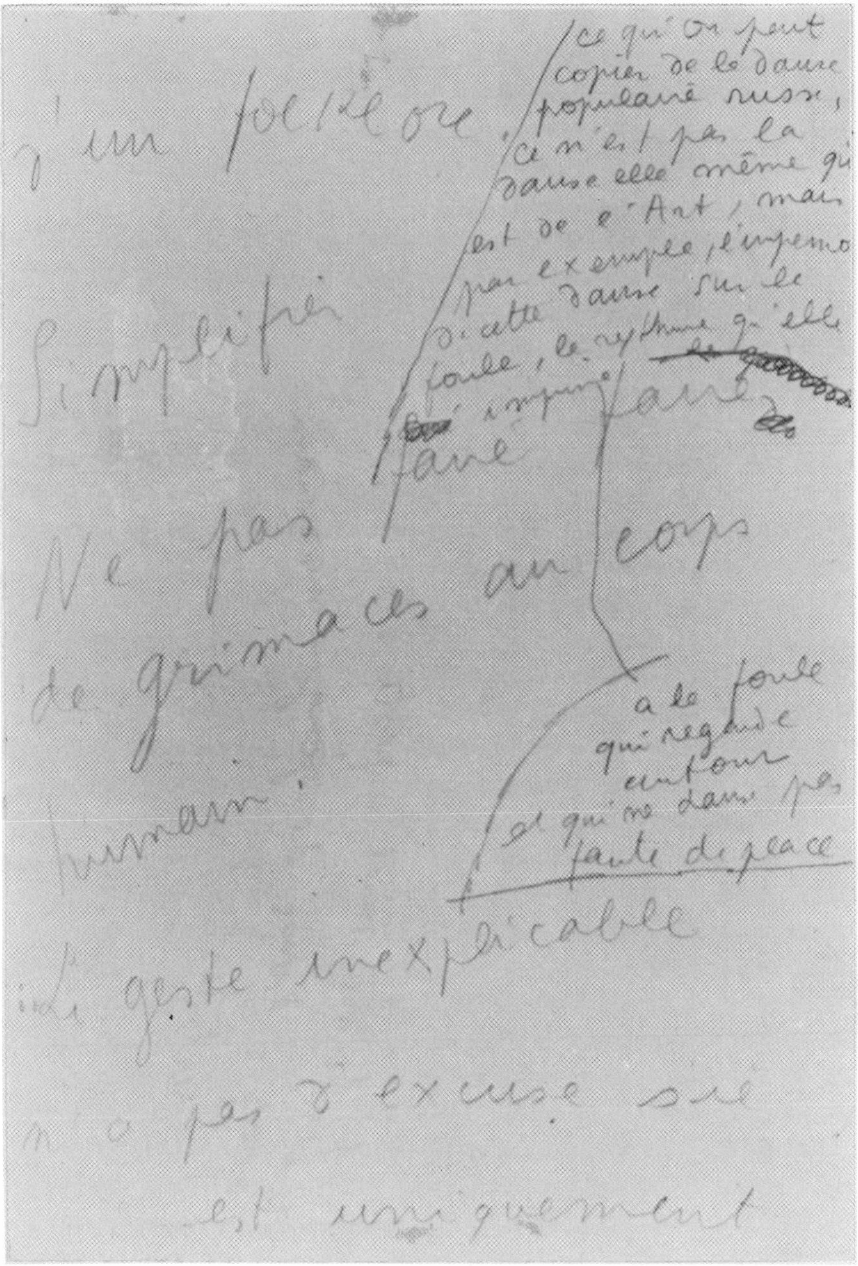

Fig. 102.--Cocteau, _Le Cahier romain_, 1917.

Fig. 103.--Cocteau, Le Cahier romain, 1917.

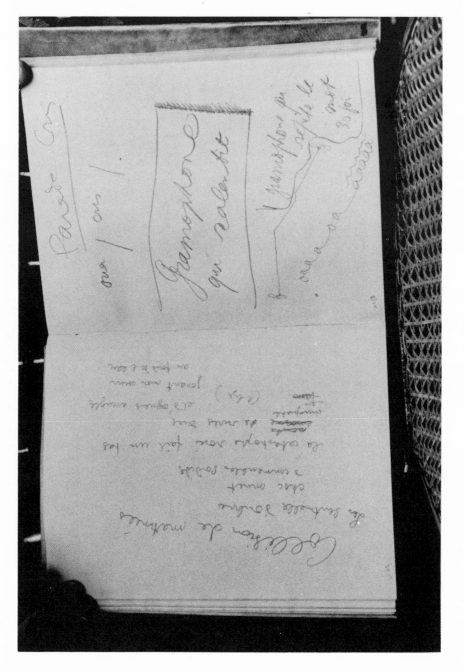

Fig. 104.--Cocteau, Le Cahier romain, 1917.

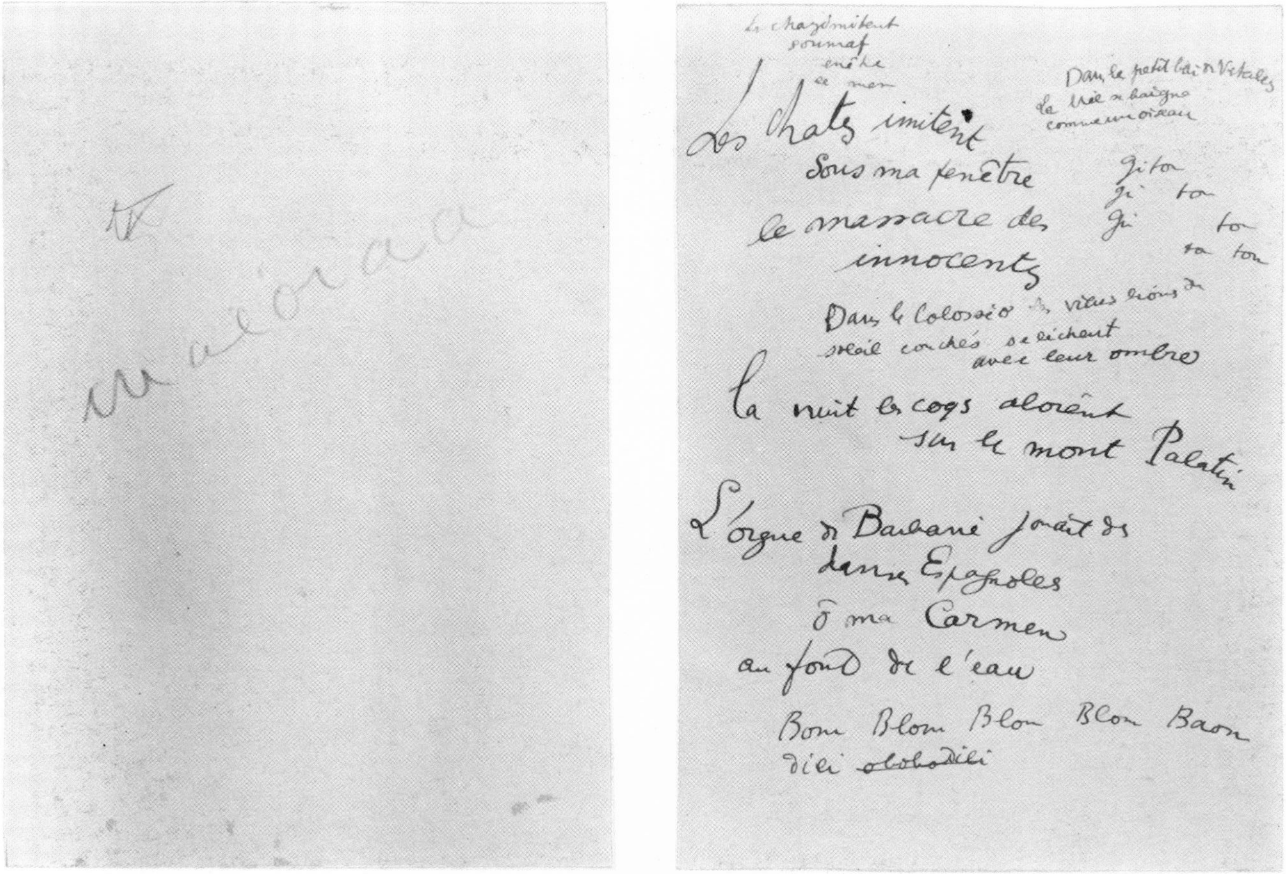

Fig. 105.--Cocteau, _Le Cahier romain_, 1917.

342

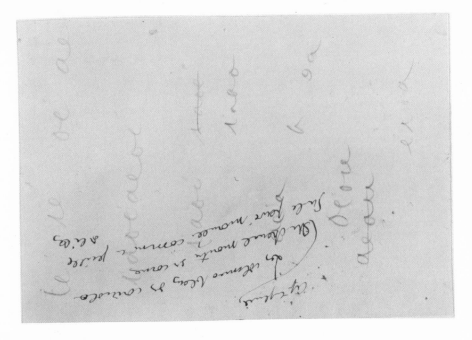

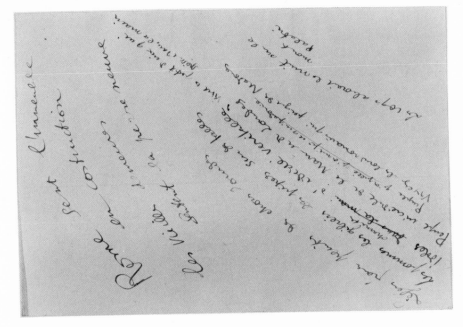

Fig. 106.--Cocteau, Le Cahier romain, 1917.

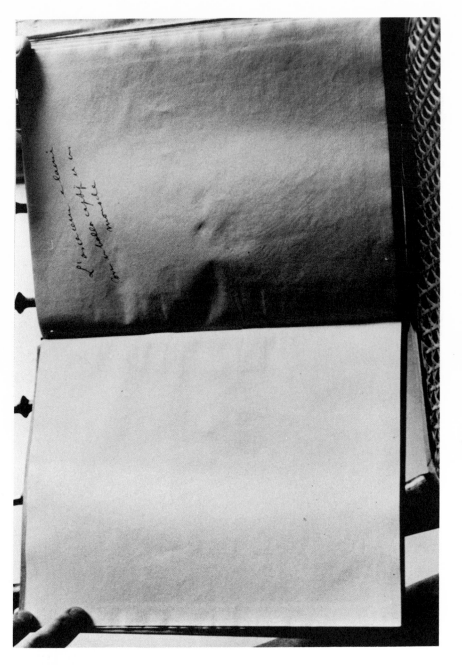

Fig. 107.--Cocteau, <u>Le Cahier romain</u>, 1917.

Fig. 108.--Cocteau, Le Cahier romain, 1917.

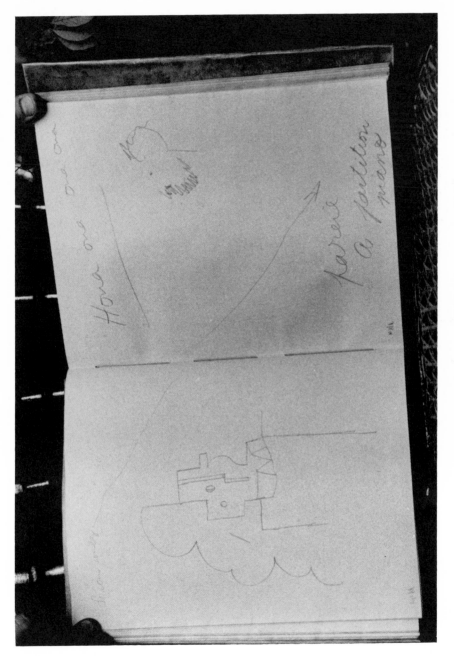

Fig. 109.--Cocteau, Le Cahier romain, 1917.

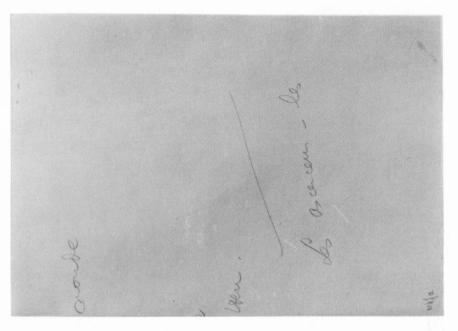

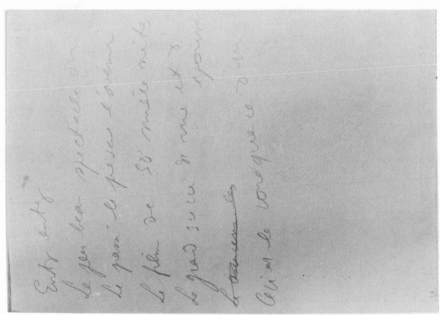

Fig. 110.--Cocteau, Le Cahier romain, 1917.

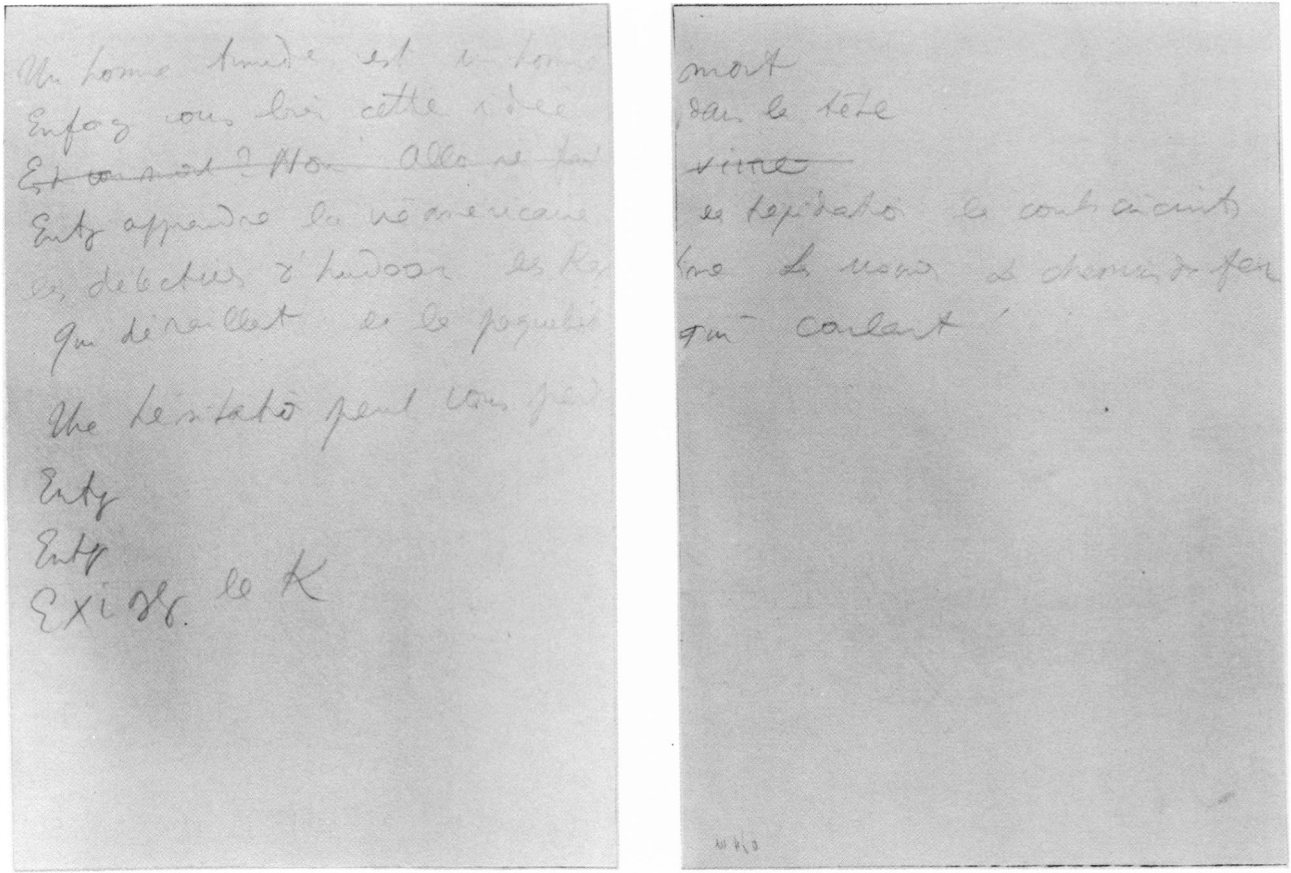

Fig. 111.--Cocteau, Le Cahier romain, 1917.

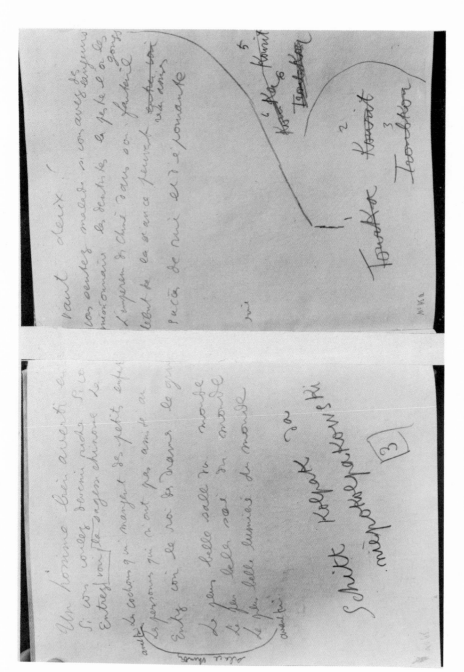

Fig. 112.--Cocteau, *Le Cahier romain*, 1917.

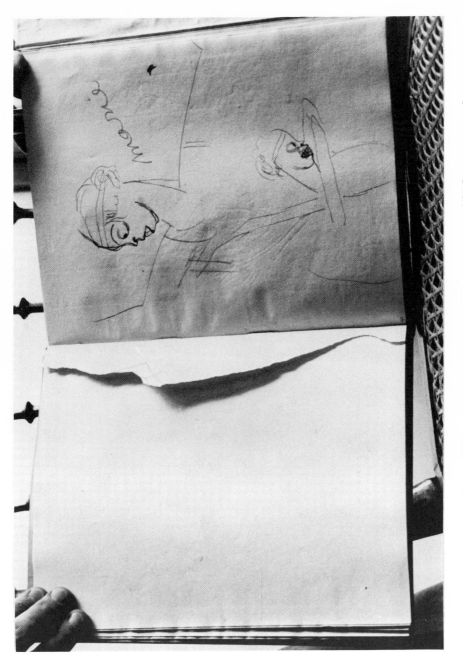

Fig. 113.--Cocteau, <u>Le Cahier romain</u>, 1917.

Fig. 114.--Cocteau, Le Cahier romain, 1917.

Fig. 115.--Cocteau, <u>Le Cahier romain</u>, 1917.

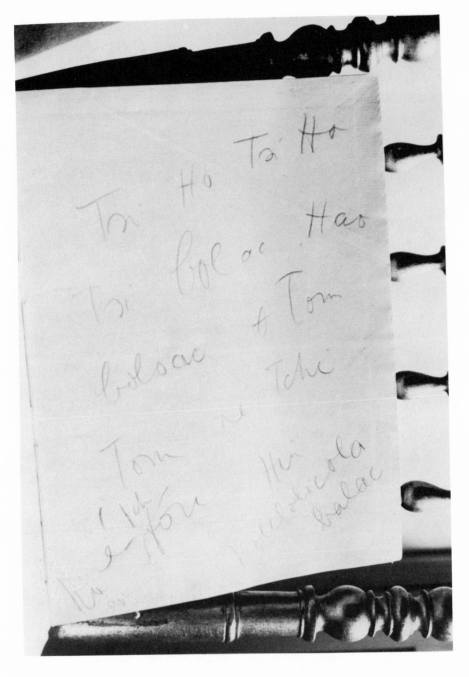

Fig. 116.--Cocteau, Loose page, 1917.

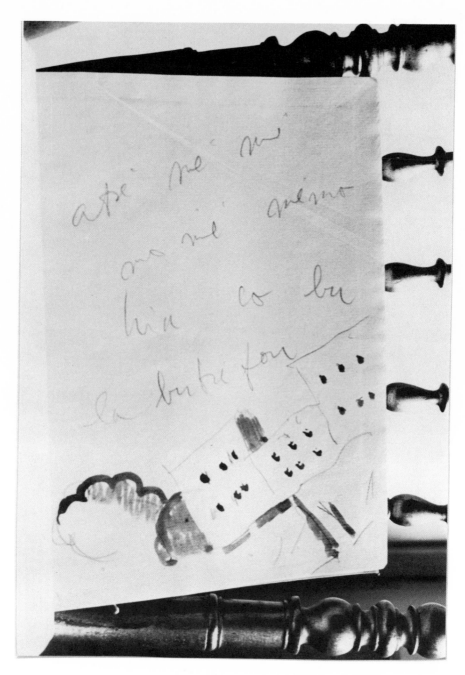

Fig. 117.--Cocteau, Loose page, 1917.

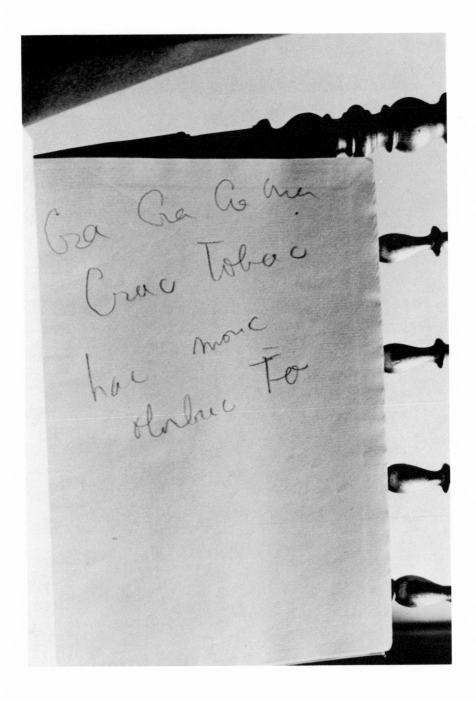

Fig. 118.--Cocteau, Loose page, 1917.

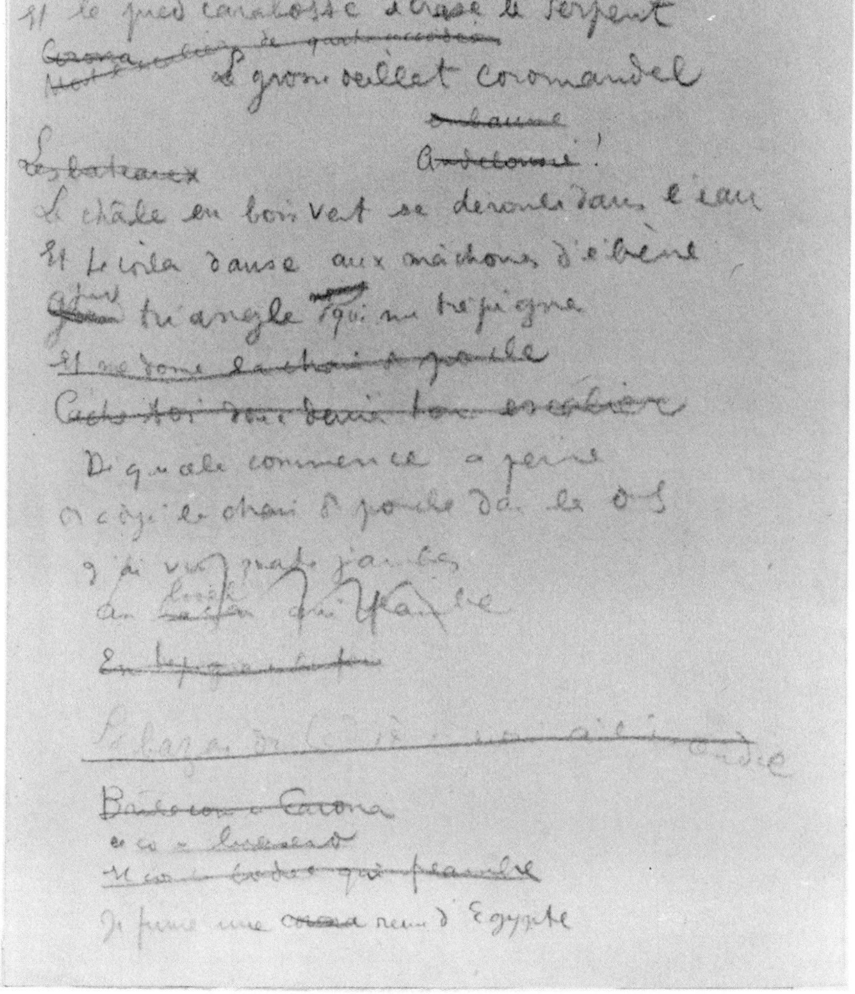

Fig. 119.--Cocteau, Loose page, 1917.

Fig. 120.--Cocteau, Loose sketch, 1917.

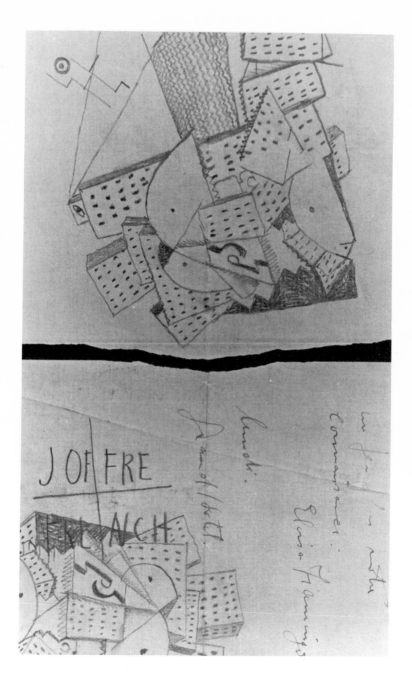

Fig. 121.--Cocteau, Loose sketch, 1917.

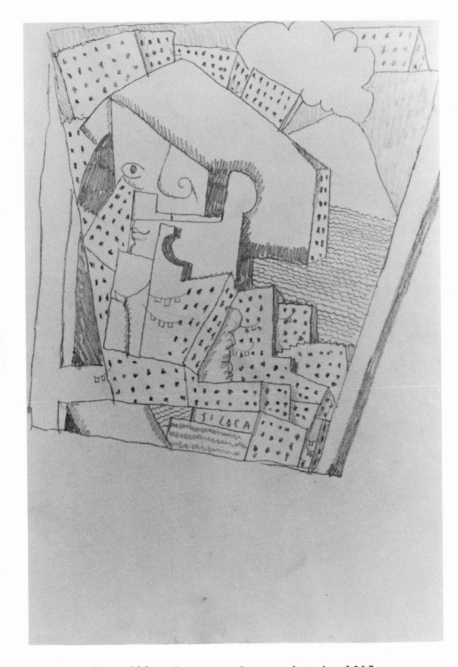

Fig. 122.--Cocteau, Loose sketch, 1917.

Fig. 123.--Cocteau, Loose sketch, 1917.

Fig. 124.--Cocteau, Loose sketch, 1917.

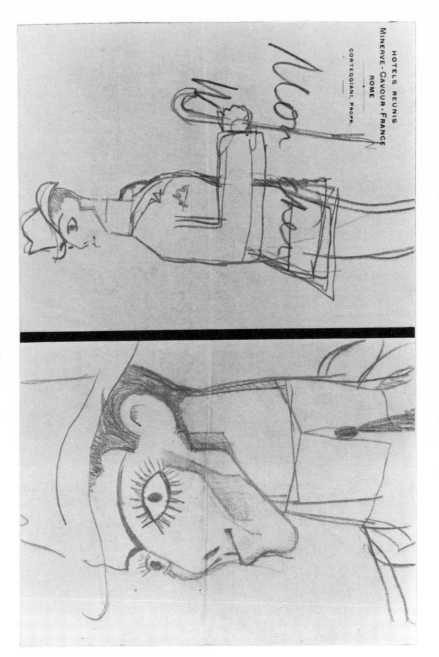

Fig. 125.--Cocteau, Loose sketch, 1917.

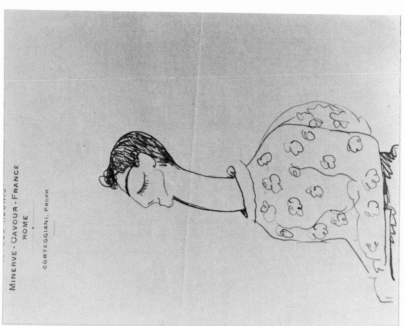

Fig. 126.--Cocteau, Loose sketch, 1917.

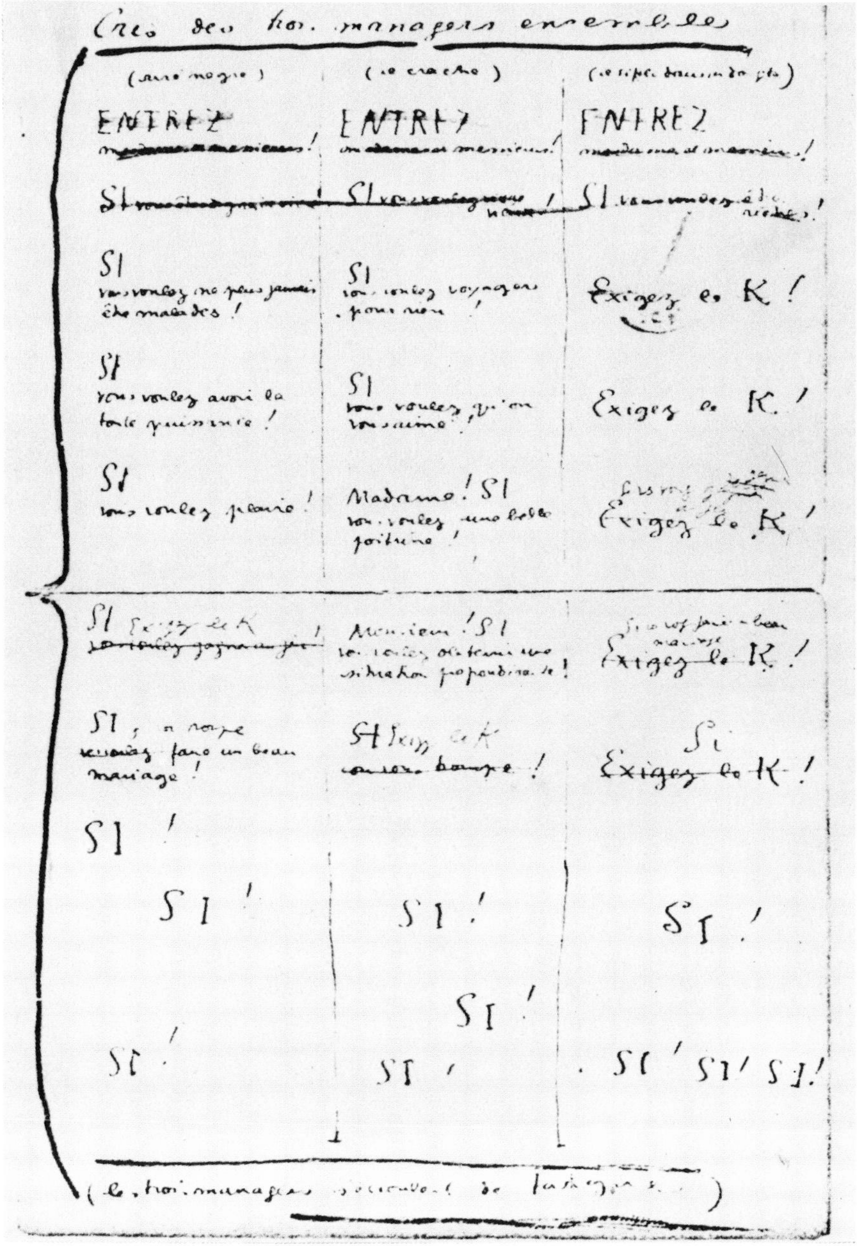

Fig. 127.--Cocteau, Loose page, 1917.